GREEN

IMPRINT

PROJECT MANAGEMENT
Florian Kobler, Cologne

COLLABORATION
Sonja Altmeppen, Berlin
Mischa Gayring, Cologne

EDITORIAL COORDINATION
Julia Krumhauer, Cologne

PRODUCTION
Ute Wachendorf, Cologne

DESIGN
Sense/Net Art Direction,
Andy Disl and Birgit
Eichwede, Cologne
www.sense-net.net

GERMAN TRANSLATION
Kristina Brigitta Köper,
Berlin

FRENCH TRANSLATION
Jacques Bosser, Paris

© VG Bild-Kunst, Bonn
2013, for the works by
Ben van Berkel

PRINTED IN CHINA
ISBN 978-3-8365-4346-0

© 2013 TASCHEN GMBH
Hohenzollernring 53
D–50672 Cologne
www.taschen.com

ORIGINAL EDITION
© 2009 TASCHEN GmbH

GREEN
ARCHITECTURE NOW!

GRÜNE *Architektur* / *L'architecture* VERTE
Philip Jodidio

TASCHEN

CONTENTS

INTRODUCTION

WAR IN THE ASPHALT JUNGLE

Green is the name of the game, no doubt about it. There has never been so much interest in the ecological impact of buildings as there is today. In the United States alone, the value of green building construction was estimated at about $100 billion in 2013; by 2016, this figure is projected to reach between $204 billion and $248 billion.[1] Nor is this a negligible fact in the struggle to control pollution and in the search for responsible "sustainable" methods of construction. Buildings are one of the heaviest consumers of natural resources and account for a significant portion of the greenhouse gas emissions that affect climate change. In the United States, buildings account for 39% of all CO_2 emissions.[2] Buildings use 40% of raw materials globally.[3] The difficulty is that green is so fashionable that everyone is jumping on the bandwagon, claiming astonishing sustainability or remarkably low-energy consumption. One effective response to the uncertainty surrounding the complex question of the environmental impact of architecture has been LEED (Leadership in Energy and Environmental Design), the accepted benchmark system of the US Green Building Council (USGBC) for the design, construction, and operation of green buildings. According to the USGBC, "LEED promotes a whole-building approach to sustainability by recognizing performance in five key areas of human and environmental health: sustainable site development, water savings, energy efficiency, materials selection, and indoor environmental quality."

TODAY CALIFORNIA, TOMORROW THE WORLD

The UK Green Building Council (UK-GBC) was launched in 2007 to bring cohesion to the green building movement in the United Kingdom. The UK government's Sustainable Buildings Task Group had earlier reported that no one body or organization concerned with sustainability was providing clear direction for the sector as a whole. The UK-GBC was established to fulfill this role. Both the American and British groups are part of the WorldGBC, which "supports national Green Building Councils whose common mission is to create a sustainable built environment …"

Although the GBC system is gaining ground and some communities or government entities are beginning to make their requirements part and parcel of the legal obligations of architects and builders, there are also doubts. Surveys show that many corporate leaders in the United States, for example, are convinced that green architecture costs more than a "normal" building. A GBC study of buildings in California found that "green improvements pay for themselves in three years." *The New York Times* recently published an article outlining a number of the ideas and issues that pose problems for the advancing green wave. One is that green buildings are ugly. This misconception is probably due to a long history of architects who felt that an environmentally friendly building had to somehow look the prickly part. Kelly Meyer, an environmentalist cited by *The New York Times*, is trying, with her husband, who is a developer, to prove that "something energy-conscious doesn't have to look as if you got it off the bottom shelf of a health-food store. It doesn't have to smell like hemp."[4]

ON A WING AND A PRAYER

The American architect David Hertz feels that the GBC LEED standards are "rigid and cumbersome" and indeed the certification process is complex and potentially costly in itself.[5] Hertz has come up with an innovative way to integrate the wings of a decommissioned 747 aircraft in a new house (747 Wing House, Santa Monica Mountains, Malibu, California, USA, 2007–09). This sort of reuse, as dramatic as it might be, may not suffice to allow Hertz to garner a precious platinum medal, but he seems set to rebel against the bureaucratic aspects

1
*Adjaye Associates, Museum of
Contemporary Art Denver, Denver,
Colorado, USA, 2004–07*

1

of the GBC rating system. Another architect quoted in the same article in *The New York Times*, Michael B. Lehrer, is predictably a bit more positive about the LEED certification process since his Water + Life Museum and Campus (Hemet, California, USA, 2001–06) recently became the first LEED Platinum museum: "They have mundane things in there that are pretty nonsensical and other things that are pretty profound. At a time when everybody and their sister and brother are saying 'We are green,' it's very important that these things be vetted in a credible way."[6]

ISLANDS IN THE STREAM

The Japanese architect Tadao Ando has long been interested in the idea of building underground, which may indeed sometimes have a bearing on the issue of "green" design. As he said in 2003: "I have an almost unconscious inclination towards underground spaces. Whatever the nature of the site, I try to create architecture that is never imposing on its environment. … Working on underground space links up with the search for the origins of architecture."[7] One of Ando's recent works is the Chichu Art Museum (Naoshima, Kagawa, Japan, 2000–04). The word *chichu* means "underground" in Japanese, and this building is almost entirely invisible from the neighboring hillsides. The luxuriant vegetation of the island assures that nothing but the skylights and open courtyards betray, at ground level, the presence of a building. Although Ando's declaration makes more reference to an architectural concept than to issues of environmental protection, the island of Naoshima in Japan's Inland Sea is now in good part a nature reserve. It may be interesting to note that Ando does not employ the newly fashionable vocabulary of "green" design very often, but the thick concrete walls he creates, and in the case of the Chichu Art Museum, a layer of earth covering the entire building, make for a very significant passive energy strategy. The inside of the museum also relies in good part on natural light.

XFROG TO THE RESCUE

The Japanese, with such figures as Itsuko Hasegawa or Toyo Ito, have long posited that architecture should engage in the creation of an artificial "nature" inspired by the forms of the natural world and yet decidedly manufactured in their aspect. The American specialist in biomimetics, Dennis Dollens, uses Xfrog software, which consists of "botanic, L-system algorithms used in computational biological simulations to grow plants and landscapes for laboratory tests and simulations." Of his various attempts to design towers or bridges that have a relation to the natural world, Dollens says: "The unifying concept behind these projects is that computational growth of architectural structures and systems can be influenced by biomimetic observations without falling into traditional categories of 'organic architecture.' In addition, the potential of biological science, biotechnology, and digital manufacturing, arriving at a union where architectural production and new possibilities for non-toxic architecture come together, begins to make sense" (see his Tree Tower, Los Angeles, California, USA, 2009). Unlike some architects, who seem content to state that a wooden house is "sustainable," Dollens is looking forward to new applications of computer science that might allow architecture itself to change, becoming somehow more like nature and thus less "toxic."

PLATINUM DREAMS

The LEED rating system addresses six major categories of questions in establishing its ratings: these are essentially judgments concerning sustainable sites, water efficiency, energy and atmosphere, materials and resources, indoor environmental quality, and, finally,

2   3

innovation and design process. There are four LEED ratings, which are determined on a basis of a total number of points, with 69 being the maximum where new construction or major renovations of commercial buildings are at issue. The ratings are Certified (26–32 points); Silver (33–38 points); Gold (39–51 points); and, finally, Platinum (52–69 points).

The Grand Rapids Art Museum (Grand Rapids, Michigan, USA, 2004–07) was designed by wHY Architecture, a firm founded in 2003 by Yo-ichiro Hakomori and Kulapat Yantrasast. Yantrasast worked before 2003 in the office of Tadao Ando, collaborating on such projects as the Fort Worth Museum of Modern Art. The Michigan Museum is an interesting case in point because a major donor for the project, local philanthropist Peter Wege, made obtaining a LEED certification a condition for giving money to the new project. With 10% of its construction materials recycled and extensive use of natural light or reuse of rainwater, the new structure is both intelligent in terms of sustainability and also boasts a strong, minimalist design that does bring to mind Yantrasast's previous working experience.

Although smaller in size, David Adjaye's first public commission in the United States, the Museum of Contemporary Art Denver (Denver, Colorado, USA, 2004–07), became the first museum to attain a LEED Gold rating. Low energy consumption, low greenhouse gas emissions, and the use of environmentally appropriate raw materials contributed to this rating. Adjaye, of course, has a considerable reputation in the United Kingdom, and his arrival in the United States for this project has been a closely watched event. Again, the combination of considerable design skills with an obvious concern for environmental issues proves that green is no longer the ugly duckling of contemporary architecture. Adjaye, though younger than Ando or Piano, for example, is certainly one of the rising stars of world architecture and his very visible participation in the movement toward sustainability is likely to influence many others.

FROM BABYLON TO THE ARCTIC

The extreme range of "green" projects that exist today might be symbolized by the selection of three works in this book, one built and two unbuilt. One unbuilt work is by the French team Agence Babylone. Their Active Nature proposal (Saclay, France, 2007, page 26) was the result of a competition launched by a group of 49 townships in the area of Paris. Although it is unlikely to be built in its proposed form, their idea consists in making radical use of the "productive capacities of nature," while preserving as much farmland as possible given predicted increases in population. Interesting because it is a combined scheme (in collaboration with architects SoA); this landscape and architecture design might well be the most reasonable path to the future, assuming the capacity of townships to impose an overall plan despite the extensive commercial interests involved. Mixing architecture and landscape design, futuristic green technology and a degree of clever presentation, the Active Nature project points, too, at the increasingly necessary collaboration between disciplines, especially when dealing with phenomena that are global rather than local.

Another recent project that illustrates a very different way to approach climate change is the Svalbard Global Seed Vault (Longyear-byen, Svalbard, Norway, 2007–08) by Peter Søderman of Barlindhaug Consult AS. Essentially a long tunnel and vault carved into a frozen mountain in Norway's Arctic north, this facility is designed to save the diversity of the world's seeds no matter what ecological or military crisis might befall the planet in the years to come. Though it is graced with a glittering work of art by Dyveke Sanne, the Svalbard Global Seed Vault has something of the Doomsday Machine about it—an icy vault that awaits a catastrophe that may well have already been announced.

2
Tadao Ando, Chichu Art Museum,
Naoshima, Kagawa, Japan, 2000–04

3
Tadao Ando, Tokyu Toyoko Line
Shibuya Station, Shibuya-ku, Tokyo,
Japan, 2005–08

It is not certain that the GBC would grant this facility a platinum rating, but it is hard to imagine a more ecological or "green" gesture in architecture. This building is a guarantee that crop diversity can be protected even as the waters rise and storms roll over the lands.

THE TIMES, THEY ARE A-CHANGIN'

The Malaysian architect Ken Yeang is one of the most committed international professionals in the area of sustainable design. His work in this area consists of very real buildings, but also of considerable thought and writing. In an essay entitled "What Is Green Design?" Yeang states: "If we integrate our business processes and design and everything we do or make in our built environment (which by definition consists of our buildings, facilities, infrastructure, products, refrigerators, toys, etc.) with the natural environment in a seamless and benign way, there will be no environmental problems whatsoever." One of Yeang's pet ideas over the years has been to bring nature into cities and buildings. Without going as far as his scheme for generalized ecomimesis, it can be admitted that his analysis of the organic and inorganic components of architecture is sensible and could lead to effective changes, short of turning cities into gurgling swamps of biological activity. "Our myriad of construction, manufacturing and other activities are, in effect, making the biosphere more and more inorganic," says Yeang. "To continue without balancing the biotic content means simply adding to the biosphere's artificiality, thereby making it increasingly more and more inorganic … This results in the biological simplification of the biosphere and the reduction of its complexity and diversity."[8]

Although Yeang's program is ambitious, he is getting to the heart of the matter. Might it be that green architecture is not so much about architecture as it is about survival? The aesthetics and internal quarreling of the architectural profession are obviously secondary considerations when it comes to finally stopping the war with nature that has resulted in the creation of "the asphalt jungle."[9] The problem, as Yeang points out, is not specific to architecture: it is systemic and concerns industry as much, if not more, than buildings. It concerns life habits and the use of resources, and the need for change before catastrophe ensues. Making green design fashionable is one tool at the disposition of architects, but it seems clear that it is now time, not to jump on the bandwagon, but to face the inevitable. With soaring gasoline prices and so much evidence of climate change, it is likely that the trend to green will be a lasting one. Architects who ignore this trend might just find they have been replaced by clever builders with a bold LEED AP stamped on their visiting card. Then again, good architecture never represented more than a small proportion of what is built in the world. The times, they are a-changin'.

Philip Jodidio, Grimentz, June 29, 2008

---

1   http://www.construction.com/about-us/press/green-building-outlook-strong-for-both-non-residential-and-residential.asp, accessed on May 3, 2013.
2   "EIA Annual Energy Review 2005," US Energy Information Administration, US Department of Energy.
3   Lenssen and Roodman, "Worldwatch Paper 124: A Building Revolution: How Ecology and Health Concerns are Transforming Construction," Worldwatch Institute, 1995. This reference, as well as the previous two, was noted in "Green Building Facts," published by the US Green Building Council (USGBC), June 2008.
4   Felicity Barringer, "The New Trophy Home, Small and Ecological," in: *The New York Times*, June 22, 2008.
5   Ibid.
6   Ibid.
7   "Reflections on Underground Space," in: *L'Architecture d'aujourd'hui*, May–June 2003.
8   Ibid.
9   *The Asphalt Jungle* is a 1950 film directed by John Huston, starring Sterling Hayden and Marilyn Monroe.

EINLEITUNG

KRIEG IM ASPHALTDSCHUNGEL

Keine Frage, „Grün" ist das Thema der Stunde. Nie gab es so viel Interesse an den ökologischen Folgen von Bauten wie heute. Allein in den Vereinigten Staaten wird das Volumen „grüner" Bauvorhaben bis 2013 auf voraussichtlich 100 Mrd. Dollar steigen und bis 2016 zwischen 204 und 248 Mrd. Dollar erreichen.[1] Dies ist kein unwesentlicher Beitrag im Kampf darum, die Umweltverschmutzung in den Griff zu bekommen, und bei der Suche nach verantwortungsvollen, „nachhaltigen" Baumethoden. Gebäude zählen zu den größten Verbrauchern von natürlichen Ressourcen und sind für einen erheblichen Teil der Treibhausgasemissionen und deren Auswirkungen auf den Klimawandel verantwortlich. In den Vereinigten Staaten verursachen Bauten 39 % aller CO_2-Emissionen.[2] Gebäude machen 40 % des globalen Verbrauchs von Rohstoffen aus.[3] Das Problem ist jedoch, dass „Grün" so in Mode gekommen ist, dass jeder versucht, auf den Zug aufzuspringen. Eine effektive Gegenreaktion auf die vagen Stellungnahmen zu den komplexen ökologischen Auswirkungen von Architektur war die Einführung von LEED (Leadership in Energy and Environmental Design). LEED ist ein anerkanntes Bewertungssystem des US Green Building Council (USGBC), mit dessen Hilfe sich Gestaltung, Bauweise und Betriebsverhalten grüner Bauten beurteilen lassen. Nach Angaben des USGBC „fördert LEED einen nachhaltigen Ansatz, der das gesamte Bauwerk im Blick hat, indem es den Leistungsstandard in fünf Schlüsselbereichen untersucht, die für Gesundheit von Mensch und Umwelt relevant sind: nachhaltige Grundstückserschließung, sparsamer Wasserverbrauch, Energieeffizienz, Materialauswahl sowie das Raumklima im Bau."

HEUTE KALIFORNIEN, MORGEN DIE WELT

2007 wurde der UK Green Building Council (UK-GBC) gegründet, um auch in Großbritannien Einheitlichkeit in das ökologische Bauen zu bringen. Ein von der Regierung berufenes Komitee für nachhaltiges Bauen hatte zuvor festgestellt, dass keine der mit Nachhaltigkeit befassten Körperschaften oder Organisationen klare Vorgaben für den gesamten Bereich bot. Diese Rolle sollte nun der UK-GBC übernehmen; sowohl die amerikanische Organisation als auch ihr britisches Pendant gehören zum Dachverband WorldGBC.

Obwohl sich das GBC-System zunehmend ausbreitet und manche Gemeinden und Regierungskörperschaften begonnen haben, entsprechende Anforderungen zum festen Bestandteil ihrer Vertragsvereinbarungen mit Architekten und Bauunternehmern zu machen, gibt es auch Zweifel. Umfragen zufolge sind zahlreiche führende Industrievertreter in den USA überzeugt, „grüne" Architektur sei teurer als ein „normales" Gebäude. Eine GBC-Studie zu Bauten in Kalifornien zeigte jedoch, dass sich „grüne Optimierungen innerhalb von drei Jahren amortisieren". Kürzlich veröffentlichte die *New York Times* einen Artikel über verschiedene Vorurteile und Thesen, die der Verbreitung der grünen Welle im Weg stehen — etwa das Vorurteil, grüne Gebäude seien hässlich. Diese Vorstellung ist vermutlich auf eine lange Tradition von Architekten zurückzuführen, die offenbar glaubten, umweltfreundliche Bauten müssten aus irgendeinem Grund unansehnlich sein. Kelly Meyer, eine von der *New York Times* zitierte Umweltschützerin, bemüht sich mit ihrem Mann, einem Bauunternehmer, zu zeigen, dass „etwas Energieeffizientes nicht so aussehen muss, als hätte man es aus dem untersten Regal eines Bioladens gefischt. Es muss nicht zwangsläufig nach Hanf riechen."[4]

FLUGEXPERIMENTE

Der amerikanische Architekt David Hertz bezeichnet die LEED-Richtlinien des GBC als „unflexibel und schwerfällig". Tatsächlich ist der Zertifizierungsprozess komplex und potenziell kostenaufwendig.[5] Hertz ist es gelungen, die Tragflächen einer ausgemusterten Boeing 747

4
*Michael B. Lehrer, Water + Life
Museum and Campus, Hemet,
California, USA, 2001–06*

4

auf innovative Weise in einen Neubau zu integrieren (747 Wing House, Santa Monica Mountains, Malibu, Kalifornien, 2007–09). Diese Art von Recycling dürfte ihm trotz ihrer Dramatik kaum eine der begehrten LEED-Platinmedaillen bescheren, dennoch scheint er entschlossen, sich gegen die bürokratischen Richtlinien des GBC aufzulehnen. Ein anderer, im gleichen Artikel der *New York Times* zitierter Architekt, Michael B. Lehrer, äußert sich erwartungsgemäß positiver über den Zertifizierungsprozess; schließlich wurde sein Water + Life Museum and Campus (Hemet, Kalifornien, 2001–06) unlängst als erstes Museum mit einer LEED-Platinmedaille ausgezeichnet.

INSELN IM FLUSS

Der japanische Architekt Tadao Ando interessiert sich schon lange für unterirdisches Bauen, was durchaus einen Bezug zu „grüner" Architektur haben kann. 2003 äußerte er: „Ich habe eine fast unbewusste Neigung zu unterirdischen Räumen. Wie auch immer das Grundstück aussehen mag, versuche ich Architektur zu schaffen, die nie dominanter ist als ihre Umgebung … An unterirdischen Räumen zu arbeiten, schlägt den Bogen zurück zu den Ursprüngen der Architektur."[6] Eines der jüngsten Projekte Andos ist das Chichu Art Museum/Naoshima (Naoshima, Kagawa, Japan, 2000–04). Das japanische Wort „chichu" bedeutet „unterirdisch", und das Gebäude selbst lässt sich von den Hügeln der Umgebung aus kaum ausmachen. Dank der üppigen Vegetation auf der Insel lassen nur die Oberlichter und offenen Innenhöfe ahnen, dass sich hier ein Gebäude verbirgt. Obwohl sich Andos Kommentar eher auf ein architektonisches Konzept als auf Umweltfragen bezieht, ist die im Seto-Binnenmeer gelegene Insel Naoshima zum Großteil Naturschutzgebiet. Früher wurde hier Bergbau betrieben. Es ist interessant, dass Ando nur selten auf das neuerdings in Mode gekommene Vokabular „grünen" Designs zurückgreift. Dennoch sind die massiven Betonmauern, die er entwirft und – im Fall des Chichu Art Museum – die Erdschicht, die das gesamte Gebäude bedeckt, eine bemerkenswerte Passivenergiestrategie. Hinzu kommt, dass die Innenräume des Museums zum Großteil natürlich belichtet werden.

EINSATZ VON XFROG

Die Japaner vertreten mit Persönlichkeiten wie Itsuko Hasegawa oder Toyo Ito schon lange die These, dass sich Architektur mit der Schaffung einer künstlichen „Natur" befassen sollte. Diese lässt sich zwar von Formen der Natur inspirieren, ist aber dennoch eindeutig künstlich. Dennis Dollens, ein amerikanischer Biometrikspezialist, arbeitet mit Xfrog, einer Software mit „botanischen L-System-Algorithmen, die bei biologischen Computersimulationen zum Einsatz kommen, um das Wachstum von Pflanzen und Landschaften für Labortests und Simulationen darzustellen". Dollens sagt über seine verschiedenen Versuche, Hochhäuser zu entwerfen, die von der Natur inspiriert sind: „Das gemeinsame Prinzip hinter diesen Projekten ist, dass computergeneriertes Wachstum von architektonischen Strukturen und Systemen von biomimetischen Erkenntnissen befruchtet werden kann, ohne in die traditionelle Kategorie ‚organische Architektur' zu fallen. Hinzu kommt, dass es sinnvoll ist, die Potenziale von Biowissenschaft, Biotechnologie und digitalen Fertigungsmethoden an einem Punkt zusammenzuführen, an dem sich architektonische Produktion und neue Optionen für nicht toxische Architektur kreuzen" (vgl. Dollens' Tree Tower, Los Angeles, Kalifornien, 2009). Anders als Architekten, die sich mit der Annahme zu begnügen scheinen, ein Haus aus Holz sei „nachhaltig", blickt Dollens voraus auf neue Anwendungen der Computerwissenschaften, die es der Architektur möglicherweise erlauben werden, sich fundamental zu verändern, in gewisser Weise naturähnlicher zu werden und damit weniger „toxisch".

5
*Barlindhaug Consult AS, Svalbard
Global Seed Vault, Longyearbyen,
Svalbard, Norway, 2007–08*

5

PLATINTRÄUME

Das LEED-Bewertungssystem berücksichtigt sechs Hauptkategorien: Diese befassen sich mit grundlegenden Fragen der Nachhaltigkeit der Grundstückserschließung, der Effizienz der Wassernutzung, mit Energie und Atmosphäre, Materialien und Ressourcen, dem Raumklima im Bau sowie Innovation und Entwurf. Es gibt vier LEED-Bewertungen, die je nach erlangter Gesamtpunktzahl ermittelt werden, wobei für Neubauten und umfassende Sanierungen von Gewerbebauten 69 Punkte die erreichbare Höchstzahl ist. Die Bewertungsstufen lauten: Zertifikat (26–32 Punkte), Silber (33–38 Punkte), Gold (39–51 Punkte) und schließlich Platin (52–69 Punkte).

Das Grand Rapids Art Museum (Grand Rapids, Michigan, 2004–07) wurde von wHY Architecture entworfen, einem 2003 von Yo-ichiro Hakomori und Kulapat Yantrasast gegründeten Büro. Vor 2003 war Yantrasast für Tadao Ando tätig und hatte an solchen Projekten wie dem Museum of Modern Art in Fort Worth mitgearbeitet. Das Museum in Michigan ist ein interessantes Beispiel, denn der Hauptsponsor des Projekts, der ortsansässige Philanthrop Peter Wege, hatte die LEED-Zertifizierung des Baus zur Bedingung für seine Spende gemacht.

David Adjayes erster öffentlicher Bauauftrag in den USA, das Museum of Contemporary Art/Denver (Denver, Colorado, 2004–07), ist zwar kleiner, aber dennoch das erste Museum, das mit einer LEED-Goldmedaille ausgezeichnet wurde. Adjaye hat sich in Großbritannien bereits einen Namen gemacht, und so wurde sein Einstand in den Vereinigten Staaten aufmerksam beobachtet. Auch hier ist es wieder die Kombination von außerordentlicher gestalterischer Begabung mit einem offensichtlichen Bewusstsein für Umweltbelange, die zeigt, dass „Grün" inzwischen keineswegs mehr das hässliche Entlein der Architektur ist. Auch wenn Adjaye jünger als etwa Ando oder Piano ist, darf man ihn sicherlich zu den aufstrebenden Stars der Architekturwelt rechnen.

VON BABYLON BIS IN DIE ARKTIS

Die extreme Bandbreite „grüner" Projekte heutzutage lässt sich anhand dreier Beispiele aus diesem Band veranschaulichen, eines davon gebaut, zwei bisher nicht realisiert. Eines der nicht gebauten Projekte stammt von dem französischen Team Agence Babylone. Ihr Entwurf Nature Active (Seite 26) war das Ergebnis eines Wettbewerbs, den 49 Stadtgemeinden im Pariser Umland ausgelobt hatten. Die Idee beruht im Wesentlichen darauf, die „produktiven Kapazitäten der Natur" angesichts eines prognostizierten Bevölkerungswachstums radikal zu nutzen und so viel Ackerland wie möglich zu erhalten. Der Landschafts- und Bauentwurf ist auch deshalb interessant, weil es sich um eine kombinierte Planung handelt (eine Zusammenarbeit mit den Architekten von SoA). Möglicherweise sieht so der sinnvollste Weg in die Zukunft aus, wenn man davon ausgeht, dass Gemeinden weiterhin befugt sein werden, Gesamtbebauungspläne zu beschließen.

Ein weiteres Projekt, der Global Seed Vault (Longyearbyen, Norwegen, 2007–08) von Peter Søderman (Barlindhaug Consult AS), zeigt eine völlig andere Herangehensweise an den Klimawandel. Im Grunde handelt es sich um einen langen Tunnel und einen Tresorraum, die in einen frostsicheren Berg geschlagen wurden. Zweck der Einrichtung ist es, die Vielfalt des globalen Saatguts zu schützen, ungeachtet aller ökologischen oder militärischen Krisen, die unseren Planeten in den kommenden Jahren heimsuchen mögen. Trotz des glitzernden Kunstwerks von Dyveke Sanne, das den Global Seed Vault auf Spitzbergen schmückt, scheint der Bau eher ein Weltuntergangsszenario heraufzubeschwören – eine eisige Gruft, die auf eine möglicherweise bereits angekündigte Katastrophe wartet. Es bleibt zu bezweifeln, dass der GBC der Einrichtung eine Platinauszeichnung zuerkennt, dennoch lässt sich kaum eine ökologischere oder „grünere" Geste in der Architektur vorstellen.

6
Ken Yeang, Mewah Oils Headquarters,
Pulau Indah Park, Port Klang,
Selangor, Malaysia, 2001–03

6

DIE ZEITEN ÄNDERN SICH

Der malaysische Architekt Ken Yeang zählt zu den weltweit engagiertesten Spezialisten im Bereich nachhaltiges Design. Seine Arbeit manifestiert sich ebenso in realen Bauten wie auch in seinen umfangreichen Thesen und Schriften. In seinem Aufsatz „What Is Green Design?" führt Yeang aus: „Wenn wir unsere Geschäftsprozesse und unser Design und alles, was in unserem baulichen Umfeld (das per definitionem aus Gebäuden, Anlagen, Infrastruktur, Produkten, Kühlschränken, Spielzeug etc. besteht) tun oder fertigen, nahtlos und auf positive Weise in das natürliche Umfeld integrieren, wird es keine Umweltprobleme geben." Eine von Yeangs Lieblingsideen im Lauf der Jahre war, die Natur in Städte und Gebäude zurückzuholen. Ohne dabei so weit zu gehen wie sein Plädoyer für eine allumfassende Ökomimesis, lässt sich durchaus einräumen, dass seine Analyse organischer und anorganischer Komponenten in der Architektur Sinn macht und einen effektiven Wandel bewirken würde, ohne unsere Städte gleich in gurgelnde Sümpfe biologischer Prozesse zu verwandeln. „Unsere zahllosen Bau-, Produktions- und anderen Aktivitäten machen die Atmosphäre im Grunde immer anorganischer", meint Yeang. „So weiterzumachen, ohne die biotischen Umweltfaktoren in ein Gleichgewicht zu bringen, trägt nur dazu bei, die Künstlichkeit der Biosphäre zu verstärken und sie immer anorganischer zu machen, diese und andere umweltschädigende Vorgänge wie etwa die Abholzung und Umweltverschmutzung also zu verschlechtern. Dies führt zu einer Simplifizierung der Biosphäre, der Minderung ihrer Komplexität und Vielfalt."[7]

Obwohl Yeangs Programm ehrgeizig ist, trifft es den Kern des Ganzen. Könnte es sein, dass es bei grüner Architektur im Grunde weniger um Architektur und vielmehr ums Überleben geht? Ästhetik und interne Streitigkeiten in der architektonischen Berufswelt sind offensichtlich sekundär, wenn es darum geht, endlich den Krieg mit der Natur zu beenden, der erst zur Entstehung des „Asphaltdschungels"[8] geführt hat. Das Problem, wie Yeang deutlich macht, ist kein spezifisch architektonisches, es ist ein systemisches Problem und betrifft die Industrie ebenso sehr (wenn nicht sogar stärker) wie unsere Bauten. Es geht um Lebensgewohnheiten, die Nutzung von Ressourcen und die Notwendigkeit eines Wandels, um einer Katastrophe zuvorzukommen. Grünes Design begehrenswert zu machen, ist ein Mittel, das Architekten zur Verfügung steht. Dennoch ist klar, dass es darum geht, nicht einfach auf den Trendzug aufzuspringen, sondern sich vielmehr dem Unausweichlichen zu stellen. Bei rasant steigenden Benzinpreisen und einer Vielzahl von Anzeichen für den Klimawandel ist damit zu rechnen, dass der grüne Trend von Dauer sein wird. Architekten, die diese Entwicklung ignorieren, werden bald feststellen müssen, dass sie von cleveren Bauunternehmern mit einer stolzen LEED-Akkreditierung auf ihrer Visitenkarte verdrängt worden sind. Andererseits war gute Architektur ohnehin nie mehr als ein kleiner Bruchteil dessen, was weltweit gebaut wird. Nun, die Zeiten ändern sich.

Philip Jodidio, Grimentz, 29. Juni 2008

1   http://www.construction.com/about-us/press/green-building-outlook-strong-for-both-non-residential-and-residential.asp, Zugriff am 3. Mai 2013.
2   „EIA Annual Energy Review 2005", US Energy Information Administration, US Department of Energy.
3   Lenssen und Roodman, „Worldwatch Paper 124: A Building Revolution: How Ecology and Health Concerns are Transforming Construction", Worldwatch Institute, 1995. Auf diese Quelle, ebenso wie die beiden vorigen, wird in „Green Building Facts" verwiesen, herausgegeben vom US Green Building Council (USGBC), Juni 2008.
4   Felicity Barringer, „The New Trophy Home, Small and Ecological", in: *New York Times*, 22. Juni 2008.
5   Ebd.
6   „Reflections on Underground Space", in: *L'Architecture d'aujourd'hui*, Mai–Juni 2003.
7   Ebd.
8   Der Film „Asphalt-Dschungel" unter der Regie von John Huston erschien 1950, in den Hauptrollen waren Sterling Hayden und Marilyn Monroe zu sehen.

INTRODUCTION

LA JUNGLE DE L'ASPHALTE EN QUESTION

Le vert est à la mode. Sans aucun doute. On ne s'est jamais autant intéressé à l'impact de la construction sur l'écologie. Rien qu'aux États-Unis, le poids économique de ce secteur en plein développement devrait représenter 100 milliards de dollars en 2013 et jusqu'à 2016 de 204 à 248 milliards de dollars.[1] C'est un fait qui n'est pas à négliger dans la bataille pour la réduction de la pollution et les recherches sur des méthodes de construction durables. Le bâti est l'un des plus gros consommateurs de ressources naturelles et participe dans une proportion significative aux émissions de gaz à effets de serre qui affectent le changement climatique. Aux États-Unis, il représente 39 % de toutes les émissions de CO_2.[2] Les bâtiments consomment globalement 40 % des matières premières.[3] La difficulté est que le « vert » est si à la mode que tout le monde saute dans le train et annonce des niveaux étonnants de durabilité ou de réduction de la consommation d'énergie. Une des réponses efficaces aux incertitudes qui entourent la question complexe de l'impact environnemental de l'architecture est le LEED (Leadership in Energy and Environmental Design), le système de référence de l'US Green Building Council (USGBC) pour la conception, la construction et la réalisation de bâtiments « verts ». Selon l'USGBC : « LEED permet une approche de la durabilité qui concerne la totalité du bâtiment par l'identification de ses performances dans cinq domaines clés de la santé humaine et environnementale : traitement écologique du site, économie dans l'utilisation de l'eau, efficacité de la consommation énergétique, sélections des matériaux et qualité environnementale intérieure. » L'USGBC certifie non seulement les constructions mais aussi les professionnels.

AUJOURD'HUI LA CALIFORNIE, DEMAIN LE MONDE

Le UK Green Building Council (UK-GBC) a été lancé en février 2007, pour coordonner les initiatives en faveur du mouvement de la construction écologique au Royaume-Uni. Le Sustainable Buildings Task Group du Gouvernement avait auparavant publié un rapport montrant qu'aucun des organismes ou agences concernés par l'écologie ne fournissait d'orientations claires à ce secteur en tant que tel. Le UK-GBC a donc été créé pour remplir ce rôle. Les deux conseils – américain et britannique – font partie du WorldGBC qui « assiste les conseils *Green Building* nationaux dont la mission commune est de créer un environnement bâti durable par des actions de transformation du marché ».

Si le système de notation des GBC commence à s'implanter sérieusement et que certaines administrations locales ou gouvernementales commencent à intégrer ses contraintes dans les cahiers des charges des architectes et des constructeurs, quelques doutes s'élèvent cependant. Des études montrent que beaucoup de responsables d'entreprises aux États-Unis, par exemple, sont convaincus que l'architecture « verte » est plus coûteuse que les méthodes traditionnelles. Une étude, commandée par le GBC en Californie, montre cependant que « les améliorations dues à la conception écologique se remboursent d'elles-mêmes en trois ans ». Le *New York Times* a récemment publié un article soulignant un certain nombre d'idées et d'enjeux qui ralentissent la progression de la vague verte. L'une est que les bâtiments écologiques sont laids. Cette vision fausse est probablement due à une longue histoire d'architectes qui pensaient qu'une construction écologique devait d'une certaine façon montrer ses secrets. Kelly Meyer, une environnementaliste citée par le quotidien, essaie avec son mari, qui est promoteur, de prouver « qu'un projet conscient des problèmes énergétiques ne doit pas avoir l'air d'avoir été trouvé sur l'étagère du bas d'une épicerie bio. Il n'a pas à sentir le chanvre ».[4]

7
wHY Architecture, Grand Rapids Art Museum, Grand Rapids, Michigan, USA, 2004–07

L'ESPOIR FAIT VIVRE

L'architecte americain David Hertz pense que les standards GBC LEED sont « rigides et gênants », et il est certain que ce processus de certification est complexe et coûteux.[5] Hertz a proposé une façon originale d'intégrer les ailes d'un vieux Boeing 747 dans une maison qu'il est en train de réaliser (747 Wing House, Malibu, Californie, 2007–09). Ce type de réutilisation, aussi spectaculaire puisse-t-il paraître, peut ne pas lui garantir de gagner la précieuse médaille de platine, mais il semble rebelle aux aspects bureaucratiques du système GBC. Un autre architecte, cité dans le même article du *New York Times*, Michael Lehrer, est sans doute un peu plus positif sur le processus de certification LEED depuis que son Water + Life Museum and Campus à Hemet en Californie (2001–06) est récemment devenu le premier musée à obtenir le LEED Platine.

ÎLES DANS LE COURANT

L'architecte japonais Tadao Ando s'est longtemps intéressé à l'idée de construire sous terre, ce qui peut en effet parfois répondre à des enjeux écologiques. Comme il le disait en 2003 : « J'ai un penchant presque inconscient pour les espaces souterrains. Quelle que soit la nature du site, j'essaie de créer une architecture qui ne s'impose jamais dans son environnement … Travailler sur un espace souterrain est lié à la recherche des origines de l'architecture. »[6] Ando a récemment construit le Musée d'art Chichu (Naoshima, Kagawa, Japon, 2000–04). Le terme « chichu » signifie « souterrain » en japonais et ce bâtiment est quasiment invisible des collines voisines. La luxuriante végétation de l'île fait que rien, si ce n'est des verrières et des cours, ne trahira au niveau du sol la présence d'une construction. Bien que les déclarations d'Ando se réfèrent davantage à un concept architectural qu'aux enjeux de la protection environnementale, l'île de Naoshima dans la Mer intérieure du Japon, est maintenant en grande partie une réserve naturelle après avoir été longtemps livrée à l'exploitation minière. Il est intéressant de noter qu'Ando n'emploie pas très souvent le nouveau vocabulaire à la mode de « conception verte », mais les épais murs de béton qu'il dessine et, dans le cas de ce musée, la couche de terre qui recouvre l'intégralité du bâtiment sont des stratégies d'énergie passive très efficaces.

XFROG À LA RESCOUSSE

Les Japonais, dont de grandes figures comme Itsuko Hasegawa ou Toyo Ito, affirment depuis longtemps que l'architecture doit s'engager dans la création d'une « nature » artificielle inspirée par les formes du monde naturel, mais cependant « fabriquées ». Le spécialiste américain de la biomimétique, Dennis Dollens, se sert du logiciel Xfrog qui consiste en « algorithmes botaniques inspirés de systèmes L, utilisés en simulations biologiques computationnelles pour des tests et des travaux en laboratoire sur la croissance des plantes et l'évolution des paysages ». De ses divers projets de tours et de ponts en relation avec l'univers naturel, Dollens précise : « Le concept unificateur derrière ces concepts est que la croissance computationnelle des structures et des systèmes architecturaux peut être influencée par des observations biomimétiques, sans tomber dans les catégories traditionnelles de "l'architecture organique". » Par ailleurs, le potentiel de la science de la biologie, des biotechnologies et de la fabrication assistée par ordinateur en arrive à une fusion à travers laquelle se dessinent et commencent à faire sens conjointement la production architecturale et de nouvelles possibilités d'architecture non toxique (voir sa Tree Tower, Los Angeles, Californie, 2007). À la différence de certains architectes qui semblent se satisfaire de dire qu'une maison en bois est « durable », Dollens regarde plus avant vers de nouvelles applications des sciences de l'informatique qui pourraient permettre à l'architecture elle-même de changer.

8

RÊVES DE PLATINE

Le système de notation LEED concerne six grandes catégories de problématiques. Ce sont essentiellement le terrain, l'utilisation efficace de l'eau, l'énergie, l'atmosphère, les matériaux et les ressources, la qualité environnementale intérieure et enfin l'innovation et le processus de conception. Il existe quatre niveaux de notation LEED déterminés par des points, 69 points étant le maximum accordé pour la construction neuve ou la rénovation d'immeubles commerciaux. Les certifications attribuées sont : Certifié (26–32 points), Argent (33–38 points), Or (39–51 points) et enfin Platine (52–69 points).

Le Grand Rapids Art Museum (Grand Rapids, Michigan, États-Unis, 2004–07) a été conçu par wHY Architecture, une agence fondée en 2003 par Yo-ichiro Hakomori et Kulapat Yantrasast qui avait auparavant travaillé chez Tadao Ando et collaboré à des projets comme le Museum of Modern Art de Fort Worth. Le musée du Michigan est intéressant en ce qu'un des principaux mécènes du projet, le philanthrope local Peter Wege, a fait de l'obtention de la certification LEED la condition d'un don pour le projet.

Bien que de dimensions plus réduites, la première commande publique reçue par David Adjaye aux États-Unis, le Museum of Contemporary Art/Denver (Denver, Colorado, États-Unis, 2004–07) a été le premier musée à obtenir la certification LEED Or. Adjaye jouit déjà d'une réputation considérable au Royaume-Uni et son arrivée aux États-Unis pour ce projet a été un événement particulièrement suivi. Là encore, la combinaison de son énorme talent et de ses préoccupations affichées pour les enjeux environnementaux prouvent que le vert n'est plus le vilain petit canard de l'architecture contemporaine. Adjaye, bien que plus jeune qu'Ando ou Piano, par exemple, est certainement l'une des étoiles montantes de l'architecture internationale.

DE BABYLONE À L'ARCTIQUE

La gamme extrêmement variée des projets « verts » qui existe aujourd'hui peut être symboliquement représentée par trois des projets montrés dans cet ouvrage, un réalisé, deux non construits. Française, l'agence Babylone a signé une proposition qui n'a pas encore passé le cap du chantier. Sa proposition intitulée « Nature Active » (Saclay, France, 2007, page 26) est née d'un concours lancé par un territoire de 49 municipalités de l'Ouest parisien. Elle consiste en un recours radical aux « capacités productives de la nature », tout en préservant au maximum les terres arables en prévision de l'accroissement attendu de la population. Intéressant parce qu'il est global (en coopération avec les architectes SoA), ce projet d'architecture et de paysagisme pourrait être la voie la plus raisonnable vers le futur, à condition que les municipalités aient le pouvoir d'imposer un tel plan d'ensemble malgré l'importance des intérêts commerciaux engagés.

Un autre projet récent qui illustre une approche très différente du changement climatique est le Svalbard Global Seed Vault ou « Caveau international de conservation de semences » (Longyearbyen, Spitzberg / Svalbard, Norvège, 2007–08) de Peter Søderman de Barlindhaug Consult AS. Consistant essentiellement en un long tunnel et une chambre forte creusés dans une montagne du nord de l'Arctique norvégien, cette installation a pour objectif de préserver la diversité des semences du monde entier, si une crise écologique ou militaire devait ravager la planète dans les années à venir. Bien qu'il soit décoré d'une œuvre d'art lumineuse de Dyveke Sanne, ce caveau glacé, en attente d'une catastrophe qui semblerait avoir déjà été annoncée, fait un peu penser à un prélude du Jugement dernier. Il n'est pas certain que cette réalisation puisse s'assurer une certification Platine, mais il est difficile d'imaginer geste plus écologique en architecture.

9
Dennis Dollens, Tree Tower,
Los Angeles, California, USA, 2009

9

LES TEMPS CHANGENT

L'architecte malaisien Ken Yeang est l'un des professionnels internationaux qui s'implique le plus dans la conception durable. Son œuvre dans ce domaine consiste à la fois en constructions réalisées, mais aussi en une réflexion approfondie et des écrits. Dans un article intitulé « What Is Green Design ? » (Qu'est-ce que la conception verte ?), Yeang écrit : « Si nous intégrons nos processus de travail, de conception et tout ce que nous faisons ou fabriquons dans notre environnement bâti (qui par définition comprend nos bâtiments, nos équipements, nos infrastructures, nos produits, réfrigérateurs, jouets, etc.) à l'environnement naturel de façon non agressive et sans rupture, il n'y aura plus de problème environnemental. L'une des idées préférées de Yeang au cours des années a été de faire entrer la nature dans les villes et les bâtiments. Sans aller aussi loin que son projet d'écomimesis généralisée, on peut admettre que son analyse des composants organiques et non organiques de l'architecture est sensible et pourrait apporter des changements effectifs, à condition de ne pas transformer les villes en marais bouillonnants d'activités biologiques. « Nos myriades de constructions, fabrications et autres activités rendent en effet la biosphère de moins en moins organique », explique Yeang. « Continuer ainsi sans rééquilibrer le contenu biotique signifie simplement renforcer le caractère artificiel de notre biosphère et donc la rendre de plus en plus inorganique, en exacerbant des actions destructrices de l'environnement comme la déforestation et la pollution. Ceci aboutit à la simplification biologique de la biosphère et à la réduction de sa complexité et de sa diversité », affirme-t-il.[7]

Bien que le programme de Yeang soit ambitieux, il est au cœur du sujet. Et si l'architecture verte n'était pas tant un problème d'architecture que de survie ? Les querelles esthétiques et internes de la profession architecturale sont à l'évidence secondaires lorsqu'il s'agit de mettre un terme à la guerre contre la nature qui a abouti à la création d'une « jungle d'asphalte »[8]. Le problème, comme insiste Yeang, n'est pas spécifique à l'architecture, il est de nature systémique et concerne autant si ce n'est plus l'industrie que la construction. Il concerne les habitudes de vie et l'utilisation des ressources et le besoin de changer les choses avant que ne se produise une catastrophe. Faire de la conception verte, ou écoconception, une mode est un outil à la disposition des architectes, mais il semble clair que le temps est venu non pas de sauter dans le train, mais de faire face à l'inévitable. Avec l'augmentation des prix de l'essence et de multiples preuves du changement climatique, il est probable que la tendance écologique durera. Les architectes qui l'ignorent risquent de se retrouver bientôt remplacés par des constructeurs plus intelligents dont la carte de visite arborera l'accréditation LEED AP. Mais là encore, la bonne architecture n'a jamais représenté plus qu'une petite partie de ce qui se construit dans le monde. Les temps vont changer.

Philip Jodidio, Grimentz, 29 juin 2008

1   http://www.construction.com/about-us/press/green-building-outlook-strong-for-both-non-residential-and-residential.asp, mis en ligne le 3 mai 2013.
2   « EIA Annual Energy Review 2005 », US Energy Information Administration, US Department of Energy.
3   Lenssen and Roodman, « Worldwatch Paper 124 : A Building Revolution : How Ecology and Health Concerns are Transforming Construction », Worldwatch Institute, 1995. Cette référence et les deux précédentes sont tirées de « Green Building Facts », publié par le US Green Building Council (USGBC), juin 2008.
4   Felicity Barringer, « The New Trophy Home, Small and Ecological », dans : *New York Times*, 22 juin 2008.
5   *Ibid.*
6   « Réflexions sur les espaces souterrains », dans : *L'Architecture d'aujourd'hui*, mai–juin 2003.
7   *Ibid.*
8   *The Asphalt Jungle (Quand la ville dort)* est un film réalisé par John Huston en 1950, avec Sterling Hayden et Marilyn Monroe.

ADJAYE ASSOCIATES

Adjaye Associates
23–28 Penn Street
London N1 5DL, UK

Tel: +44 20 77 39 49 69
Fax: +44 20 77 39 34 84
E-mail: info@adjaye.com
Web: www.adjaye.com

DAVID ADJAYE was born in 1966 in Dar es Salaam, Tanzania. He studied at the Royal College of Art in London (M.Arch, 1993), and worked in the offices of David Chipperfield and Eduardo Souto de Moura, before creating his own firm Adjaye Associates in London in 2000. He has been widely recognized as one of the leading architects of his generation in the United Kingdom, in part because of the talks he has given in various locations such as the Architectural Association, the Royal College of Art, and Cambridge University, as well as Harvard, Cornell, and the Universidade Lusíada in Lisbon. He was also the co-presenter of the BBC's six-part series on modern architecture "Dreamspaces." His Idea Store library in East London was selected by Deyan Sudjic for the exhibition highlighting "100 Projects that are Changing the World" at the 8th Venice Biennale of Architecture in 2002. His office employs a staff of 35, and some of his key works are: a house extension (Saint John's Wood, 1998); studio/home for Chris Ofili (1999); SHADA Pavilion (2000, with artist Henna Nadeem), Siefert Penthouse (2001); Elektra House (2001); and a studio/gallery/home for Tim Noble and Sue Webster (2002), all in London. Other work includes the Nobel Peace Center (Oslo, Norway, 2002–05); Bernie Grant Performing Arts Centre (London, 2001–06); Stephen Lawrence Centre (London, 2004–06); a visual arts building for the London-based organizations Iniva and Autograph ABP at Rivington Place (London, 2003–07); and the Museum of Contemporary Art Denver (Denver, Colorado, USA, 2004–07, published here), all in the UK unless stated otherwise.

DAVID ADJAYE wurde 1966 in Daressalam, Tansania, geboren. Er studierte am Royal College of Art in London (M.Arch., 1993) und arbeitete für David Chipperfield und Eduardo Souto de Moura, bevor er 2000 in London sein eigenes Büro Adjaye Associates gründete, das heute 35 Mitarbeiter beschäftigt. Er gilt weithin als einer der führenden Architekten seiner Generation in Großbritannien, u. a. wegen seiner Vorträge an so verschiedenen Institutionen wie der Architectural Association, dem Royal College of Art, der Universität Cambridge, der Harvard und der Cornell University sowie der Universidade Lusíada in Lissabon. Darüber hinaus war Adjaye Komoderator der sechsteiligen BBC-Serie „Dreamspaces" über moderne Architektur. Seine Bibliothek „Idea Store" in Ost-London wurde von Deyan Sudjic für die Ausstellung „100 Projekte, die die Welt verändern" für die 8. Architekturbiennale 2002 in Venedig ausgewählt. Zu seinen wichtigsten Projekten zählen: eine Hauserweiterung (St. John's Wood, 1998), eine Atelierwohnung für Chris Ofili (1999), der SHADA-Pavillon (2000, mit der Künstlerin Henna Nadeem), das Siefert-Penthouse (2001), das Elektra House (2001) und eine Kombination aus Atelier, Galerie und Wohnraum für Tim Noble und Sue Webster (2002), alle in London. Weitere Arbeiten sind das Nobel-Friedenszentrum (Oslo, Norwegen, 2002–05), das Bernie Grant Performing Arts Centre (London, 2001–06), das Stephen Lawrence Centre (London, 2004–06), ein Haus für visuelle Künste für die Londoner Organisationen Iniva (Institute of International Visual Arts) und Autograph ABP am Rivington Place (London, 2003–07) sowie das Museum of Contemporary Art Denver (Denver, Colorado, USA, 2004–07, hier vorgestellt), alle in Großbritannien, sofern nicht anders angegeben.

DAVID ADJAYE est né en 1966 à Dar es-Salaam, Tanzanie. Après des études au Royal College of Art à Londres (M.Arch, 1993), il travaille auprès de David Chipperfield et d'Eduardo Souto de Moura, avant de créer sa propre agence Adjaye Associates à Londres en 2000 et qui emploie actuellement 35 collaborateurs. Il est reconnu comme l'un des plus brillants architectes de sa génération au Royaume-Uni, en partie du fait des conférences qu'il a données au sein de divers lieux comme l'Architectural Association, le Royal College of Art et Cambridge University, mais aussi Harvard, Cornell et l'Universidade Lusíada à Lisbonne. Il a aussi été coprésentateur d'une série télévisée de la BBC en six parties sur l'architecture moderne *Dreamspaces*. Sa bibliothèque Idea Store dans l'est de Londres a été sélectionnée par Deyan Sudjic pour l'exposition « 100 Projets qui changent le monde » à la VIIIe Biennale d'architecture de Venise en 2002. Parmi ses réalisations les plus notables : l'extension d'une maison (Saint John's Wood, 1998) ; le studio-maison pour Chris Ofili (1999) ; le pavillon SHADA (2000, avec l'artiste Henna Nadeem) ; la Siefert Penthouse (2001) ; la maison Elektra (2001) et un studio-galerie-résidence pour Tim Noble et Sue Webster (2002), le tout à Londres. D'autres travaux comprennent le Centre Nobel de la Paix (Oslo, Norvège, 2002–05) ; le Bernie Grant Performing Arts Centre (Londres, 2001–06) ; le Stephen Lawrence Centre (Londres, 2004–06) ; un bâtiment pour les arts plastiques pour Iniva et Autograph ABP à Rivington Place (Londres, 2003–07) et le Musée d'art contemporain Denver (Denver, Colorado, États-Unis, 2004–07, publié ici), tous réalisés en Grande-Bretagne sauf exception.

MUSEUM OF CONTEMPORARY ART DENVER

Denver, Colorado, USA, 2004–07

Total floor area: 2320 m². Client: Museum of Contemporary Art Denver.
Cost: not disclosed. Project Director: Joe Franchina. Architect of Record: Davis Partnership

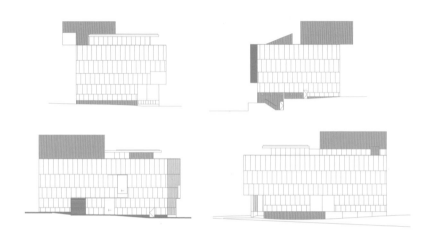

This is the first public commission of Adjaye Associates in the United States. Located on a prominent site, the new museum is at the corner of 15th and Delgany Street. The structure is due to be the first LEED Gold certified museum, thanks to its low energy consumption, greenhouse gas emissions, and use of environmentally appropriate raw materials. The new building includes 1858 square meters of exhibition, education, and lecture spaces, a bookshop, and a roof garden for outdoor art. The announced intention of the building is that it should "support rather than define the museum's mission." The architect has chosen to employ "a limited number of monochromes and textures" because of the "kunsthalle" or temporary-exhibition function to which most of the building is put. With respect to its immediate architectural environment, the structure has four stories in its main volume. As the architects explain: "In order to establish a visual relationship with the traffic moving in and out of the downtown area, the northeast façade is set at a slight angle to 15th Street. The southeastern corner of the building has been pulled forward so that it's visible from the metro station on Delgany Street." Thanks to its sincere modesty and its environmental credentials, the Museum of Contemporary Art Denver contributes to the emergence of a new generation of cultural facilities in the United States, perhaps less flamboyant but more responsible than its predecessors.

Dieses Museum ist der erste öffentliche Auftrag für Adjaye Associates in den USA und liegt prominent an der Ecke 15th Street und Delgany Street. Das Projekt wurde als erstes Museum mit einer LEED-Goldmedaille ausgezeichnet, was es seinem niedrigen Energieverbrauch, den geringen Treibhausgasemissionen und dem Einsatz umweltgerechter Rohmaterialien verdankt. Der Neubau umfasst 1858 m² Fläche für Ausstellungen, Bildungsprogramme und Vorträge, eine Buchhandlung sowie einen Dachgarten für Außenrauminstallationen. Ziel des Baus ist erklärtermaßen, das Museum in seinem Auftrag „zu unterstützen, statt diesen zu definieren". Der Architekt entschied sich für „eine begrenzte Farb- und Materialauswahl", da der Großteil des Baus für temporäre Kunstausstellungen vorgesehen ist. Mit Rücksicht auf das unmittelbare Umfeld präsentiert sich der Hauptbau als vierstöckiges Volumen. Der Architekt führt aus: „Um einen visuellen Bezug zum vorbeifließenden Zentrumsverkehr herzustellen, wurde die Nordostfassade leicht zur 15th Street versetzt. Die südöstliche Ecke des Gebäudes wurde vorgezogen, sodass sie von der U-Bahnstation an der Delgany Street aus zu sehen ist." Dank seiner Bescheidenheit und ökologischen Stärken trägt das Museum of Contemporary Art Denver unmittelbar dazu bei, dass in den Vereinigten Staaten eine neue Generation kultureller Einrichtungen entsteht, die möglicherweise weniger extravagant, dafür aber verantwortungsbewusster als ihre Vorläufer auftreten.

Il s'agit de la première commande américaine reçue par Adjaye Associates. Ce nouveau musée occupe un site très en vue à l'angle de 15ᵗʰ Street et de Delgany Street à Denver. Il est le premier musée certifié LEED Or, pour sa faible consommation énergétique, son bas niveau d'émissions de gaz à effet de serre et son utilisation de matériaux bruts écologiques. Il comprend 1858 m² de salles pour expositions, conférences et activités éducatives, une librairie et un jardin sur le toit pour l'exposition de sculptures. L'intention affichée est que ce bâtiment « soutienne plutôt que définisse la mission du musée ». L'architecte a choisi d'utiliser « un nombre limité de couleurs et de textures » pour s'adapter à la fonction principale de *Kunsthalle* du musée, c'est-à-dire d'accueil d'expositions temporaires. Respectant son environnement architectural immédiat, le bâtiment ne compte que quatre niveaux dans son volume principal. « Afin de créer une relation visuelle avec l'axe de circulation qui le longe, la façade nord-est est légèrement inclinée par rapport à 15ᵗʰ Street. L'angle sud-est a été tiré vers l'avant pour être visible de la station de métro de Delgany Street », explique l'architecte. Grâce à sa modestie, sa sincérité et sa valeur environnementale, ce musée participe à l'émergence d'une nouvelle génération d'équipements culturels aux États-Unis, peut-être moins flamboyante, mais plus consciente de ses responsabilités que ses prédécesseurs.

Sections, a plan, and images clearly indicate that the museum is made up of basic, rather austere forms, translating a willful modesty and rendering its green program easier to implement than extravagant glass forms might have, for example.

Schnitte, Grundriss und Fotos zeigen deutlich die schlichten, vergleichsweise strengen Formen des Museums. Dies zeugt von bewusster Bescheidenheit und macht es einfacher, das grüne Programm umzusetzen, als dies bei extravaganten Glasformen der Fall gewesen wäre.

Coupes, plan et photographies montrent que le musée est composé de formes basiques assez austères, qui traduisent une modestie volontaire mais facilitent la mise en œuvre de son programme de développement durable par rapport à des formes en verre extravagantes, par exemple.

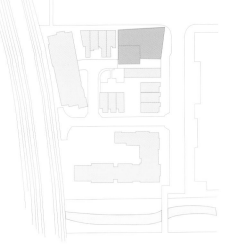

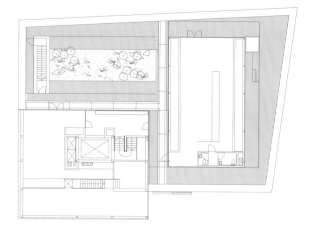

Interior views and a plan confirm the impression of strict, efficient geometry announced by the façades of the building. Natural light is ample where possible.

Innenansichten und Grundriss bestätigen den Eindruck einer strengen, effizienten Geometrie, den schon die Fassaden des Baus vermitteln. Wo immer möglich, fällt großzügig natürliches Licht ein.

Les vues de l'intérieur et ce plan confirment l'impression de géométrie stricte et efficace donnée par les façades. La lumière naturelle pénètre en abondance dans les volumes en fonction de l'éclairage souhaité.

AGENCE BABYLONE

Agence Babylone
56 rue de Paradis
75010 Paris
France

Tel: +33 1 49 23 51 01
Fax: +33 1 43 40 31 31
E-mail: contact@agencebabylone.com
Web: www.agencebabylone.com

Jeoffroy de Castelbajac was born in 1957. He obtained his degree in Landscape Architecture from the École Nationale Supérieure du Paysage de Versailles in 2003. He worked from 1980 to 2000 as a composer. Henri de Dreuzy was born in 1974, and also obtained his Landscape Architecture degree in 2003 from the Versailles school. Adrien Fourès was born in 1978, and completed the same studies as Castelbajac and Dreuzy the same year. This is also the case of Vincent Léger, born in 1978. The four landscape architects are co-managers of **AGENCE BABYLONE**. As they explain their work, Agence Babylone "intervenes essentially in the urban environment, be it on the scale of a town square or an entire region, with a passion for ecology that guides them in the development of new synergies between the city and nature." Along with their winning project Active Nature (Saclay, 2007, published here), their current work includes a park in Cormeilles-en-Parisis (2004–09); an avenue, gardens, and a square in Liévin (2006–09); gardens for the ZAC des Ponts Jumeaux (Toulouse, 2006–10); a redesign of public spaces in Rouen (2005–10), Villeneuve-le-Roi (2006–10), and in Chauray (2007–10); and the Saint-Louis Square in Choisy-le-Roi (2007–10), all in France.

Jeoffroy de Castelbajac wurde 1957 geboren. Er schloss sein Studium der Landschaftsarchitektur 2003 an der École Nationale Supérieure du Paysage de Versailles ab. Von 1980 bis 2000 arbeitete er als Komponist. Henri de Dreuzy wurde 1974 geboren und beendete sein Studium der Landschaftsarchitektur ebenfalls 2003 an der École National Supérieure du Paysage de Versailles. Adrien Fourès wurde 1978 geboren und schloss den gleichen Studiengang wie Castelbajac und Dreuzy im selben Jahr ab. Dasselbe gilt für Vincent Léger, der 1978 geboren wurde. Gemeinsam leiten die vier Landschaftsarchitekten die **AGENCE BABYLONE**. Nach eigener Aussage „greift [die Agence Babylone] im Grunde in die urbane Umwelt ein, sei es nun in der Größenordnung eines Marktplatzes oder einer ganzen Region, und zwar mit einer Leidenschaft für Ökologie, die ihr Leitschnur bei der Entwicklung neuer Synergien zwischen Stadt und Natur ist." Neben ihrem preisgekrönten Projekt Nature Active (Saclay, 2007, hier vorgestellt) gehören zu ihren derzeitigen Aufträgen ein Park in Cormeilles-en-Parisis (2004–09), eine Allee, Gärten und ein Platz in Liévin (2006–09), Gärten für die ZAC des Ponts Jumeaux (Toulouse, 2006–10), Umgestaltungen des öffentlichen Raums in Rouen (2005–10), in Villeneuve-le-Roi (2006–10) und in Chauray (2007–10) sowie die Place Saint-Louis in Choisy-le-Roi (2007–10), alle in Frankreich.

Né en 1957, Jeoffroy de Castelbajac est paysagiste DPLG de l'École nationale supérieure du Paysage de Versailles (2003). Il a été compositeur de musique de 1980 à 2000. Henri de Dreuzy, né en 1974, est également paysagiste DPLG de l'École nationale supérieure du Paysage de Versailles (2003). Adrien Fourès, né en 1978, a accompli les mêmes études que Castelbajac et Dreuzy et a été diplômé la même année. C'est également le cas de Vincent Léger, né en 1978. Les quatre architectes paysagistes dirigent ensemble l'**AGENCE BABYLONE**. Celle-ci, expliquent-ils, « intervient essentiellement en milieu urbain, de l'échelle du square à celle du territoire, avec une passion pour l'écologie qui nous guide dans le développement de nouvelles synergies, pérennes et actives, entre ville et nature ». En dehors du projet Nature Active (Saclay, 2007, publié ici), leurs réalisations, toutes en France, comprennent un parc à Cormeilles-en-Parisis (2004–09) ; une avenue, des jardins et une place à Liévin (2006–09) ; des jardins pour la ZAC des Ponts-Jumeaux (Toulouse, 2006–10) ; la remise en forme d'espaces publics à Rouen (2005–10), Villeneuve-le-Roi (2006–10) et Chauray (2007–10) ainsi que la place Saint-Louis à Choisy-le-Roi (2007–10), toutes en France.

ACTIVE NATURE

Saclay, France, 2007

Site area: 360 km². Client: OIN Massy Palaiseau, Saclay, Versailles, Saint-Quentin-en-Yvelines.
Cost: not disclosed. Collaboration: SoA architects, Alter Développement, Biodiversita

The OIN (Opération d'Intérêt National) or Operation of National Interest, a grouping of 49 towns in the suburbs of Paris, launched a competition in 2007 for ideas concerning its development over the next 30 years. With a projected increase in population of 350 000 people during the period, the region has placed a clear emphasis on sustainable development and ecology. Participants were asked to envisage the creation of 5000 homes per year over the 30-year span, while conserving 2000 hectares of existing farmland. Agence Babylone, with an emphasis on landscape design and urban development, worked on this competition with SoA architects, Biodiversita ecological engineers, and Alter Développement engineers. The team won the competition in the category for best use of the resources and natural patrimony of the site. Their idea was to make the maximum possible use of the "productive capacities of nature." Rather than imagining only the overall situation, they used a principle of successively larger zones, each responsible for its own resources. Existing forest areas would be preserved, and agricultural areas for fruit and vegetables added to urban zones. Agricultural zones, crossed by "ecological corridors" intended to protect the natural environment, would be used only for local production. A system of "green batteries" (*piles vertes*) produces energy in the process of treating waste water and garbage. New housing, coupled with retail and office space, would be concentrated in dense 120 x 160 meter "islands," allowing the overall population density of the region not to exceed 41 inhabitants per hectare.

OIN (Opération d'intérêt national) oder Operation im nationalen Interesse, ein Zusammenschluss von 49 Stadtgemeinden im Umland von Paris, schrieb 2007 einen Wettbewerb aus, um Ideen für die kommenden 30 Jahre zu entwickeln. Prognosen sagen für diese Zeitspanne ein Wachstum der dortigen Bevölkerung um 350 000 Menschen voraus, weshalb die Region besonderen Wert auf eine nachhaltige, ökologische Entwicklung legt. Prämisse für die Wettbewerbsteilnehmer war die Schaffung von 5000 Wohnungen innerhalb der kommenden 30 Jahre und zugleich die Erhaltung von 2000 ha Agrarland. Die Agence Babylone, mit ihrem Schwerpunkt auf Landschaftsgestaltung und Stadtentwicklung, arbeitete für diesen Wettbewerb mit SoA architectes, dem ökologischen Ingenieurbüro Biodiversita und dem Ingenieurbüro Alter Développement zusammen. Die Gruppe gewann den Wettbewerb in der Kategorie beste Nutzung von Ressourcen und des landschaftlichen Erbes des Areals. Ihre Idee war es, die „produktiven Kapazitäten der Natur" maximal zu nutzen. Statt nur die Gesamtsituation zu betrachten, arbeiteten sie nach einem Prinzip immer größer werdender Zonen, von denen jede für ihre eigenen Ressourcen verantwortlich ist. Bestehende Waldgebiete sollen erhalten, urbane Zonen um landwirtschaftliche Nutzflächen für Obst und Gemüse ergänzt werden. Landwirtschaftszonen, die ausschließlich der lokalen Versorgung dienen, werden von „ökologischen Korridoren" zum Schutz der Umwelt durchzogen. Ein System „grüner Batterien" („piles vertes") erzeugt Energie durch die Aufbereitung von Brauchwasser und Abfall. Die neuen Wohnanlagen, kombiniert mit Geschäfts- und Büroflächen, sollen sich auf „Inseln" von 120 x 160 m konzentrieren, sodass die Bevölkerungsdichte der Region 41 Bewohner pro Hektar nicht übersteigt.

L'OIN (Opération d'intérêt national) de Massy-Palaiseau, Saclay, Versailles et Saint-Quentin-en-Yvelines regroupant 49 communes de l'ouest de la banlieue parisienne a lancé un concours d'idées en 2007 pour préfigurer l'aménagement de son territoire sur les 30 prochaines années. Pour répondre à un accroissement prévu de la population de 350 000 personnes, l'accent a été mis sur le développement durable. Les participants devaient envisager la création de 5000 logements par an, tout en conservant 2000 ha de terres agricoles. L'agence, spécialisée dans le paysage et le développement urbains, a travaillé pour cette compétition en collaboration avec SoA architectes, les ingénieurs en écologie Biodiversita et les ingénieurs d'Alter Développement. L'équipe a remporté le concours dans la catégorie de la mise en valeur des ressources et du patrimoine naturel. Leur idée était d'utiliser au maximum « les capacités productives de la nature ». Plutôt que de n'imaginer que la situation globale, ils ont défini un principe de zones de plus en plus grandes, chacune en charge de ses propres ressources. Les zones forestières existantes seraient préservées et des secteurs agricoles de maraîchage créés à proximité des zones urbaines. Les terres agricoles, traversées par des « corridors écologiques », protégeraient l'environnement naturel et seraient cultivées pour la consommation locale. Un système de « piles vertes » produirait de l'énergie par le traitement des eaux et des déchets. Les nouveaux logements couplés à des bureaux et des commerces seraient concentrés en « îles » de 120 x 160 m permettant de ne pas dépasser une densité globale de population de 41 habitants par hectare.

An aerial view of the project shows its scale and also the close integration of green areas into and around the built-up zones.

Eine Luftaufnahme des Projekts macht dessen Dimensionen sowie die enge Integration der Grünflächen in und um die bebauten Zonen deutlich.

Une vue aérienne du projet montre son échelle et l'intégration étroite des espaces verts dans et autour du bâti.

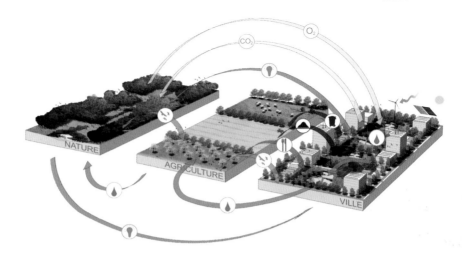

les processus écologiques pour développer la ville
nature active

A diagram and a rendering emphasize the close connection of the complex to nature. In the diagram, the flow of energy and sustenance from field and forest to built-up areas is depicted as a natural cycle.

Diagramm und Rendering veranschaulichen die Anbindung des Projekts an die Natur. Das Diagramm stellt den Energie- und Versorgungsfluss zwischen Feld und Wald und bebauten Zonen als natürlichen Zyklus dar.

Ce schéma et l'image de synthèse montrent les interactions entre le projet et la nature. Ci-dessus, les flux d'énergie et de production des cultures et de la forêt vers les zones construites sont représentés comme un cycle naturel.

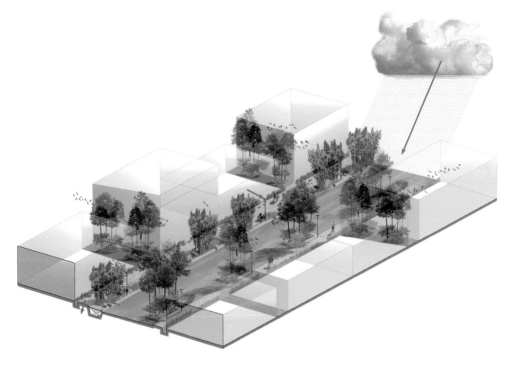

The biodiverse green areas surrounding the city can assimilate part of the CO_2 it produces and generate 34% of the oxygen needs. Forests and farms can provide food for 350 000 people, becoming an "agricultural garden."

Die biologisch vielfältigen Grünflächen um die Stadt absorbieren einen Teil des dort ausgestoßenen CO_2 und produzieren 34% des benötigten Sauerstoffs. Wälder und Bauernhöfe liefern Lebensmittel für 350 000 Menschen und werden zum „landwirtschaftlichen Garten".

Les zones vertes de biodiversité entourant la ville peuvent absorber une partie du CO_2 qu'elle émet et produire 34% de sa consommation d'oxygène. Des forêts et des fermes produisent la nourriture pour 350 000 habitants et deviennent un « jardin agricole ».

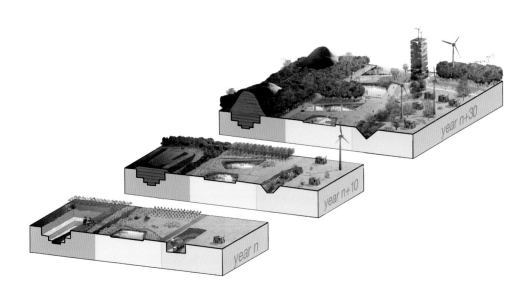

TADAO ANDO

Tadao Ando Architect & Associates
5–23 Toyosaki 2-Chome Kita-ku
Osaka 531, Japan

Tel: +81 6 6375 1148
Fax: +81 6 6374 6240

Born in Osaka in 1941, **TADAO ANDO** was self-educated as an architect, largely through his travels in the United States, Europe, and Africa (1962–69). He founded Tadao Ando Architect & Associates in Osaka in 1969. He has received the Alvar Aalto Medal, Finnish Association of Architects (1985); the Medaille d'or, French Academy of Architecture (1989); the 1992 Carlsberg Prize; and the 1995 Pritzker Prize. He has taught at Yale (1987), Columbia (1988), and Harvard (1990). Notable buildings include: Rokko Housing (Kobe, 1983–93); Church on the Water (Hokkaido, 1988); Japan Pavilion Expo '92 (Seville, Spain, 1992); Forest of Tombs Museum (Kumamoto, 1992); and Suntory Museum (Osaka, 1994), all in Japan unless stated otherwise. Other work includes the Awaji Yumebutai (Awajishima, Hyogo, Japan, 1997–2000); the Pulitzer Foundation for the Arts (St. Louis, Missouri, USA, 1997–2000); and the Modern Art Museum of Fort Worth (Texas, 1999–2002). He completed the Chichu Art Museum on the island of Naoshima in the Inland Sea in 2004 (published here), part of the continuing project that led him to create the Benesse House Museum and Hotel there beginning in the early 1990s. More recent work includes the Omotesando Hills complex (Tokyo, 2006); 21_21 Design Sight (Tokyo, 2004–07); and Tokyu Toyoko Line Shibuya Station (Shibuya-ku, Tokyo, 2005–08, also published here), and the Punta della Dogana for François Pinault (Venice, Italy, 2007–2009). Tadao Ando is working on an expansion of the Clark Art Institute (Williamstown, Massachusetts); the Abu Dhabi Maritime Museum (Abu Dhabi, UAE, 2006–); and a house for the designer Tom Ford near Santa Fe, New Mexico.

TADAO ANDO wurde 1941 in Osaka geboren. Als Architekt ist er Autodidakt und bildete sich in erster Linie durch seine Reisen in den USA, Europa und Afrika zwischen 1962 und 1969. 1969 gründete er in Osaka das Büro Tadao Ando Architect & Associates. 1985 erhielt er die Alvar-Aalto-Medaille des finnischen Architektenverbands, 1989 die Medaille d'Or der französischen Académie d'Architecture, 1992 den Carlsberg-Preis sowie 1995 den Pritzker-Preis. Er lehrte an den Universitäten Yale (1987), Columbia (1988) und Harvard (1990). Zu seinen beachtenswerten Bauten zählen: die Rokko-Wohnanlage (Kobe, 1983–93), die Kirche auf dem Wasser (Hokkaido, 1988), der japanische Pavillon auf der Expo '92 (Sevilla, Spanien, 1992), das Museum im Gräberwald (Kumamoto, 1992) und das Suntory Museum (Osaka, 1994), alle in Japan, sofern nicht anders vermerkt. Weitere Bauten sind u. a. das Awaji Yumebutai (Awajishima, Hyogo, Japan, 1997–2000), die Pulitzer Foundation for the Arts (St. Louis, Missouri, USA, 1997–2000) und das Modern Art Museum in Fort Worth (Texas, 1999–2002). 2004 konnte das Chichu Art Museum auf der Insel Naoshima im Seto-Binnenmeer fertiggestellt werden (hier vorgestellt), Teil eines fortlaufenden Projekts, für das er Anfang der 1990er-Jahre das Benesse House (Museum und Hotel) realisiert hatte. 2007–09 führte er im Auftrag von François Pinault den Umbau der Punta della Dogana in Venedig durch. Andere Projekte sind der Omotesando-Komplex (Tokio, 2006), das 21_21 Design Sight (Tokio, 2004–07) sowie der U-Bahnhof Shibuya der Tokyu-Toyoko-Linie (Shibuya-ku, Tokio, 2005–08, hier vorgestellt). Tadao Ando arbeitet derzeit an einer Erweiterung des Clark Art Institute (Williamstown, Massachusetts), dem Meeresmuseum von Abu Dhabi (VAE, 2006–) sowie an einem Haus für den Modedesigner Tom Ford unweit von Santa Fe, New Mexico.

Né à Osaka en 1941, **TADAO ANDO** est un architecte autodidacte formé en grande partie par ses voyages aux États-Unis, en Europe et en Afrique (1962–69). Il fonde Tadao Ando Architect & Associates à Osaka en 1969. Parmi ses prix et distinctions : la médaille Alvar Aalto de l'Association finlandaise des architectes (1985) ; la médaille d'or de l'Académie d'architecture (Paris, 1989) ; le Prix Carlsberg (1992) et le Prix Pritzker (1995). Il a enseigné à Yale (1987), Columbia (1988) et Harvard (1990). Il a notamment réalisé : les immeubles d'appartements Rokko (Kobé, Japon, 1983–93) ; l'église sur l'eau (Hokkaido, Japon, 1988) ; le pavillon japonais d'Expo '92 (Séville, Espagne, 1992) ; le musée de la Forêt des tombes (Kumamoto, Japon, 1992) et le musée Suntory (Osaka, Japon, 1994). D'autres réalisations comprennent le Awaji Yumebutai (Awajishima, Hyogo, Japon, 1997–2000) et la Fondation Pulitzer pour les Arts (St. Louis, Missouri, 1997–2000) et le Musée d'art moderne de Fort Worth (Texas, 1999–2002). En 2004, il a achevé le Musée d'art Chichu sur l'île de Naoshima en Mer intérieure du Japon, dans le cadre d'un projet à long terme pour lequel il avait déjà conçu le musée et l'hôtel de la maison Benesse au début des années 1990. Il a travaillé sur la rénovation de la Punta della Dogana pour François Pinault (Venise, 2007–09). D'autres interventions comprennent : le complexe Omotesando Hills (Tokyo, 2006) ; le 21_21 Design Sight (Tokyo, 2004–07) ; la station Shibuya/ligne Tokyu Toyoko (Shibuya-ku, Tokyo, 2005–08, publiée ici). Tadao Ando travaille actuellement à l'extension du Clark Institute (Williamstown, Massachusetts), au musée maritime d'Abu Dhabi (Abu Dhabi, EAU, 2006–) ainsi qu'une maison pour le créateur Tom Ford près de Santa Fe, au Nouveau-Mexique.

CHICHU ART MUSEUM

Naoshima, Kagawa, Japan, 2000–04

Site area: 9990 m². Floor area: 2573 m².
Client: Naoshima Fukutake Art Museum Foundation. Cost: not disclosed

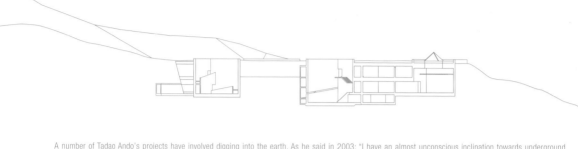

A number of Tadao Ando's projects have involved digging into the earth. As he said in 2003: "I have an almost unconscious inclination towards underground spaces. Whatever the nature of the site, I try to create architecture that is never imposing on its environment…. Working on underground space links up with the search for the origins of architecture."[1] Located on a hillside just opposite Benesse House (the Naoshima Contemporary Art Museum), the Chichu Art Museum was intended for a small number of works of art, some of which were designed specifically for the spaces. As the client describes it, the central work of the new Chichu Art Museum is a remarkable six-meter-long *Water Lily* painting by Claude Monet. A large-scale installation by Walter De Maria (*Time/Timeless/No Time*, 2004, granite, mahogany, gold leaf, concrete) has a place of honor here, together with three works by James Turrell: *Afrum, Pale Blue* (1968, projector); *Open Field* (2000, fluorescent light, neon tube); and *Open Sky* (2004, LED, xenon lamp), one of his famous "sky spaces" with an opening to the exterior. Once within the Chichu Art Museum, visitors are invited to follow a circuitous route past strong concrete walls alternating with open courtyards in the purest style of Tadao Ando. The only view to the exterior (aside from the sky seen in the courtyards and in Turrell's installation) comes at the end of the visit in a magnificent café looking out to the Inland Sea. Ando collaborated closely with the client, the curator Yuji Akimoto, Turrell, and De Maria. The result is one of the most astonishing and spiritual of Tadao Ando's works, where architecture, art, and nature truly come together. [1] "Reflections on Underground Space," in: *L'Architecture d'Aujourd'hui*, May–June 2003.

Bei mehreren Projekten Tadao Andos musste teilweise in die Erde hineingegraben werden. 2003 bemerkte er: „Ich habe eine fast unbewusste Neigung zu unter-irdischen Räumen. Wie auch immer das Grundstück aussehen mag, versuche ich Architektur zu schaffen, die nie dominanter ist als ihre Umgebung … An unterirdischen Räumen zu arbeiten, schlägt den Bogen zurück zu den Ursprüngen der Architektur."[1] Das Chichu Art Museum liegt auf einem Hügel unmittelbar gegenüber dem Benesse House (in dem sich das Naoshima Contemporary Art Museum befindet) und war für die Anzahl von Kunstwerken vorgesehen, von denen einige speziell für die neuen Räume geschaffen wurden. Laut Auftraggeber ist das zentrale Werk des neuen Chichu Art Museum ein beeindruckendes 6 m langes Seerosenbild von Claude Monet. Einen Ehrenplatz haben eine großformatige Installation von Walter De Maria („Time/Timeless/No Time", 2004, Granit, Mahagoni, Blattgold, Beton) sowie drei Arbeiten von James Turrell, „Afrum, Pale Blue" (1968, Projektor), „Open Field" (2000, fluoreszierendes Licht, Neonröhre) und „Open Sky" (2004, LED, Xenonleuchte), eines seiner berühmten „Skyspaces" mit Öffnung nach außen. Haben die Besucher das Chichu Art Museum betreten, werden sie eingeladen, einem kreisförmigen Rundgang zu folgen, der sich an den für Tadao Ando so typischen Betonmauern und offenen Innenhöfen entlangzieht. Der einzige Blick nach draußen (abgesehen vom Himmel, der in den Innenhöfen und in Turrells Installation zu sehen ist) bietet sich am Ende des Rundgangs in einem atemberaubenden Café mit Aussicht auf das Binnenmeer. Ando arbeitete eng mit dem Auftraggeber, dem Kurator Yuji Akimoto, mit Turrell und De Maria zusammen. Das Ergebnis ist eines der erstaunlichsten und spirituellsten Werke Andos, in dem Architektur, Kunst und Natur wahrhaft zueinander finden. [1] „Reflections on Underground Space", in: *L'Architecture d'Aujourd'hui*, Mai–Juni 2003.

Un certain nombre de projets de Tadao Ando ont déjà impliqué le creusement du sol et l'enfouissement. Comme il disait en 2003 : « J'ai un penchant presque inconscient pour les espaces souterrains. Quelle que soit la nature du site, j'essaie de créer une architecture qui ne s'impose jamais dans son environnement … Travailler sur un espace souterrain est lié à la recherche des origines de l'architecture. »[1] Situé à flanc de colline, juste en face de la maison Benesse (Musée d'art contemporain de Naoshima), le Musée d'art Chichu a été conçu pour ne présenter qu'un nombre d'œuvres réduit dont certaines ont été spécialement réalisées pour ses salles. Son commanditaire précise que l'œuvre centrale de ce nouveau musée est un superbe *Nymphéas* de Claude Monet de 6 m de long. Une grande installation de Walter De Maria (*Time/Timeless/No Time*, 2004, granit, acajou, feuille d'or, béton) occupe la place d'honneur, ainsi que trois œuvres de James Turrell, *Afrum, Pale Blue* (1968, projecteur), *Open Field* (2000, lumière fluorescente) et *Open Sky* (2004, LED, lampe xénon) et l'un de ses fameux *sky spaces* qui s'ouvrent sur l'extérieur. Une fois entrés dans le musée, les visiteurs sont invités à suivre un parcours qui se déroule entre de puissants murs de béton alternant avec des cours ouvertes du plus pur style Ando. La seule vue sur l'extérieur (en dehors du ciel visible de la cour et de l'installation de Turrell) est un panorama sur la mer du Japon que l'on admire du magnifique café situé en fin de visite. Ando a étroitement collaboré avec le conservateur, Yuji Akimoto, Turrell et De Maria. C'est l'une de ses réalisations les plus étonnantes et les plus empreintes de spiritualité : l'architecture fusionne ici l'art et la nature. [1] « Reflections on Underground Space », dans : *L'Architecture d'Aujourd'hui*, mai–juin 2003.

A section (above) shows that the volumes of the museum lie essentially below grade. A view of the hill on which it is sited (top right) shows just how little of the architecture protrudes, but openings still allow light to penetrate the complex.

Ein Schnitt (oben) verrät, dass die Baukörper des Museums zum Großteil unter der Erde liegen. Ein Blick über den Hügel (rechts oben) zeigt, wie geringfügig das Gebäude aus dem Boden hervorragt, wenngleich Öffnungen Licht einfallen lassen.

La coupe ci-dessus montre que les salles du musée sont essentiellement situées en sous-sol. Une vue du sommet de la montagne (en haut à droite) montre à quel point l'architecture se fait discrète. Les ouvertures sont des capteurs de lumière.

The plan of the museum shows its
skewed, yet geometric lines. Open
courtyards allow for light and air to
penetrate the entrance sequence
(below).

Le plan du musée est géométrique-
ment articulé en oblique. Les cours
ouvertes laissent pénétrer l'air et la
lumière dans la séquence de l'entrée
(ci-dessous).

Anhand des Grundrisses wird die
schiefe und doch geometrische
Linienführung des Museums deutlich.
Offene Innenhöfe lassen Licht und
Luft in den Eingangsbereich hinein
(unten).

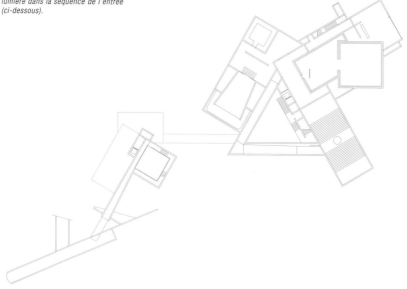

Above, the space designed in a collaboration between the architect, the artist, and the curator houses Walter De Maria's Time/Timeless/No Time. Below, an opening toward the sea, and a plan showing the museum with the outline of former salt pans leading down the hill to the sea.

Der Raum (oben) wurde in enger Zusammenarbeit zwischen Architekt, Künstler und Kurator gestaltet und präsentiert Walter De Marias Installation Time/Timeless/No Time. Unten ein Durchblick auf das Meer und ein Grundriss, der das Museum und den Verlauf alter Salzpfannen den Hügel hinunter bis zum Meer zeigt.

Ci-dessus, un espace conçu en collaboration entre l'architecte, l'artiste et le conservateur du musée accueille Time/Timeless/No Time, œuvre de Walter De Maria. Ci-dessous, une ouverture vers la mer et un plan montrent le musée et les contours d'anciens marais salants descendant de la colline vers la mer.

TOKYU TOYOKO LINE SHIBUYA STATION

Shibuya-ku, Tokyo, Japan, 2005–08

Floor area: 27 725 m². Client: Tokyu Corporation. Cost: not disclosed

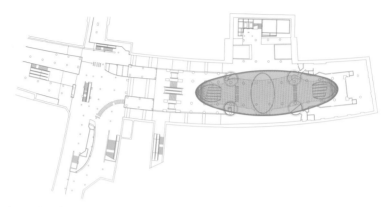

As Tadao Ando points out, the architectural design of subway stations is usually a minimal affair undertaken after the engineering has been completed. In this instance, the architect was able to work with the engineering team from the outset. The resulting project is described as a "hypogenous ship floating deep under the ground." The unusual use of the botanical term "hypogenous," meaning "growing on the underside of something such as a leaf," gives both a natural and a physical context to the design. A void in an egg-shaped shell with an oval plan runs through the site from the second to the fifth levels below grade. This station might be imagined as the first "underground landmark" of contemporary architecture. Ando has also created a natural ventilation system for the space, another unusual feature in subway design. Glass fiber reinforced concrete (GFRC) was used as the material for the shell. Lighter than Ando's favorite concrete, it also allows the use of a panel cooling system consistent with natural ventilation. Shibuya Station, which includes other areas not designed by Tadao Ando, serves three million travelers a day, which means that his facility will be widely seen and used. As the architect says: "Shibuya Station is a major public space within the city and because of this important public nature we wanted to create an urban infrastructure that transcends its functionality, offering people a timeless spatial experience that will remain in their minds and will be embedded in the urban memory."

Tadao Ando weist darauf hin, dass die architektonische Gestaltung von U-Bahnstationen normalerweise ein Minimaleingriff ist, der nach Abschluss der technischen Planung stattfindet. In diesem Fall jedoch konnte der Architekt von Anfang an mit den Ingenieuren zusammenarbeiten. Das so gewachsene Projekt beschreibt er als „hypogenes Schiff, das tief unter der Erde schwebt". Der ungewöhnliche Gebrauch des botanischen Begriffs „hypogen", der soviel bedeutet wie „an der Unterseite von etwas wachsend" (etwa an einem Blatt), ordnet den Entwurf in einen natürlichen und physischen Kontext ein. Durch das gesamte zweite bis fünfte Untergeschoss zieht sich eine schalenartige, eiförmige Aussparung mit ovalem Grundriss. Dieser Bahnhof ist vielleicht der erste „unterirdische Meilenstein" der zeitgenössischen Architektur. Darüber hinaus entwickelte Ando ein natürliches Belüftungssystem, ein weiteres ungewöhnliches Element bei der Gestaltung von U-Bahnhöfen. Für die Schale wurde Glasfaserbeton (GFB) verwendet. Leichter als Andos bevorzugter Beton, erlaubt er den Einsatz einer Deckenkühlung, was einer natürlichen Belüftung entspricht. Der Bahnhof Shibuya, der auch Abschnitte umfasst, die nicht von Ando entworfen wurden, wird täglich von drei Millionen Fahrgästen genutzt, was dem Bau breite Aufmerksamkeit bescheren dürfte. Der Architekt führt aus: „Der Bahnhof Shibuya ist ein wichtiger öffentlicher Raum in der Stadt und gerade wegen seiner bedeutenden öffentlichen Funktion wollten wir eine Infrastruktur schaffen, die über die reine Funktionalität hinausgeht, wollten den Menschen ein zeitloses Raumerlebnis bieten, an das sie sich erinnern und das sich in das urbane Gedächtnis einprägt."

Comme le fait remarquer Tadao Ando, la conception architecturale des stations de métro est généralement une petite intervention entreprise une fois les problèmes d'ingénierie résolus. Ici, l'architecte a pu travailler avec l'équipe d'ingénierie dès le départ. Le résultat de leurs travaux est décrit comme « un bateau symbiotique en suspension dans les profondeurs de la terre ». L'utilisation rare du terme de botanique « symbiotique » qui signifie « pousser en symbiose » fournit à la fois le contexte naturel et physique du projet. Un vide de plan ovale dans une coque ovoïde traverse le site entre les deuxième et cinquième niveaux en sous-sol. Cette station pourrait être qualifiée de premier « monument souterrain » de l'architecture contemporaine. Ando a également créé un système de ventilation naturelle pour ces volumes, autre élément inhabituel dans un projet souterrain. La coque est en béton renforcé de fibre de verre (GFRC). Plus léger que le béton habituel de l'architecte, il permet d'utiliser un système de panneaux refroidissant l'air en conjonction avec la ventilation naturelle. Cette station, qui comprend d'autres parties non conçues par Ando, accueille 3 millions de voyageurs par jour. « La station Shibuya est un espace public majeur à l'intérieur de la ville et du fait de cette nature publique très présente, nous souhaitions créer une infrastructure urbaine qui transcende sa fonctionnalité, offrant aux usagers une expérience spatiale intemporelle qui restera dans leur esprit, comme une incarnation de la mémoire urbaine. »

A plan above shows the oblong form of the new station while the image to the right shows the reality of Ando's soaring curves—an uncommon sight in the subways of Tokyo.

Der Grundriss oben zeigt die längliche Form der neuen Station, während die Abbildung rechts die Wirkung der hohen Bögen vermittelt – ein für Tokios U-Bahnsystem untypischer Anblick.

Le plan ci-dessus montre la forme oblongue de la nouvelle gare. À droite, le jaillissement des courbes d'Ando offre une vision étonnante dans le métro de Tokyo.

Oval forms characterize the space,
as seen in the openings between the
various levels, assisting in the natural
flow of air that is part of the design.

Ovale Formen dominieren den Raum,
wie sich an den Öffnungen zwischen
den Geschossebenen zeigt. Zugleich
fördern sie die natürliche Ventilation,
die im Entwurf eingeplant wurde.

Les espaces se caractérisent par des
formes ovales, à l'instar des ouvertures pratiquées entre les niveaux
qui facilitent la ventilation naturelle
prévue dans le projet.

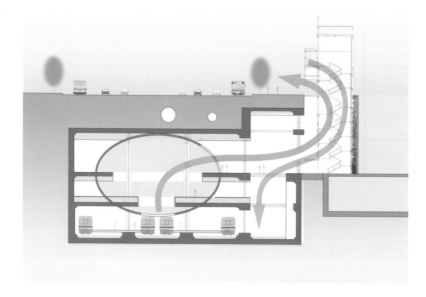

SHIGERU BAN

Shigeru Ban Architects / 5–2–4 Matsubara / Setagaya-ku
Tokyo 156–0043 / Japan
Tel: +81 3 3324 6760 / Fax: +81 3 3324 6789
E-mail: tokyo@shigerubanarchitects.com / Web: www.shigerubanarchitects.com

Born in 1957 in Tokyo, **SHIGERU BAN** studied at SCI-Arc from 1977 to 1980. He attended the Cooper Union School of Architecture, where he studied under John Hejduk (1980–82). He worked in the office of Arata Isozaki (1982–83), before founding his own firm in Tokyo in 1985. His work includes numerous exhibition designs (including the Alvar Aalto show at the Axis Gallery, Tokyo, 1986). His buildings include the Odawara Pavilion (Kanagawa, 1990); the Paper Gallery (Tokyo, 1994); the Paper House (Lake Yamanaka, 1995); and the Paper Church (Takatori, Hyogo, 1995), all in Japan. He has also designed ephemeral structures, such as his Paper Refugee Shelter made with plastic sheets and paper tubes for the United Nations High Commissioner for Refugees (UNHCR). He designed the Japanese Pavilion at Expo 2000 in Hanover. He installed his Paper Temporary Studio on top of the Centre Georges Pompidou in Paris to work on the new Centre Pompidou in Metz (France, 2004–09). Other recent work includes the Papertainer Museum (Seoul Olympic Park, Songpa-Gu, South Korea, 2003–06, published here); the Nicolas G. Hayek Center (Tokyo, 2005–07); the Takatori Church (Kobe, Hyogo, 2005–07), the last two in Japan; and the disaster relief Post-Tsunami Rehabilitation Houses (Kirinda, Hambantota, Sri Lanka, 2005–07). Current work includes a small museum of canal history in Pouilly-en-Auxois (France); the Schwartz Residence (Sharon, Connecticut); Forest Park Pavilion, Bamboo Gridshell-02 (St. Louis, Missouri); Mul(ti)houses (Mulhouse, France); Sagaponac House, Furniture House-05 (Long Island, New York); and Hanegi Forest Annex (Setagaya, Tokyo).

SHIGERU BAN, 1957 in Tokio geboren, studierte von 1977 bis 1980 am Southern California Institute of Architecture (SCI-Arc). 1980 bis 1982 besuchte er die Cooper Union School of Architecture in New York, wo er bei John Hejduk studierte. Bevor er 1985 sein eigenes Büro in Tokio gründete, arbeitete er bei Arata Isozaki (1982–83). Sein Werk umfasst zahlreiche Ausstellungsarchitekturen (etwa für die Alvar-Aalto-Ausstellung in der Axis Gallery, Tokio, 1986). Zu seinen Bauten zählen zudem der Odawara-Pavillon (Kanagawa, 1990), die Paper Gallery (Tokio, 1994), das Paper House (Yamanaka-See, 1995) sowie die Paper Church (Takatori, Hyogo, 1995), alle in Japan. Darüber hinaus entwarf Ban temporäre Konstruktionen wie Flüchtlingsquartiere aus Papier, die er aus Plastikplanen und Papphröhren für den UN-Flüchtlingskommissar (UNHCR) realisierte. Für die Expo 2000 in Hannover entwarf er den japanischen Pavillon. Auf dem Dach des Centre Georges Pompidou in Paris hat Ban sich ein temporäres Atelier aus Papier eingerichtet, um dort am neuen Centre Pompidou für Metz arbeiten zu können (2004–09). Andere jüngere Arbeiten sind u. a. das Papertainer Museum (Olympiapark Seoul, Songpa-Gu, Südkorea, 2003–06, hier vorgestellt), das Nicolas G. Hayek Center (Tokio, 2005–07) und die Takatori-Kirche (Kobe, Hyogo, 2005–07), beide in Japan, sowie Einrichtungen für die Katastrophenhilfe nach dem großen Tsunami (Kirinda, Hambantota, Sri Lanka, 2005–07). In Arbeit sind derzeit ein kleines Museum für Kanalgeschichte in Pouilly-en-Auxois (Frankreich), die Schwartz Residence (Sharon, Connecticut), der Forest Park Pavilion, das Bamboo Gridshell-02 (St. Louis, Missouri), die Mul(ti)houses (Mulhouse, Frankreich), das Sagaponac House oder Furniture House-05 (Long Island, New York) sowie ein Anbau im Hanegi-Wald (Setagaya, Tokio).

Né en 1957 à Tokyo, **SHIGERU BAN** a étudié à SCI-Arc de 1977 à 1980 et à la Cooper Union School of Architecture, auprès de John Hejduk (1980–82). Il a travaillé dans l'agence d'Arata Isozaki (1982–83), avant de fonder la sienne à Tokyo en 1985. Son œuvre comprend de nombreuses installations d'expositions (Alvar Aalto Show à la Axis Gallery, Tokyo, 1986) et des bâtiments comme le pavillon Odawara (Kanagawa, 1990) ; la Paper Gallery (Tokyo, 1994) ; la Paper House (Lake Yamanaka, 1995) et la Paper Church (Takatori, Hyogo, 1995), tous au Japon. Il a également conçu des structures éphémères comme un abri en carton pour réfugiés, constitué de films plastiques et de tubes en carton pour le Haut-Commissariat des Nations unies pour les Réfugiés (HCR). Il a dessiné le Pavillon japonais pour l'Expo 2000 à Hanovre. Son Atelier de carton temporaire a été installé au sommet du Centre Georges Pompidou à Paris comme annexe de son agence pour le nouveau Centre Pompidou à Metz (France, 2004–09). Parmi d'autres réalisations récentes : Le Papertainer Museum (Séoul, Parc olympique, Songpa-Gu, Corée du Sud, 2003–06, publié ici) ; le Nicolas G. Hayek Center (Tokyo, 2005–07) ; l'église de Takatori (Kobé, Hyogo, 2005–07), tous deux au Japon, et les maisons de reconstruction post-tsunami (Kirinda, Hambantota, Sri Lanka, 2005–07). Actuellement, il travaille sur le projet d'un petit musée sur l'histoire d'un canal à Pouilly-en-Auxois (France) ; la résidence Schwartz (Sharon, Connecticut) ; le Forest Park Pavilion, Bamboo Gridshell-02 (St. Louis, Missouri) ; les Mul(ti)houses (Mulhouse, France) ; la maison Sagaponac ou Furniture House-05 (Long Island, New York) et l'annexe de la forêt d'Hanegi (Setagaya, Tokyo).

PAPERTAINER MUSEUM

Seoul Olympic Park, Songpa-Gu, South Korea, 2003–06

Floor area: 3454 m². Client: Designhouse Inc. Cost: not disclosed.
Collaboration: Shigeru Ban Architects + KACI International (Kyeong-Sik Yoon, Principal)

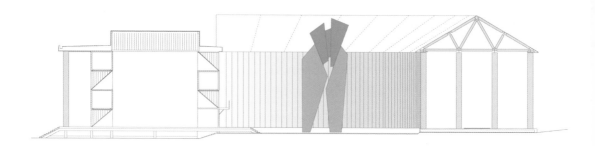

This unusual project involves the combination of two of Shigeru Ban's favorite construction elements—structural paper tubes and used shipping containers—both of which represent a significant contribution to the reduction of the overall ecological impact of such a structure. Ban had already designed a temporary art-exhibition facility with these elements (Nomadic Museum, Pier 54, New York, 2005). Composed of a colonnaded, rectangular container structure ten meters high and a semicircular "Paper Gallery" enclosing an arc-shaped inner courtyard, this was a temporary exhibition pavilion for the celebration of the 30th anniversary of the Korean publisher Designhouse. The forested 14 214-square-meter site is located in the Olympic Park of Seoul. The first "container wall" was intended for exhibition booths, while the sec-ond housed office and storage areas. The alternating placement of the containers, with regular voids, animated the main façade, while the paper tube colonnade in front of the structure lent it a gravitas that it might have lacked given the use of such industrial materials. The semicircular Paper Gallery was made of two walls composed of 75-centimeter-diameter paper tube poles, with a roof truss made of 30-centimeter paper tubes.

Dieses ungewöhnliche Projekt kombiniert zwei bevorzugte Bauelemente des Architekten – konstruktive Röhren aus Papier und gebrauchte Schiffscontainer. Beide tragen entscheidend dazu bei, die negativen ökologischen Folgen eines solchen Bauwerks zu reduzieren. Ban hatte aus denselben Elementen schon einmal eine temporäre Kunsthalle errichtet (Nomadic Museum, Pier 54, New York, 2005). Der zum 30. Geburtstag des koreanischen Verlags Designhouse realisierte temporäre Ausstellungsraum bestand aus einer 10 m hohen, mit Säulen umstandenen rechteckigen Containerkonstruktion und einer halbkreisförmigen „Papiergalerie", die einen bogenförmigen Innenhof umschloss. Das bewaldete 14 214 m² große Grundstück liegt im Olympiapark von Seoul. Die erste „Containerwand" war für Ausstellungsräume vorgesehen, in der zweiten befanden sich Büro- und Lagerräume. Die rhythmische Anordnung der Container mit regelmäßigen Aussparungen belebte die Hauptfassade. Zugleich verliehen die vorgelagerten Kolonnaden aus Papierröhren dem Bau eine Würde, die er wegen der industriellen Baumaterialien sonst wohl nicht gehabt hätte. Die halbrunde Papiergalerie bestand aus zwei Wänden, die wiederum aus Papierröhren mit 75 cm Durchmesser konstruiert waren. Seinen Abschluss fand das Ganze mit einem Dachstuhl aus Papierröhren mit 30 cm Durchmesser.

Cet étonnant projet combine deux des matériaux de construction favoris de Shigeru Ban, les tubes de carton et les conteneurs de transport qui, tous deux, représentent une contribution significative à la réduction de l'impact écologique global de ce bâtiment. Ban avait antérieurement conçu des installations d'expositions temporaires à partir d'éléments semblables (Nomadic Museum, Pier 54, New York, 2005). Ce pavillon temporaire, doté d'une structure composée de conteneurs rectan-gulaires empilés sur 10 m de haut et d'une « Paper Gallery » semi-circulaire fermant une cour intérieure en demi-cercle, a été construit pour la célébration du trentième anniversaire de la maison d'édition coréenne Designhouse. Son terrain boisé de 14 214 m² se trouve dans le Parc olympique de Séoul. Le premier « mur de conteneurs » servait aux guichets d'entrée, le second abritait bureaux et stockages. La disposition alternée de conteneurs et de vides réguliers animait la façade principale, tandis que la colonnade en tubes de carton lui donnait une *gravitas* qui ne devait *a priori* rien à ce type de matériaux industriels. La Paper Gallery, semi-circulaire, était faite de deux colonnades de piliers de carton de 75 cm de diamètre sur lesquelles venait se poser une ferme de charpente en tubes de carton de 30 cm de diamètre.

The Papertainer Museum, as its name implies, employs both paper tube columns and shipping containers— two elements that Shigeru Ban has employed with success in the past few years.

Das Papertainer Museum besteht, wie schon der Name andeutet, aus Papierröhren und Schiffscontainern – zwei Elemente, die Shigeru Ban in den vergangenen Jahren immer wieder erfolgreich eingesetzt hat.

Ce musée, comme son nom l'indique, utilise à la fois des tubes de carton et des conteneurs d'expédition, deux éléments utilisés avec succès par Shigeru Ban depuis plusieurs années.

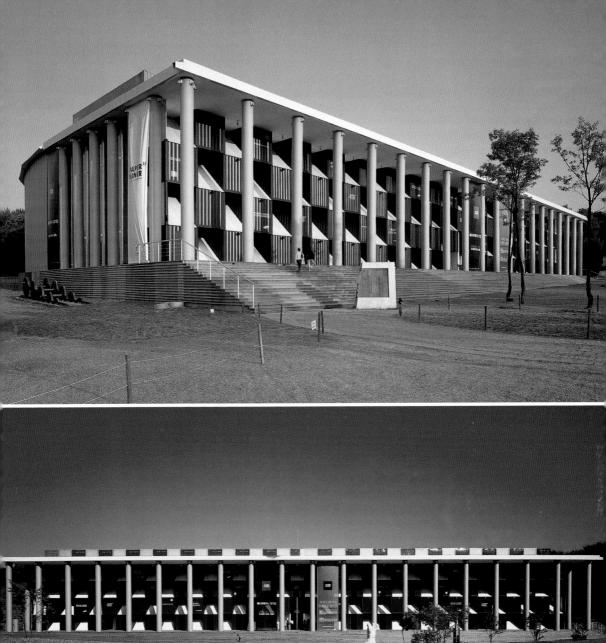

Shigeru Ban's mastery of the use of paper tubes as structural elements in his architecture is visible in this image of the columns and beams that support this building.

Shigeru Bans meisterhafter Einsatz von Papierröhren als konstruktives Element zeigt sich auf dieser Aufnahme: Säulen und Träger stützen den Bau.

La maîtrise dans l'utilisation des tubes de carton comme éléments structurels se constate dans cette image de colonnes et de poutres qui soutiennent le bâtiment.

The stunning form of the Papertainer
Museum has a processional or volun-
tarily repetitive rhythm that lends it
grandeur precisely because industrial
elements are used.

Die atemberaubende formale Gestaltung des Papertainer Museum ist von
feierlichem, bewusst von Wieder-
holungen geprägtem Rhythmus. Die
resultierende Erhabenheit bildet
einen Kontrapunkt zu den industriellen Bauelementen.

La forme étonnante du musée suit
un rythme processionnel ou volontairement répétitif qui confère une
certaine grandeur à cette utilisation
d'éléments industriels.

BARLINDHAUG CONSULT AS

Barlindhaug Consult AS
Sjølundveien 2
9291 Tromsø
Norway

Tel: +47 77 62 26 00
Fax: +47 77 62 26 99
E-mail: peter.w.soderman@barlindhaug.no
Web: www.barlindhaug.no

The chief architect of this project was Peter Wilhelm Søderman, who works with the firm **BARLINDHAUG CONSULT AS** in Tromsø, Norway. He was born in Vasa, Finland, in 1960, and received his M.Arch degree from the Helsinki University of Technology in 1990. From 1985 to the present, he has worked on public and private projects with Marja & Kari Kyyhkynen Architects, Vasa, Finland; Nyréns Architecture, Stockholm, Sweden; Anderssen+Fremming Architects, Tynset and Hamar, Norway; Hille+Melbye architects and HRTB architects, both Oslo, Norway; Sigurd Hamran architects, Tromsø; Contur Architects, Tromsø; and, most recently, Barlindhaug Consult AS, Tromsø. Recent projects by Peter Søderman include the Reinen Elementary School (Tromsø, 2002); Først og fremst Housing Project (Hammerfest, 2004); Vestre Mortensnes Housing Project (Tromsø, 2004); Breivang High School (Tromsø, 2005); and the Svalbard Global Seed Vault (Longyearbyen, Svalbard, 2007–08, published here), all in Norway. Barlindhaug Consult AS provides engineering services to the Norwegian and international markets. The company's scope of services includes engineering and construction, Arctic technology, energy conservation planning, and impact assessments.

Leitender Architekt des Projekts war Peter Wilhelm Søderman vom Büro **BARLINDHAUG CONSULT AS** in Tromsø, Norwegen. Er wurde 1960 in Vasa, Finnland, geboren und erhielt seinen M.Arch. 1990 an der Technischen Universität Helsinki. Seit 1985 arbeitet er an öffentlichen und privaten Projekten, u. a. für Marja & Kari Kyyhkynen Architekten, Vasa, Finnland, für Nyréns Architecture, Stockholm, für Anderssen+Fremming Architekten, Tynset und Hamar, Norwegen, für Hille+Melbye Architekten und HRTB Architekten, beide Oslo, für Sigurd Hamran Architekten und Contur Architekten sowie in jüngster Zeit für Barlindhaug Consult AS, alle Tromsø. Zu den jüngeren Projekten von Peter Søderman zählen die Grundschule Reinen (Tromsø, 2002), die Wohnanlagen Først og fremst (Hammerfest, 2004) und Vestre Mortensnes (Tromsø, 2004), die Breivang-Schule (Tromsø, 2005) sowie der Global Seed Vault (Longyearbyen, Spitzbergen, 2007–08, hier vorgestellt), alle in Norwegen. Barlindhaug Consult AS bietet ingenieurtechnische Dienstleistungen für den norwegischen und internationalen Markt an. Das Leistungsspektrum der Firma umfasst technische Planung und Bauausführung, Technologie für arktisches Klima, Planung von Energiesparmaßnahmen und Umweltverträglichkeitsprüfungen.

Peter Wilhelm Søderman, architecte responsable du projet de Svalbard, travaille pour l'agence norvégienne **BARLINDHAUG CONSULT AS** installée à Tromsø. Né à Vasa, Finlande, en 1960, il est architecte diplômé de l'université de Technologie d'Helsinki (1990). De 1985 à aujourd'hui, il a travaillé sur des projets tant privés que publics avec Marja & Kari Kyyhkynen Architects, à Vasa, Finlande ; Nyréns Architecture, Stockholm, Suède ; Anderssen+Fremming Architects, Tynset et Hamar, Norvège ; Hille+Melbye Architects et HRTB Architects à Oslo, Norvège ; Sigurd Hamran Architects, Tromsø ; Contur Architects, Tromsø, et, plus récemment, Barlindhaug Consult AS. Parmi ses réalisations récentes figurent l'école élémentaire de Reinen (Tromsø, 2002) ; les logements Først og fremst (Hammerfest, 2004) et Vestre Mortensnes (Tromsø, 2004) ; le collège Breivang (Tromsø, 2005) et le Svalbard Global Seed Vault (Longyearbyen, Spitzberg / Svalbard, 2007–08, publié ici), toutes en Norvège. Barlindhaug Consult AS est une agence d'ingénierie qui intervient aussi bien en Norvège qu'à l'international. Elle propose des services dans les domaines de la construction, de la technologie arctique, de l'énergie et des études d'impact.

SVALBARD GLOBAL SEED VAULT

Longyearbyen, Svalbard, Norway, 2007–08

*Site area: 1720 m². Client: Statsbygg, Norwegian Ministry of Government Administration and Reform.
Cost: $880 000. Collaboration: Peter W. Søderman, Louis Lunde, Trond Hansen (Architects),
Sverre Barlindhaug (Engineer)*

The long, rectangular form of the entrance to the Seed Vault is highlighted by a glittering work imagined by the artist Dyveke Sanne.

Die gestreckte Rechteckform des Eingangs zum Seed Vault wird von einem glitzernden Werk der Künstlerin Dyveke Sanne unterstrichen.

Le volume rectangulaire allongé de l'entrée du Seed Vault est signalé par une œuvre scintillante de l'artiste Dyveke Sanne.

Located on a remote island in the Arctic Circle, the Svalbard Global Seed Vault was designed to conserve 100 million seeds of 268 000 plants originating in 100 different countries, making it the largest collection of food crop seeds anywhere in the world. As the Norwegian government's declaration on the occasion of the opening of the vault in February 2008 read: "The seed vault is part of an unprecedented effort to protect the planet's rapidly diminishing biodiversity. The diversity of our crops is essential for food production, yet it is being lost." This "fail-safe" facility, dug deep into the frozen rock of an Arctic mountain, is intended to secure for centuries, or longer, seeds representing every important crop variety available in the world today. As well as protecting against the daily loss of diversity, the vault could also prove indispensable for restarting agricultural production at the regional or global level in the wake of a natural or man-made disaster. Even in the worst-case scenarios of global warming, the vault rooms will remain naturally frozen for up to 200 years. The Global Crop Diversity Trust (www.croptrust.org) is providing support for the ongoing operations of the vault, which has the capacity to store up to 4.5 million samples or some two billion seeds. The vault consists of three secure rooms located at the end of a 125-meter-long tunnel blasted out of the mountain site. The seeds are stored at a temperature of -18°C in foil pouches, allowing some samples to be usable for as long as 2000 years or more. The artist Dyveke Sanne and KORO, the Norwegian agency overseeing art in public spaces, created a work made of reflective steel, mirrors, and prisms that "acts as a beacon, reflecting polar light in the summer months."

Der Global Seed Vault liegt auf Spitzbergen, einer entlegenen Insel im Polarkreis, und wurde realisiert, um 100 Millionen Arten von Saatgut von 268 000 Nutzpflanzen aus 100 verschiedenen Ländern einlagern zu können – die größte Sammlung von Nutzpflanzensaatgut weltweit. Anlässlich der Einweihung der Einrichtung im Februar 2008 erklärte die norwegische Regierung: „Der Saatguttresor ist Teil einer nie dagewesenen Anstrengung, die rasch schwindende Biodiversität dieses Planeten zu erhalten. Die Vielfalt unserer Nutzpflanzen ist unerlässlich für unsere Nahrungsmittelproduktion und doch verlieren wir sie." Diese tief in den frostsicheren Felsen eines arktischen Bergs geschlagene Sicherheitseinrichtung soll das Saatgut sämtlicher bedeutender, heute weltweit existierender Nutzpflanzenarten jahrhundertelang, wenn nicht gar länger, erhalten. Doch der Tresor ist nicht nur eine Sicherung gegen den täglich wachsenden Verlust an Biodiversität, er könnte sich auch als notwendig erweisen, sollte es je nötig sein, die landwirtschaftliche Produktion regional oder global nach einer von der Natur oder dem Menschen verursachten Katastrophe wieder aufzunehmen. Selbst bei Eintreten der schlechtest denkbaren Prognose hinsichtlich der Erderwärmung dürften die Tresorräume noch bis zu 200 Jahre frostsicher bleiben. Der Global Crop Diversity Trust (www.croptrust.org) unterstützt den aktuellen Betrieb des Tresors, dessen Kapazität auf die Lagerung von bis zu 4,5 Millionen Musterspezies oder etwa 2 Milliarden Samen angelegt ist. Der Tresor besteht aus drei Sicherheitsräumen am Ende eines 125 m langen Tunnels, der in den Berg hineingesprengt wurde. Das Saatgut wird bei einer Temperatur von –18 °C in Folie verpackt gelagert, was es erlaubt, die Proben bis zu 2000 Jahre oder länger nutzbar zu erhalten. In Kooperation mit der norwegischen Behörde für Kunst im öffentlichen Raum, KORO, konnte die Künstlerin Dyveke Sanne eine Arbeit aus Spiegelstahl, Spiegeln und Prismen realisieren, die „wie ein Leuchtfeuer wirkt und das polare Licht in den Sommermonaten reflektiert".

Implanté sur une île lointaine de l'intérieur du Cercle arctique, le Svalbard Global Seed Vault (Caveau international de conservation de semences de Spitzberg / Svalbard) a été conçu pour la conservation de 100 millions de semences de 268 000 plantes alimentaires originaires de 100 pays différents ce qui en fait la plus importante collection de ce type dans le monde. La déclaration du gouvernement norvégien, publiée à l'occasion de l'inauguration des installations en 2008, précisait : « Ce caveau de semences fait partie d'un effort sans précédent pour protéger la planète de la diminution rapide de la diversité. Celle-ci qui est essentielle pour la production d'aliments est en cours d'appauvrissement dramatique. » Ces installations à toute épreuve, creusées dans la roche gelée d'une montagne de l'Arctique, devraient protéger pour des siècles ou plus des semences représentant toutes les variétés végétales exploitables importantes existant dans le monde. Leur contenu pourrait se révéler indispensable pour le redémarrage de productions agricoles au niveau régional ou global à la suite de désastres naturels ou provoqués par l'homme. Même dans le pire des scenarii de réchauffement global, les salles devraient rester naturellement gelées pendant au moins deux cents ans. Le Global Crop Diversity Trust (www.croptrust.org) finance les opérations qui consistent à engranger plus de 4,5 millions d'échantillons et quelque 2 milliards de semences. Le caveau se compose de trois salles de sécurité à l'extrémité d'un tunnel de 125 m de long creusé à l'explosif dans la montagne. Les semences sont stockées à -18 °C dans des emballages spéciaux. L'artiste Dyveke Sanne et l'agence norvégienne KORO en charge de l'installation d'œuvres d'art dans des lieux publics ont créé, à l'entrée, une œuvre en acier réfléchissant, miroirs et prises, qui « agit comme un phare, reflétant la lumière polaire pendant les mois d'été ».

The architecture of the Seed Vault is as simple as its function—to provide a protected environment for the seeds of the world, potentially a key to the survival of the human race in the case of some future catastrophe.

Die Architektur des Seed Vault ist ebenso einfach wie sein Zweck – er dient als Schutzraum für Saatgut aus aller Welt – im Falle zukünftiger Katastrophen ein potenzieller Schlüssel zum Überleben der Menschheit.

L'architecture du Seed Vault est aussi simple que sa fonction : offrir un environnement protégé à la conservation de semences venues du monde entier, pour la survie de la race humaine en cas de future catastrophe.

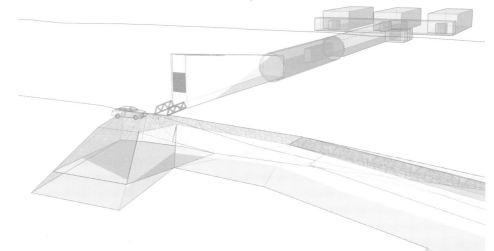

The vault burrows deep into a mountain to ensure the stability of the collections in terms of temperature, even if global warming should begin to change exterior conditions.

Der Seed Vault reicht tief in den Berg hinein, wohin er verlegt wurde, um Temperaturstabilität für die Bestände zu gewährleisten, selbst bei Veränderung der äußeren klimatischen Gegebenheiten durch die globale Erwärmung.

Le caveau est creusé au plus profond de la montagne pour garantir la constance thermique de la collection de semences, même si le réchauffement climatique doit entraîner la modification des conditions extérieures.

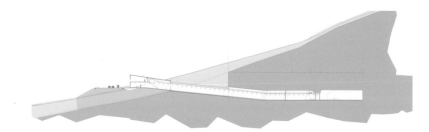

Above, vials and pouches containing seeds and the stacked sample collections.

Oben Ampullen und Beutel mit Saatgut, unten die gestapelten Lagerbestände.

Ci-dessus, ampoules et poches contenant les semences. Ci-dessous, le stockage des collections.

BARTON WILLMORE

Barton Willmore
7 Soho Square
London W1D 3QB
UK

Tel: +44 20 74 46 68 88
Fax: +44 20 74 46 68 89
E-mail: info@bartonwillmore.co.uk
Web: www.bartonwillmore.co.uk

BARTON WILLMORE presents itself as the "UK's leading independent integrated planning and design consultancy." The firm was originally established as an architectural practice in 1947. Nick Sweet was born in London in 1957. He studied Landscape Architecture at Thames Polytechnic (now the University of Greenwich, 1981), and worked with the Omrania / Buro Happold / Frei Otto joint venture for the Tuwaiq Palace (Riyadh, Saudi Arabia). He returned to his studies at the University of Westminster, London, obtaining an M.A. in Urban Design (1992–95) while working at Aukett Fitzroy Robinson. He took up an equity partnership at Barton Willmore in 2005. He continues to work in collaboration with such firms as Omrania and Buro Happold. Nick Sweet has obtained a number of commissions through design competitions, including the Salam Park project (Riyadh, Saudi Arabia, 1996); the European Parliament Quarter (Brussels, Belgium, 1998); and the King Abdullah International Gardens project (Riyadh, Saudi Arabia, 2008–11, published here). Further Barton Willmore buildings include Clearwater Court (Reading, 1998); the Honda UK Headquarters (Berkshire, 2002); and the Tonbridge Conference Centre in Kent (2003), all in the UK. In addition, the firm is developing proposals for the new city of Beitun in western China.

BARTON WILLMORE, nach eigener Aussage „die führende, unabhängige und integrierte Beratungsfirma für Planung und Entwurf in Großbritannien", wurde 1947 ursprünglich als Architekturbüro gegründet. Nick Sweet wurde 1957 in London geboren. Er studierte Landschaftsarchitektur an der Thames Polytechnic (heute University of Greenwich, 1981) und arbeitete mit Omrania / Buro Happold / Frei Otto am Tuwaiq-Palast (Riad, Saudi-Arabien). Anschließend nahm er sein Studium an der University of Westminster, London, wieder auf und erwarb einen M. A. in Stadtplanung (1992–95), während er parallel bei Aukett Fitzroy Robinson arbeitete. 2005 wurde er Partner bei Barton Willmore. Sweet kooperiert nach wie vor mit Firmen wie Omrania und Buro Happold. Verschiedene Aufträge erhielt er durch Entwurfswettbewerbe, darunter das Salam-Park-Projekt (Riad, Saudi-Arabien, 1996), das Quartier des Europaparlaments (Brüssel, Belgien, 1998) sowie das King-Abdullah-International-Gardens-Projekt (Riad, Saudi-Arabien, 2008–11, hier vorgestellt). Zu den Bauten von Barton Willmore zählen außerdem die Clearwater Court (Reading, 1998), die britische Firmenzentrale von Honda (Berkshire, 2002) sowie das Tonbridge Conference Centre in Kent (2003), alle in Großbritannien. Darüber hinaus entwickelt das Büro Entwürfe für die Planstadt Beitun in Westchina.

BARTON WILLMORE se présente comme « la première agence indépendante d'urbanisme et de conception intégrée ». À l'origine, en 1947, c'était une agence d'architecture. Nick Sweet, né à Londres en 1957, a étudié l'architecture du paysage à Thames Polytechnic (aujourd'hui université de Greenwich, 1981), et travaillé avec la *joint venture* Omrania/Buro Happold/Frei Otto pour le Tuwaiq-Palace (Riyad, Arabie saoudite). Il est revenu aux études et a obtenu son M. A. en urbanisme de l'université de Westminster à Londres (1992–95), tout en travaillant chez Aukett Fitzroy Robinson. Il s'est associé à Barton Willmore en 2005, mais continue à collaborer avec des agences comme Omrania et Buro Happold. Il a gagné un certain nombre de concours dont le projet de Salam Park (Riyad, Arabie saoudite, 1996) ; le quartier du Parlement européen (Bruxelles, Belgique, 1998) et les jardins internationaux du roi Abdallah (Riyad, Arabie saoudite, 2008–11, publiés ici). Parmi les autres réalisations de Barton Willmore figurent Clearwater Court (Reading, 1998) ; le siège de Honda UK (Berkshire, 2002) et le centre de conférences Tonbridge dans le Kent (2003), toutes en Grande-Bretagne sauf exception. Par ailleurs, l'agence développe des propositions pour la nouvelle ville de Beitun dans l'ouest de la Chine.

KING ABDULLAH INTERNATIONAL GARDENS

Riyadh, Saudi Arabia, 2008–11

Site area: 170 ha. Floor area: 60 000 m². Client: Riyadh Municipality. Cost: $280 million.
Collaboration: Buro Happold (Consulting Engineers), The Eden Project, The Natural History Museum

Borrowing its sweeping forms from the crescent of Islam, the gardens and greenhouses are intended to be carbon neutral. .

Die Gärten und Gewächshäuser, formal in Anlehnung an den islamischen Halbmond gestaltet, sind CO_2-neutral konzipiert.

Empruntant leur forme incurvée au croissant islamique, les jardins et les serres présentent une empreinte carbone neutre.

This project involves the creation of a master plan, and an architectural and landscape design concept for the Saudi Arabian city of Riyadh. The brief called for a botanical garden seed bank, visitor attractions, and back-of-house facilities sufficient to accommodate up to 45 000 visitors per day. As the architects explain: "The team's response challenged the idea of creating a conventional botanical collection…. Our response proposed a paleo-botanic timeline, creating authentic interpretations of ecosystems that existed on this precise site in past epochs. The scheme aims to become a unique educational device in the explanation of global climate change and desertification." Seven controlled environments representing past local ecosystems and a final "garden of choices, an exploration of the options available to produce genuinely sustainable development in the future," are contained in a 22-hectare zone. The entire project is to be carbon neutral, using stone, gravel, rainwater, and sun power to sustain the development and operation of the facility.

Das Projekt umfasst einen Masterplan und ein Entwurfskonzept für die Bebauung und Landschaftsgestaltung der saudi-arabischen Stadt Riad. Gefragt waren eine Saatgutbank für einen botanischen Garten, Attraktionen für Besucher und Versorgungseinrichtungen für bis zu 45 000 Besucher pro Tag. Der Architekt führt aus: „Der Entwurf des Teams hinterfragte die Vorstellungen von einem konventionellen botanischen Garten … Unser Entwurf sah eine paläobotanische Zeitleiste vor, die die verschiedenen Ökosysteme, die in vergangenen Epochen an diesem Ort existierten, authentisch illustriert. Der Ansatz ist eine einzigartige Methode, anhand derer sich der globale Klimawandel und die globale Versteppung veranschaulichen lassen." Das 22 ha große Areal umfasst sieben steuerbare Biosphären, die vergangene Ökosysteme repräsentieren, sowie einen „Garten der Möglichkeiten, der auslotet, wie sich eine wirklich nachhaltige Entwicklung in Zukunft gestalten lassen könnte". Das gesamte Projekt ist CO_2-neutral und nutzt Stein, Kies, Regenwasser und Solarenergie für eine nachhaltige Bauerschließung und den umweltgerechten Betrieb der Anlage.

Ce projet porte sur la création d'un plan directeur et un concept d'architecture et d'aménagements paysagers pour Riyad, la capitale saoudienne. L'appel d'offre concernait une banque de semences, des attractions pour visiteurs et des installations techniques prévues pour 45 000 visiteurs quotidiens. Comme l'expliquent les architectes : « La réponse de l'équipe a remis en question l'idée de créer une collection botanique conventionnelle… Notre réponse est de proposer un parcours temporel paléobotanique, et de créer des interprétations authentiques d'écosystèmes ayant jadis existé sur ce site précis. Le projet devient ainsi un outil éducatuf unique qui explique les changements climatiques globaux et la désertification. » Sept environnements contrôlés représentent ces écosystèmes disparus et un dernier « jardin des choix, exploration des options possibles en faveur d'un développement durable future authentique », occupent une surface d'environ 22 ha. Le projet tout entier n'émettra pas de CO_2 et utilisera la pierre, le gravier, l'eau de pluie et le soleil pour assurer le fonctionnement des installations.

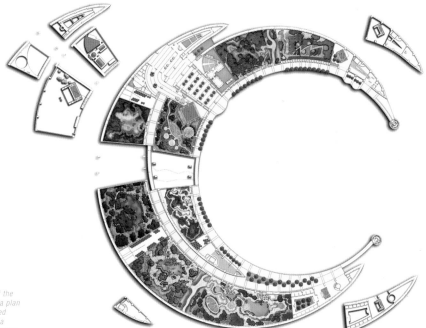

To the left, the entrance level of the covered gardens. On this page, a plan showing the layout of the covered areas, and a perspective giving a sense of the soaring interior volumes.

Links der Eingangsbereich der überdachten Gärten. Auf dieser Seite ein Grundriss der überdachten Zonen und eine Innenansicht, die einen Eindruck von der Höhe der Räume vermittelt.

À gauche, le niveau d'entrée des jardins couverts. Le plan de cette page montre la disposition des zones couvertes et une perspective des énormes volumes intérieurs.

VINCENT CALLEBAUT ARCHITECTURES

Vincent Callebaut Architectures
119 rue Manin
75019 Paris
France

Tel: +33 1 42 45 11 10
E-mail: vincent@callebaut.org
Web: www.vincent.callebaut.org

VINCENT CALLEBAUT was born in 1977 in Belgium. He graduated from the Institut Victor Horta in Brussels in 2000, where he received the René Serrure Prize for the best diploma project, a proposal for the "Metamuseum of Arts and Civilizations, Quai Branly." He worked as an intern in the offices of Odile Decq and Massimiliano Fuksas in Paris, before opening his own firm in Brussels and Paris. He has collaborated with Jakob + MacFarlane, Claude Vasconi, and Jacques Rougerie. Callebaut seeks to contribute to a "new Ecopolis via 'parasitical' strategies for an investigative architecture, mixing biology with information and communications technologies." His projects (all unbuilt) include Underwater Venice of Beirut, a Master Plan for Martyrs' Square (Beirut, 2004); Fractured Monolith, Hotel and Congress Center (Brussels, 2004); Eye of the Storm, a performing arts center for Seoul (South Korea, 2005); Red Baobab, a project for the New National Library in Prague (2006); as well as Anti-Smog (Paris, 2007); and Perfumed Jungle (Hong Kong, 2007), the last two published here.

VINCENT CALLEBAUT wurde 1977 in Belgien geboren. Sein Studium schloss er 2000 am Institut Victor Horta in Brüssel ab, wo er mit dem René-Serrure-Preis für das beste Diplomprojekt ausgezeichnet wurde, seinen Entwurf „Metamuseum of Arts and Civilizations, Quai Branly". Er war als Praktikant in den Büros von Odile Decq und Massimiliano Fuksas in Paris tätig, bevor er sein eigenes Büro mit Sitz in Brüssel und Paris gründete. Er kooperierte mit Jakob + MacFarlane, Claude Vasconi und Jacques Rougerie. Callebaut geht es darum, zu einer „neuen Ökopolis beizutragen" und zwar „durch ‚parasitäre' Strategien für eine investigative Architektur, in der sich Biologie, Informations- und Kommunikationstechnologien miteinander verbinden". Zu seinen (sämtlich ungebauten) Projekten zählen u. a. ein „Unterwasser-Venedig" in Beirut, ein Masterplan für einen Märtyrerplatz (Beirut, 2004), das Hotel- und Kongresszentrum Fractured Monolith (Brüssel, 2004), Eye of the Storm, ein Zentrum für darstellende Künste in Seoul (Südkorea, 2005), Red Baobab, ein Projekt für die Neue Nationalbibliothek in Prag (2006), sowie seine Projekte Anti-Smog (Paris, 2007) und Perfumed Jungle (Hongkong, 2007), beide hier vorgestellt.

VINCENT CALLEBAUT, né en 1977 en Belgique, est diplômé de l'Institut Victor Horta à Bruxelles en 2000, qui lui a accordé le prix René Serrure pour le meilleur projet de diplôme avec son « Metamuseum des arts et civilisations, quai Branly ». Il a été stagiaire chez Odile Decq et Massimiliano Fuksas à Paris, avant d'ouvrir sa propre agence à Bruxelles et Paris. Il a collaboré avec Jakob + MacFarlane, Claude Vasconi et Jacques Rougerie. Callebaut cherche à contribuer à la création d'une « nouvelle Ecopolis *via* des stratégies "parasitaires" d'architecture de recherche, mêlant biologie et technologies de l'information et de la communication ». Ses projets (aucun réalisé pour l'instant) comprennent « Underwater Venice of Beirut », un plan directeur pour la place des Martyrs (Beyrouth, 2004) ; Fractured Monolith, Hotel and Congress Center (Bruxelles, 2004) ; Eye of the Storm, un centre pour les arts de la scène à Séoul (Corée du Sud, 2005) ; Red Baobab, projet pour la Bibliothèque nationale de Prague (2006), ainsi que Anti-Smog (Paris, 2007) et Jungle parfumée (Hong Kong, 2007), ces deux derniers publiés dans ces pages.

ANTI-SMOG

Paris, France, 2007

Floor area: 2065 m². Client: City of Paris. Cost: not disclosed

The architect describes Anti-Smog as an "Innovation Center in Sustainable Development" to be located near the Canal de l'Ourq in the 19th arrondissement of Paris. The complex would make use of "all available renewable energy forms to fight against the Parisian smog." Two distinct museum structures would produce more energy than they consume—the Solar Drop with a superstructure covered in polyester fiber and 250 square meters of photovoltaic cells, and the Wind Tower, a "helical structure incrusted with wind machines." The Solar Drop would be covered with a layer of titanium dioxide (TiO_2) in the form of anatase, "which, by reacting to ultra-violet rays, allows the reduction of air pollution." Planted arches would allow the collection of rainwater for the complex. As Callebaut describes it: "Below this thermo-regulating solar roof, there is a huge exhibition and meeting room organized around a central garden, a phyto-purified aquatic lagoon. It is a didactic place dedicated to new ecological urbanities and renewable energies." The Wind Tower, 45 meters tall, would be topped by a suspended garden with spectacular views of the city. The architect imagines that it might be used to house the "Vélib" bicycles, introduced to Paris by its mayor, or solar cars, in a silo configuration. "This," says Vincent Callebaut, "is a play project, an urban and truly living graft. In osmosis with its surroundings, it is an architecture that interacts with its surroundings in climatic, chemical, kinetic, and social ways to better reduce our ecological footprint in the urban area."

Der Architekt beschreibt Anti-Smog als „Innovationsprojekt für nachhaltige Entwicklung", das in der Nähe des Canal de l'Ourq im 19. Arrondissement von Paris angesiedelt sein soll. Der Komplex soll „alle verfügbaren Formen erneuerbarer Energien nutzen, um den Pariser Smog zu bekämpfen". Zwei separate Museumsbauten würden mehr Energie produzieren als sie verbrauchen – der sogenannte Solar Drop mit einem Überbau aus Polyesterfaser und 250 m² Solarmodulen sowie der Wind Tower, eine „mit Windrädern besetzte Helixkonstruktion". Der Solar Drop würde mit einer Anatasmodifikation von Titandioxid (TiO_2) überzogen werden, „das dank seiner Reaktion mit ultravioletter Strahlung Luftverschmutzung reduzieren" würde. Begrünte Bögen würden Regen für den Komplex sammeln. Callebaut beschreibt sein Projekt wie folgt: „Unter dem wärmeregulierenden Solardach befindet sich ein riesiger Ausstellungs- und Konferenzraum, der um einen zentral angelegten Garten mit einem Teich organisiert ist, dessen Wasser biologisch geklärt wird. Es ist ein didaktischer Ort, der sich mit neuen ökologischen Urbanitäten und erneuerbaren Energien auseinandersetzt." Der 45 m hohe Wind Tower soll oben mit einem hängenden Garten abschließen, der beeindruckende Ausblicke über die Stadt bieten würde. Der Architekt hofft, hier auch die vom Pariser Bürgermeister eingeführten „Vélib"-Fahrräder oder solarbetriebene Autos unterzubringen. Laut Vincent Callebaut handelt es sich um „eine Projektspielerei, ein urbanes und wahrhaft lebendiges Transplantat. Es ist eine Architektur, die in einer Form von Osmose mit ihrem Umfeld in klimatischer, chemischer, kinetischer und sozialer Weise interagiert, um unseren ökologischen Fußabdruck in der Stadt wirksamer zu reduzieren."

L'architecte présente Anti-Smog comme un « prototype didactique d'expérimentations écologiques » qui pourrait être installé près du canal de l'Ourcq dans le 19e arrondissement de Paris. Ce complexe utiliserait « toutes les formes disponibles d'énergies renouvelables pour combattre le *smog* parisien ». Deux structures muséales distinctes devraient produire davantage d'énergie qu'elles n'en consomment : la *Solar drop* dont la superstructure est recouverte de fibre de polyester et de 250 m² de cellules photovoltaïques, et la *Wind Tower*, une « structure hélicoïdale incrustée de turbines à vent ». La *Solar Drop* serait recouverte d'une couche de dioxyde de titane (TiO_2) sous forme d'anatase « qui, en réagissant aux rayons ultraviolets, permet de réduire la pollution de l'air ». Des arches plantées permettraient de collecter l'eau de pluie réutilisée par le complexe. « Sous cette couverture solaire thermorégulatrice, se trouve une énorme salle d'expositions et de réunions organisée autour d'un jardin central, un lagon aquatique phyto-épuré. C'est un lieu didactique consacré aux nouvelles urbanités écologiques et aux énergies renouvelables. » La *Wind Tower*, de 45 m de haut, serait surmontée d'un jardin suspendu offrant de superbes vues sur la ville. L'architecte a aussi imaginé abriter les « Vélib' » ou des voitures à énergie solaire dans une configuration de silo. « Il s'agit, précise Callebaut, d'un projet ludique, une greffe urbaine et vivante. En osmose avec son milieu, c'est une architecture qui interagit complètement avec son contexte qu'il soit climatique, chimique, cinétique ou social pour mieux réduire notre empreinte écologique en milieu urbain. »

The Anti-Smog complex takes the idea of the "green" building a step further than usual: the architect proposes to reduce ambient pollution rather than simply taking care not to contribute to energy waste.

Der Anti-Smog-Komplex spinnt das Konzept „grüner" Bauten ein Stück weiter: Der Architekt plant, Umweltverschmutzung aktiv zu reduzieren, statt lediglich Energieverschwendung zu vermeiden.

En proposant de diminuer concrètement la pollution ambiante plutôt que de simplement ne pas contribuer au gaspillage de l'énergie, le complexe Anti-Smog fait progresser le concept de bâtiment « vert ».

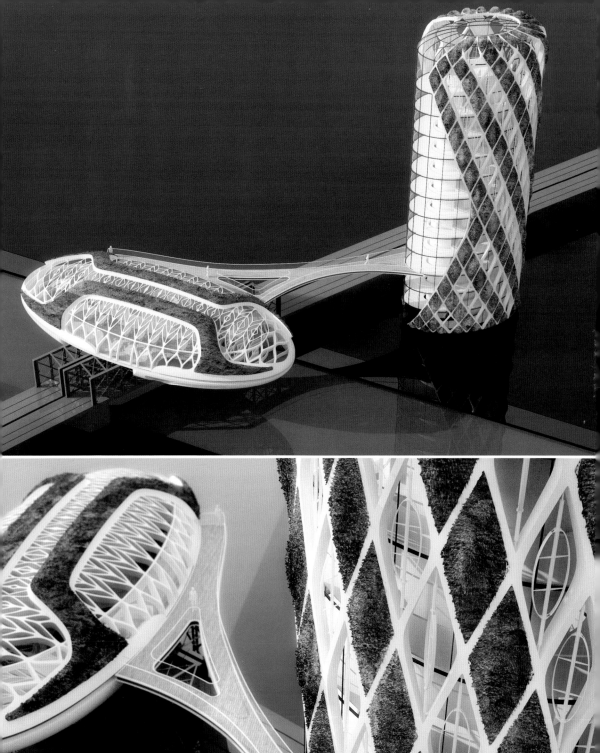

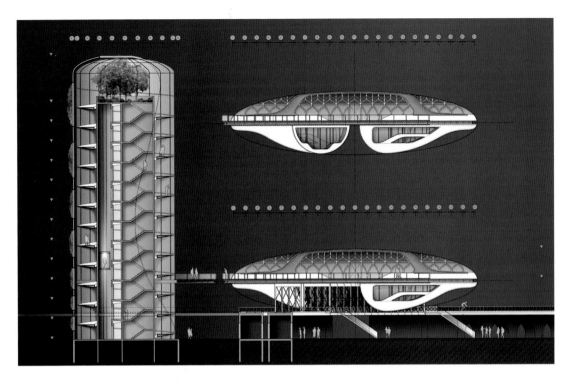

The rather futuristic forms proposed by Vincent Callebaut confirm the visionary aspect of his design. Light and open space are grafted onto the existing, less modern environment.

Die vergleichsweise futuristischen Formen von Vincent Callebauts Entwurf betonen seinen visionären Ansatz. Helle und offene Räume werden in das weniger moderne Umfeld eingeschrieben.

Les formes futuristes proposées par Vincent Callebaut confirment l'aspect visionnaire de son projet. L'espace ouvert et lumineux se greffe sur un environnement moins moderne.

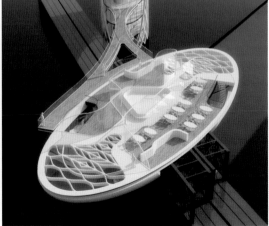

PERFUMED JUNGLE

Hong Kong, China, 2007

Site area: 2.7 km². Client: City of Hong Kong. Cost: not disclosed. Collaboration: Vincent Callebaut, Arnaud Martinez, Maguy Delrieu

This is a "Master Plan for the Eco-Design of the Central Waterfront of the Business District of Hong Kong." The architect explains: "Hong Kong is one of the more populated territories in the world with a density of 30 000 inhabitants / per square kilometer. To respond to this overpopulation, the 'Urban Jungle' proposes to re-tame nature and to widen the territory of the ultra-contemporary city." Any new built spaces would be self-sufficient, producing more energies and biodiversity than they consume. A "mesh of irregular cells" brings water into the entire new district, forming open-air swimming pools, marinas, new quays, or lagoons for biological purification. "In front of the skyline of the Kowloon peninsula," says Callebaut, "a true cascade of aquatic and vegetable terraces like the ones of a rice terrace are laid out on this fifth façade. This new topography, without any wall, thus without any limit, is not only meant to be inhabited by the citizens of Hong Kong, but is also designed to be infiltrated, crossed and printed by the numerous species of the fauna and local flora or in migration that will come to install themselves." The towers the architect proposes are modeled on arborescent development and have fishnet skin "closed on a random basis with cushions of substrate and vegetable fertilizers enabling the development of luxuriant vegetation."

Das Projekt ist ein „Masterplan für die ökologische Gestaltung des zentralen Uferabschnitts im Geschäftsviertel von Hongkong". Der Architekt führt aus: „Hongkong zählt mit 30 000 Bewohnern pro Quadratkilometer zu den am dichtest bevölkerten Gegenden der Welt. Um dieser Überbevölkerung entgegenzutreten, geht es dem ‚urbanen Dschungel' darum, die Natur aufs Neue zu zähmen und neues Territorium für eine ultra-zeitgenössische Stadt zu erschließen." Sämtliche Neubauten wären autark und würden mehr Energie und Biodiversität produzieren, als sie verbrauchen. Ein „Geflecht aus unregelmäßigen Zellen" würde Wasser in das gesamte neue Stadtviertel holen, aus denen Freibäder, Jachthäfen, neue Kaianlagen oder Lagunen für biologische Wasseraufbereitung entstehen könnten. „Vor der Skyline der Halbinsel Kowloon", beschreibt Callebaut, „würde eine Kaskade von wassergefüllten oder mit Gemüsekulturen bepflanzten Terrassen, ähnlich wie Reisterrassen, entstehen, die die gesamte fünfte Fassade überziehen würden. Diese neue Art von Topografie, die ohne Mauer und somit ohne Begrenzung auskommt, soll nicht nur von den Bürgern Hongkongs bewohnt werden, sondern ist auch darauf angelegt, von den verschiedenen Arten regionaler Flora und Fauna, die sich hier niederlassen, erobert und geprägt zu werden." Die vom Architekten geplanten Hochhausbauten basieren auf Wachstumsmodellen von Bäumen und sind mit einer fischnetzartigen Haut überzogen, „die nach dem Zufallsprinzip mit Kissen aus Substrat und Gemüsedünger gefüllt werden, um eine üppige Vegetation anzuregen".

Il s'agit ici d'un « plan directeur pour l'écoconception de la partie centrale du front de mer du quartier d'affaires de Hong Kong ». L'architecte explique : « Avec une densité de 30 000 habitants au km², Hong Kong est l'un des territoires les plus peuplés du monde. Pour répondre à cette surpopulation, la "Jungle urbaine" propose de redomestiquer la nature et d'agrandir le territoire de la cité ultra-contemporaine ». Cette toute nouvelle construction devrait être autosuffisante et produire plus d'énergie et de biodiversité qu'elle n'en consomme. Une « résille de cellules irrégulières » fournit l'eau au quartier tout entier, formant des piscines en plein air, des marinas, de nouveaux quais ou des lagons d'épuration biologique. « Face au panorama de la péninsule de Kowloon, explique Callebaut, une vraie cascade de terrasses aquatiques et végétalisées, comme celle des cultures rizicoles, est disposée sur cette cinquième façade. Cette topographie nouvelle, sans mur, et donc sans la moindre limite, est non seulement pensée pour les habitants de la ville, mais aussi pour être infiltrée, parcourue et appropriée par les nombreuses espèces de la faune et de la flore locale ou en migration qui viendront s'y installer. » Les tours proposées par l'architecte sont modelées sur des développements de type arborescent et présente une peau en filet « posée sur une base aléatoire avec des coussins de substrats et d'engrais permettant le développement d'une végétation luxuriante ».

The Perfumed Jungle is presented with vast open spaces that almost give the impression that these towers would not have a precise function, yet they would produce both energy and biodiversity.

Der Perfumed Jungle präsentiert sich mit riesigen Freiflächen, wodurch beinahe der Eindruck entsteht, die Türme hätten keine spezielle Funktion. Tatsächlich sollen sie Energie erzeugen und Biodiversität schaffen.

La « Jungle parfumée » se présente comme de vastes espaces ouverts donnant l'impression que ces tours n'ont pas de fonction précise, or elles produisent de l'énergie et défendent la biodiversité.

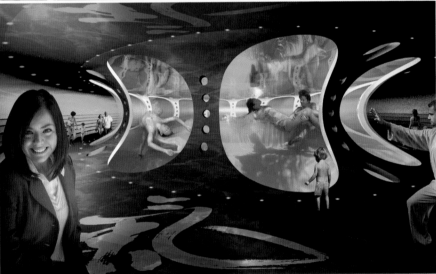

Callebaut's fantastic environment seems to suggest that architecture could become an integral part of a living environment.

Callebauts fantastische Umwelt scheint geradezu nahezulegen, dass Architektur integraler Bestandteil des gesamten Lebensraums werden könnte.

L'environnement fantastique imaginé par Callebaut suggère que l'architecture pourrait devenir partie intégrante d'un environnement vivant.

DILLER SCOFIDIO + RENFRO

Diller Scofidio + Renfro / 601 West 26th Street, Suite 1815
New York, NY 10001 / USA
Tel: +1 212 260 7971 / Fax: +1 212 260 7924
E-mail: disco@dsrny.com / Web: www.dsrny.com

ELIZABETH DILLER is Professor of Architecture at Princeton University and **RICARDO SCOFIDIO** is Professor of Architecture at the Cooper Union in New York. They founded Diller + Scofidio in 1979. **CHARLES RENFRO** is a Visiting Professor at Columbia University and became partner in 2004. According to their own description: "DS+R is a collaborative, interdisciplinary studio involved in architecture, the visual arts, and the performing arts. The team is primarily involved in thematically driven experimental works that take the form of architectural commissions, temporary installations, and permanent site-specific installations, multimedia theater, electronic media, and print." Their work includes Slither, 100 units of social housing in Gifu, Japan; and *Moving Target*, a collaborative dance work with Charleroi/Danse Belgium. Installations have been seen at the Cartier Foundation in Paris (*Master/Slave*, 1999); and the Museum of Modern Art in New York. Their completed work includes The Brasserie Restaurant (Seagram Building, New York, 1998–99); the Blur Building (Expo '02, Yverdon-les-Bains, Switzerland, 2000–02); the Institute of Contemporary Art in Boston (2004–06); and they are responsible for the Phantom House (Southwest USA, 2007, published here). They were selected as architects of the Eyebeam Institute in the Chelsea area of Manhattan and Lincoln Center (New York), and they completed the expansion of the Julliard School and Alice Tully Hall in 2009. They designed the viewing platforms at Ground Zero in Manhattan; the Brown University Creative Arts Center (Providence, Rhode Island, 2011); the High Line, a park on three kilometers of elevated train line (New York, in collaboration with Field Operations); the Hudson Riverfront Performing Arts Center (Weehawken, New Jersey); and the Mott Street (Kopp) Townhouse (New York), all in the USA.

ELIZABETH DILLER ist Professorin für Architektur an der Universität Princeton, **RICARDO SCOFIDIO** Professor für Architektur an der Cooper Union in New York. 1979 gründeten sie das Büro Diller + Scofidio. **CHARLES RENFRO** ist Gastprofessor an der Columbia University und wurde 2004 Partner. Eigener Aussage nach verstehen sich DS+R als „kooperierendes, interdisziplinäres Studio, das in den Bereichen Architektur, bildende und darstellende Künste tätig ist. Das Team beschäftigt sich in erster Linie mit thematisch ausgerichteten, experimentellen Projekten, wobei es sich um architektonische Aufträge, temporäre Installationen und permanente, ortsspezifische Installationen handeln kann, um Multimedia-Theater, elektronische Medien und Publikationen." Zu ihren Projekten zählen Slither, 100 Sozialbaueinheiten in Gifu, Japan, und „Moving Target", ein Tanzprojekt mit Charleroi/Danse Belgium. Installationen waren in der Fondation Cartier in Paris zu sehen („Master/Slave", 1999) sowie im Museum of Modern Art in New York. Zu ihren realisierten Bauten zählen das Restaurant The Brasserie (Seagram Building, New York, 1998–99), das Blur Building (Expo '02, Yverdon-les-Bains, Schweiz, 2000–02), das Institute of Contemporary Art in Boston (2004–06); außerdem zeichnen sie verantwortlich für das Phantom House (Südwesten der USA, 2007, hier vorgestellt). Sie erhielten den Auftrag für das Eyebeam Institute in Manhattan (Chelsea) und das Lincoln Center (New York) und schlossen 2009 die Erweiterung der dortigen Julliard School und Alice Tully Hall ab. Das Team entwarf die Aussichtsplattformen für Ground Zero in Manhattan und arbeitete am Brown University Creative Arts Center (Providence, Rhode Island, 2011), der High Line, einem 3 km langen Park auf einem ehemaligen Hochbahnabschnitt (New York, mit Field Operations), am Hudson Riverfront Performing Arts Center (Weehawken, New Jersey) sowie am Mott Street (Kopp) Townhouse (New York), alle in den USA.

ELIZABETH DILLER est professeur d'architecture à l'université de Princeton et **RICARDO SCOFIDIO** enseigne à Cooper Union, New York. Tous deux ont créé en 1979 l'agence Diller + Scofidio. **CHARLES RENFRO** est professeur invité a l'université Columbia et s'associe à eux en 2004. Ils se présentent comme « une agence interdisciplinaire coopérative se consacrant à l'architecture, aux arts plastiques et arts de la scène. L'équipe travaille surtout sur des recherches thématiques expérimentales : commandes architecturales, installations temporaires, installations permanentes adaptées au site, théâtres multimédia, médias électroniques et d'édition ». Parmi leurs projets : Slither, 100 logements sociaux, Gifu, Japon ; *Moving Target*, œuvre chorégraphique avec Charleroi/Danse (Belgique). Ils ont exposé leurs installations à la Fondation Cartier à Paris (*Master/Slave*, 1999) et au MoMA de New York. Autres réalisations : le restaurant The Brasserie du Seagram Building, New York (1998–99) ; le Blur Building à l'Expo '02 (Yverdon-les-Bains, Suisse, 2000–02) ; l'Institut d'Art contemporain à Boston (2004–06) et le Phantom House (sud-ouest des États-Unis, 2007, publié ici). Ils ont été sélectionnés pour l'Institut Eyebeam à Manhattan (Chelsea) et le centre Lincoln (New York), et ont achevés l'extension de l'école Julliard et de l'Alice Tully Hall en 2009. Ils ont conçu les plates-formes d'observation de Ground Zero à Manhattan et ont travaillé sur le projet du Brown University Creative Arts Center (Providence, Rhode Island, 2011) ; la High Line, un parc de 3 km de long sur une ancienne voie ferrée surélevée (avec Filed Operations, New York) ; le Hudson Riverfont Performing Arts Center (Weehawken, New Jersey) et la maison de ville de Mott Street (Kopp) à New York.

PHANTOM HOUSE

Southwest USA, 2007

Floor area: 204 m² (inside); 204 m² (outside). Client: The New York Times Magazine; Project for print
Project Leader: David Allin. Collaboration: Atelier Ten

Designed in conjunction with the May 20, 2007, issue of *The New York Times Magazine*, dedicated to the subject of "Ecotecture," this concept house draws on existing technologies and some imagined ones to create the most sustainable and ecologically conscious residence possible. An indoor, climate-controlled space is located above an outdoor one of the same dimensions. Energy produced in everyday activities is stored for later use, while "ground-coupled heating and cooling uses the steady temperature of the earth" (13°C in the imagined location of the residence) as a source of heat. Double-layer glass called OpaciView by the architects, made with a ventilated cavity between the layers and a porous film of tungsten oxide that lightens or darkens depending on the heat of the sun, is used in the house. Photovoltaic cells are aligned on the roof, and exercise equipment in active use generates electricity that can be stored. Even the mattresses on the beds are equipped with a similar system that generates and stores electricity generated by "excess human energy," as the architects put it. The house can be put in "hibernation mode" when it is not in use, reducing energy use to a bare minimum. The house would be built from "recycled, remanufactured, and renewable materials. Wood species are selected from the nearest sustainably managed forest." Water sensors on the roof double the areas able to catch rainwater when necessary, and store the water for use in toilets and the garden.

Der Konzeptentwurf für ein Wohnhaus entstand für die Ausgabe des *New York Times Magazine* vom 20. Mai 2007, die sich dem Thema „Ecotecture" widmete. Der Entwurf greift sowohl existierende als auch visionäre Technologien auf, um ein möglichst nachhaltiges und ökologisch bewusstes Wohnhaus zu gestalten. Ein klimatisierter Innenraum liegt über einem ebenso großen Außenbereich. Die bei alltäglichen Verrichtungen erzeugte Energie wird für spätere Nutzung gespeichert, während ein „geothermisches Heizungs- und Kühlsystem die konstante Temperatur des Erdreichs" (bei der geplanten Lage des Hauses 13 °C) nutzt. Im Haus kommt eine Doppelverglasung zum Einsatz, die die Architekten OpaciView nennen. Sie besteht aus zwei Schichten, zwischen denen ein belüfteter Hohlraum und ein poröser Film aus Wolframoxid liegen, der sich je nach Sonnenstrahlung heller oder dunkler tönt. Auf dem Dach sind Solarzellen installiert, Fitnessgeräte erzeugen bei aktiver Nutzung speicherbaren Strom. Selbst die Matratzen der Betten sind mit einem System ausgestattet, das (so die Architekten) „bei exzessiver menschlicher Energie" Strom erzeugt und speichert. Wird das Haus nicht genutzt, kann es in einen „Winterschlafmodus" versetzt werden, der den Energieverbrauch auf ein absolutes Minimum reduziert. Das Haus soll aus „recycelten, wiederaufbereiteten und erneuerbaren Materialien gebaut und das Holz aus möglichst nahe gelegenen und nachhaltig bewirtschafteten Wäldern bezogen werden". Wassersensoren auf dem Dach verdoppeln die Fläche, auf der sich nach Bedarf Regenwasser sammeln und für Sanitäranlagen und Bewässerung speichern lässt.

Conçue en conjonction avec la parution du numéro du 20 mai 2007 du *New York Times Magazine* consacré à l'*Ecotecture*, cette maison concept s'appuie sur des technologies existantes, et certaines encore imaginaires, pour créer la résidence la plus durable et la plus écologique possible. Le volume intérieur à climatisation contrôlée est posé sur un second volume de dimensions identiques. L'énergie produite par les activités quotidiennes est stockée pour un usage ultérieur tandis que des « systèmes de chauffage et de refroidissement utilisent la température stable de la terre » (13 °C ici) comme source de chaleur. Un vitrage double, appelé OpaciView par les architectes, aux verres séparés par une cavité d'air ventilée est enduit d'un film poreux d'oxyde de tungstène qui s'assombrit ou s'éclaircit au gré de la chaleur solaire. Des panneaux de cellules photovoltaïques équipent le toit, et les équipements de gymnastique utilisés génèrent de l'énergie qui peut être stockée. Même les matelas sont équipés pour stocker l'électricité produite par « l'énergie humaine en excès », comme le précisent les architectes. La maison peut être placée en « mode hibernation » lorsqu'elle n'est pas utilisée pour réduire au minimum la consommation énergétique. Elle sera réalisée en « matériaux recyclés, reconditionnés et renouvelables. Les variétés de bois sont choisies dans les forêts les plus proches gérées dans un esprit de développement durable ». Les capteurs d'eau du toit doublent les surfaces pouvant recueillir l'eau de pluie, qui est alors récupérée pour les toilettes et l'irrigation.

The Phantom House was designed for The New York Times Magazine as a willful exercise in maximizing environmental responsibility in architecture.

Das Phantom House wurde für das New York Times Magazine *mit dem expliziten Ziel entworfen, Umweltbewusstsein in der Architektur zu erhöhen.*

Le Phantom House a été conçue pour le New York Times Magazine *comme expérimentation pour accroître au maximum le sens de la responsabilité environnementale en architecture.*

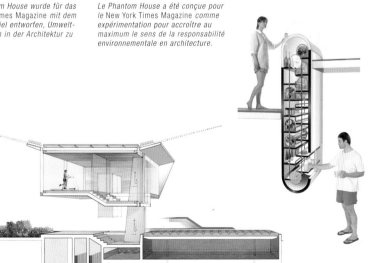

VLADIMIR DJUROVIC

Vladimir Djurovic Landscape Architecture (VDLA)
Villa Rizk
Broumana
Lebanon

Tel: +961 4 862 444/555
Fax: +961 4 862 462
E-mail: info@vladimirdjurovic.com
Web: www.vladimirdjurovic.com

VLADIMIR DJUROVIC was born to a Serb father and a Lebanese mother in 1967. He received a degree in Horticulture from Reading University in England in 1989 and his M.A. in Landscape Architecture from the University of Georgia in 1992, after having worked at EDAW in Atlanta. Vladimir Djurovic Landscape Architecture (VDLA) was created in 1995 in Beirut. The office has participated and won several international competitions, such as Freedom Park South Africa (2003). They have completed numerous private residences in Lebanon, including the F House (Dahr El Sawan, Lebanon, 2000–04, with Nabil Gholam). The firm won a 2008 Award of Honor in the residential design category from the American Society of Landscape Architects (ASLA) for its Bassil Mountain Escape project in Faqra, Lebanon. After the work on the award-winning Samir Kassir Square (Beirut, 2004, published here), current work includes the landscaping of the Wynford Drive site in Toronto, Canada, to accomodate the Aga Khan Museum by Fumihiko Maki and the Ismaili Center by Charles Correa. VDLA won the international competition for this design in 2006. Other work includes Beirut Marina, Solidere, BCD (Lebanon, architect: Steven Holl); and The Edge, a very large multiuse complex in Business Bay (Dubai, UAE, architects: RCR Arquitectes).

VLADIMIR DJUROVIC wurde 1967 als Sohn eines serbischen Vaters und einer libanesischen Mutter geboren. 1989 schloss er zunächst sein Gartenbaustudium an der Universität Reading in England ab, arbeitete für EDAW in Atlanta und absolvierte schließlich 1992 einen M.A. in Landschaftsarchitektur an der Universität von Georgia (USA). Sein Büro Vladimir Djurovic Landscape Architecture (VDLA) gründete er 1995 in Beirut. Das Büro hat mehrfach erfolgreich an internationalen Wettbewerben teilgenommen, etwa für den Freedom Park in Südafrika (2003). Das Team gestaltete zahlreiche Privatwohnbauten im Libanon, darunter das F House (Dahr El Sawan, Libanon, 2000–04, mit Nabil Gholam). Für sein Projekt Bassil Mountain Escape in Fakra, Libanon, wurde das Büro 2008 mit dem Ehrenpreis der American Society of Landscape Architects (ASLA) in der Kategorie Wohnbaugestaltung ausgezeichnet. Nach der Arbeit am preisgekrönten Samir-Kassir-Platz (Beirut, 2004, hier vorgestellt) sind aktuelle Projekte u. a. die Landschaftsgestaltung eines Grundstücks am Wynford Drive in Toronto, Kanada, für das Aga-Khan-Museum von Fumihiko Maki und das Ismaili Center von Charles Correa. Mit diesem Entwurf gewann VDLA 2006 einen internationalen Wettbewerb. Weitere Projekte sind die Beirut Marina, Solidere, BCD (Libanon, Architekt: Steven Holl), sowie The Edge, ein Mehrzweck-Großkomplex in der Business Bay von Dubai (VAE, Architekten: RCR Arquitectes).

VLADIMIR DJUROVIC est né d'un père serbe et d'une mère libanaise en 1967. Il est diplômé en horticulture de l'université Reading (G.-B.) en 1989 et a obtenu son M.A. en architecture du paysage de l'université de Géorgie (1992) après avoir travaillé pour l'agence EDAW à Atlanta. L'agence Vladimir Djurovic Landscape Architecture (VDLA) a été fondée en 1995 à Beyrouth. Elle a remporté plusieurs concours internationaux, dont celui du Freedom Park South Africa (2003), et a réalisé de nombreuses résidences privées au Liban, comme la maison F (avec Nabil Gholam, Dahr El Sawan, Liban, 2000–04). En 2008, elle a reçu un Prix d'honneur dans la catégorie « Projets résidentiels » de l'American Society of Landscape Architects (ASLA) pour le chalet de montagne Bassil à Faqra, Liban. Après avoir remporté le Prix Aga Khan pour le jardin Samir-Kassir (Beyrouth, 2004, publié ici), l'agence travaille sur les aménagements paysagers du site de Wynford Drive à Toronto, Canada, qui regroupe le Musée Aga Khan par Fumihiko Maki et le Centre ismaélien par Charles Correa. VDLA en avait remporté le concours international en 2006. D'autres projets comprennent : la Marina de Beyrouth, Solidere, BCD (Liban, architecte: Steven Holl), et The Edge, un très vaste complexe mixte à Business Bay (Dubai, EAU, architectes : RCR Arquitectes).

SAMIR KASSIR SQUARE

Beirut, Lebanon, 2004

Site area: 815 m². Client: Solidere (Société Libanaise de Développement et Reconstruction)
Cost: $322 000. Collaboration: Vladimir Djurovic (Principal), Paul De Mar Yousef (Design Architect),
Salim Kanaan (Project Architect)

Vladimir Djurovic has a decidedly minimalist style in his gardens and Samir Kassir Square is no exception. Located in the redeveloped Beirut Central District, the small park was conceived around two existing ficus trees that had somehow managed to survive the violence that wracked Beirut for years. "The challenge of this project," says Djurovic, "was to create a quiet refuge on a limited piece of land surrounded by buildings, while addressing the prominent street frontage that it occupies. In essence, to become a small escape dedicated to the city and its people." A raised "water mirror" is a central feature of the square, faced by a 20-meter-long solid stone bench. This project was a winner of the 2007 Aga Khan Award for Architecture. The jury citation reads: "The Samir Kassir Square is a restrained and serene urban public space that skillfully handles the conditions and infrastructure of its location in a city that has undergone rapid redevelopment. The Award will go to Vladimir Djurovic, the pre-eminent landscape architect working in Lebanon today."

Vladimir Djurovics Gärten zeichnen sich durch einen minimalistischen Stil aus, und der Samir-Kassir-Platz ist keine Ausnahme. Der im sanierten Zentrum von Beirut gelegene Park wurde um zwei Feigenbäume herum geplant, die erstaunlicherweise die jahrelang in Beirut wütende Gewalt überstanden haben. Djurovic zufolge lag „die Herausforderung des Projekts darin, einen Zufluchtsort auf einem engen, von Gebäuden umstandenen Grundstück zu schaffen und dabei die prominente Straßenfront des Platzes zu gestalten. Im Grunde sollte es ein kleiner Zufluchtsort für die Stadt und ihre Bewohner werden." Ein erhöhter „Wasserspiegel" ist zentraler Blickpunkt des Platzes, der von einer 20 m langen Steinbank flankiert wird. Das Projekt wurde 2007 mit dem Aga-Khan-Preis für Architektur ausgezeichnet. Die Jury merkte an: „Der Samir-Kassir-Platz ist ein zurückgenommener und heiterer öffentlicher Platz, der gekonnt mit den Bedingungen und der Infrastruktur seines Standorts in einer Stadt umgeht, die sich rasch verändert hat. Der Preis geht an Vladimir Djurovic, den herausragendsten heute im Libanon praktizierenden Landschaftsarchitekten."

Le style des jardins de Vladimir Djurovic est résolument minimaliste et le jardin Samir-Kassir n'y fait pas exception. Situé dans le centre reconstruit de Beyrouth, ce petit square a été conçu autour de deux ficus sauvés des violences qui dévastèrent la ville pendant des années. « Le défi de ce projet, explique Djurovic, était de créer un refuge sur une parcelle de terrain de dimensions limitées et entourée d'immeubles, tout en traitant son importante façade sur rue. Fondamentalement, l'idée était de réaliser un lieu dédié à la ville et à ses habitants. » Un « miroir d'eau » surélevé est l'élément central du projet, face à un banc de pierre massive de 20 m de long. Ce projet a remporté le Prix d'architecture Aga Khan 2007. La citation du jury précisait : « Le jardin Samir-Kassir est un espace public limité et serein qui s'adapte avec talent aux conditions et à l'infrastructure de sa situation dans une ville qui connaît un développement rapide. Le prix ira à Vladimir Djurovic, le plus éminent architecte paysagiste œuvrant actuellement au Liban. »

A central feature of the square are two ficus trees that symbolize the continuity of the place, in spite of all the events that have marked the history of Beirut in recent years.

Zentrale Elemente des Platzes sind zwei Feigenbäume – Symbol der Kontinuität des Ortes, allen Ereignissen zum Trotz, die die Geschichte Beiruts in den vergangenen Jahren geprägt haben.

Une des caractéristiques importantes de ce square est la présence de deux anciens ficus qui symbolisent les événements récents qui ont marqué l'histoire de Beyrouth.

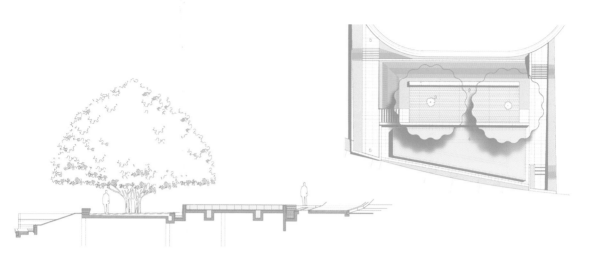

Dominated by its two old trees, the
square uses the sound of water
to create a haven of peace in the
middle of the city.

Der von den zwei Bäumen beherrschte
Platz wird dank des plätschernden
Wassers zum friedlichen Zufluchtsort
inmitten der Stadt.

Dominé par ses deux vieux arbres,
le jardin profite du bruit de l'eau,
créant un havre de paix au cœur de
la ville.

DENNIS DOLLENS

Dennis Dollens, Exodesic
40 Camino Cielo
Santa Fe, NM 87506
USA

Tel: +1 505 988 9236
Fax: +1 505 988 5820
E-mail: exodesic@mac.com
Web: www.exodesic.org

Born in Los Angeles in 1950, **DENNIS DOLLENS** has taught Design Biomimetics in the Genetic Architectures Program and in the Department of Ecology and Architecture at the Universitat Internacional de Catalunya's School of Architecture (Barcelona) since 2000. He lectures internationally on Digital-Biomimetic Architecture and his work in schools of industrial design and architecture. He is currently working on a Ph.D. at the University of Strathclyde, Glasgow. His studios are in Santa Fe, New Mexico, and Barcelona, Spain, and his most recent books are *D2A: Digital to Analog* (translated into Spanish and published as *De lo digital a lo analógico*) and *DBA: Digital-Botanic Architecture*. His current architectural work includes a 3D weaving prototype for an apartment building; a passive ventilating and self-shading 14-story tower; and the development of new sensor-embedded biomimetic exterior paneling using adobe, fiber pulp, and bio-resins. See his Tree Tower (Los Angeles, California, 2009), published here.

DENNIS DOLLENS wurde 1950 in Los Angeles geboren und unterrichtet seit 2000 biomimetisches Design im Programm für genetische Architektur an der Architekturfakultät der Universitat Internacional de Catalunya (Barcelona). Er lehrt international an Hochschulen für Industriedesign und Architektur in den Bereichen digital-biomimetische Architektur, wo er auch seine eigene Arbeit vorstellt. Derzeit arbeitet er an seiner Doktorarbeit an der Universität von Strathclyde, Glasgow. Er unterhält Büros in Santa Fe in New Mexico und in Barcelona. Seine jüngsten Publikationen sind *D2A: Digital to Analog* (auf Spanisch erschienen als *De lo digital a lo analógico*) und *DBA: Digital-Botanic Architecture*. Zu seinen aktuellen Architekturprojekten zählen ein 3-D-Gewebeprototyp für ein Apartmenthaus, ein passiv belüftetes und sich automatisch verschattendes 14-stöckiges Hochhaus und die Entwicklung einer neuartigen sensor-integrierten biomimetischen Außenverkleidung, bei der die ungebrannte Lehmziegel, Zellstoff und Bioharze zum Einsatz kommen. Vergleiche hierzu auch seinen Tree Tower (Los Angeles, Kalifornien, 2009, hier vorgestellt).

Né à Los Angeles en 1950, **DENNIS DOLLENS** a enseigné le design biomimétique dans le cadre d'un programme sur les architectures génétiques au Département d'écologie et d'architecture de l'École d'architecture de l'Université internationale de Catalogne (Barcelone) depuis 2000. Il donne de nombreuses conférences dans le monde sur « l'architecture numérique-biomimétique » et sur ses recherches dans des écoles d'architecture et de design industriel. Il prépare actuellement un Ph.D. (Université de Strathclyde, Glasgow). Ses bureaux se trouvent à Santa Fe (Nouveau-Mexique) et Barcelone, et ses livres les plus récents sont *D2A : Digital to Analog* (traduit en espagnol sous le titre *De lo digital a lo analógico*) et *DBA : Digital-Botanic Architecture*. Il travaille actuellement à un prototype weaving en 3D pour un immeuble d'appartements, une tour de quatorze niveaux à ventilation passive et autoprotection solaire ; et le développement d'un nouveau type de panneaux à capteurs incrustés extérieur biomimétique utilisant l'adobe, la pâte de fibres et des biorésines. Voir sa Tree Tower (Los Angeles, 2009), publiée ici.

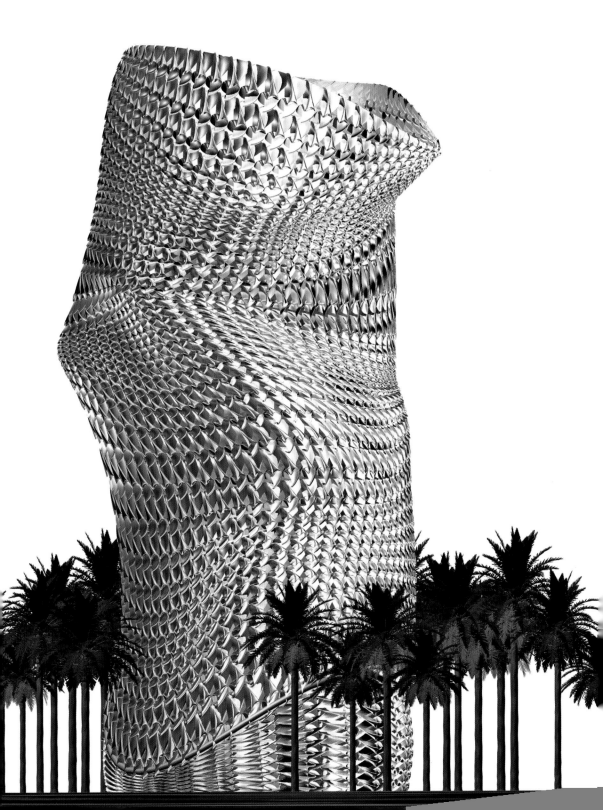

TREE TOWER

Los Angeles, California, USA, 2009

Floor area: 8919 m². Client: Lumen, Inc. Cost: $23 million

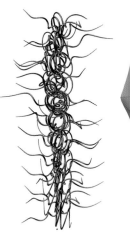 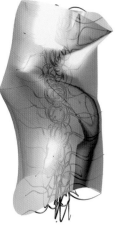  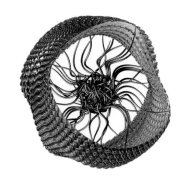

Although the final form of the tower does not really look like a tree, these drawings show how its structure evolved from its biomimetic origins.

Obwohl der Turm in seiner endgültigen Form nicht wirklich wie ein Baum wirkt, illustrieren diese Zeichnungen doch, wie sich die Struktur aus biomimetischen Ursprüngen entwickelt.

Bien que la forme finale de la tour ne soit pas celle d'un arbre, ces dessins montrent l'évolution de la structure à partir de ses origines biomimétiques.

As is the case in much of the work of Dennis Dollens, this project is based on biomimetics. The design features "digitally grown" flexible and therefore earthquake-resistant trusses. Dollens used four software programs to create these forms—Xfrog, ParaCloud, Rhinoceros, and 3DS MAX. Digital simulations of tree, branch, and root growth are the basis for the structure. The underground elements would theoretically be "bio-reactors in the form of underground pods for the harvesting of water and processing sewage with bacteria." The skin, both interior and exterior, is formed with 2200 parametrically designed monocoque panels with an interlocking leaf pattern created with ParaCloud. Each of these panels will have glass elements, though the building itself would have neither traditional windows, nor a normal door, being entered below grade. The skin serves as a sunscreen "while also allowing filtered views to the exterior—as if occupants were looking through a tree's leaves." Denis Dollens concludes: "While a first impression of the Tree Tower may not suggest that it is mimicking nature the building's digital heritage is tightly linked to functions found in plants. As the project moves into semifinal phases, environmental sensors for testing air pollution and allergens are being researched, as is the potential for the building's skin panels to filter its incoming air."

Wie viele Arbeiten von Dennis Dollens basiert auch dieses Projekt auf dem Prinzip der Biomimetik. Der Entwurf zeichnet sich durch „digital gezüchtete", flexible und damit erdbebensichere Träger aus. Dollens nutzte vier verschiedene Softwareprogramme, um diese Formen zu entwerfen – Xfrog, ParaCloud, Rhinoceros und 3DS MAX. Grundlage der Konstruktion sind digital simulierte Wachstumsprozesse von Bäumen, Ästen und Wurzeln. Bei den unterirdischen Komponenten handelt es sich um bisher hypothetische, „unterirdische, kapselartige Bio-Reaktoren, die Frischwasser sammeln und mithilfe von Bakterien Abwässer klären sollen". Die Gebäudehaut wurde innen wie außen aus 2200 parametrisch generierten Monocoque-Paneelen gestaltet, die zu einem ineinander zahnenden Blattmuster angeordnet und mit ParaCloud entwickelt wurden. Diese Paneele verfügen über integrierte Glaselemente, wobei der Bau weder traditionelle Fenster noch eine übliche Tür hat, sondern unterirdisch erschlossen wird. Die Außenhaut dient als Sonnenschutz und „filtert zugleich den Ausblick – als würden die Bewohner durch das Laub eines Baumes blicken". Dennis Dollens fasst zusammen: „Auch wenn es auf den ersten Blick nicht so scheint, als ahme der Tree Tower die Natur nach, knüpft das digitale Erbgut des Bauwerks doch eng an pflanzliche Funktionen an. Während sich das Projekt seiner Endphase nähert, experimentieren wir mit umweltsensiblen Sensoren, die Luftverschmutzung und Allergengehalte messen können, sowie mit der Option, einströmende Luft durch die Paneele der Gebäudehaut zu filtern."

Comme souvent chez Dennis Dollens, ce projet repose sur une approche biomimétique. Il présente des poutres « d'origine numérique » souples et donc résistantes aux tremblements de terre. L'architecte a utilisé quatre logiciels pour créer ces formes : Xfrog, ParaCloud, Rhinoceros et 3DS MAX. Des simulations numériques de la croissance d'arbres, de branches et de racines sont à la base de la structure. Théoriquement, des éléments, des « bioréacteurs en forme de cosses souterraines pour capter l'eau et traiter les eaux usées par bactéries », devraient être mis en place dans le sol. La peau, aussi bien externe qu'interne, se compose de 2200 panneaux monocoques de conception paramétrique à motif de feuillage entrelacé créé à l'aide de ParaCloud. Chacun de ces panneaux sera doté d'éléments en verre, bien que le bâtiment ne doive avoir ni fenêtres traditionnelles, ni porte classique et que son accès se fasse par le sous-sol. La peau sert d'écran de protection solaire « tout en autorisant des vues filtrées vers l'extérieur, comme si les occupants regardaient à travers le feuillage d'un arbre ». Denis Dollens conclut : « Si, à première vue, la Tree Tower n'imite pas la nature, le patrimoine numérique de l'immeuble est étroitement lié à des fonctions observées parmi les plantes. Le projet entre dans ses phases semi-finales, et nous étudions des capteurs environnementaux pour tester la pollution de l'air et la présence d'allergènes ainsi que le potentiel des panneaux de la peau dans la filtration de l'air entrant. »

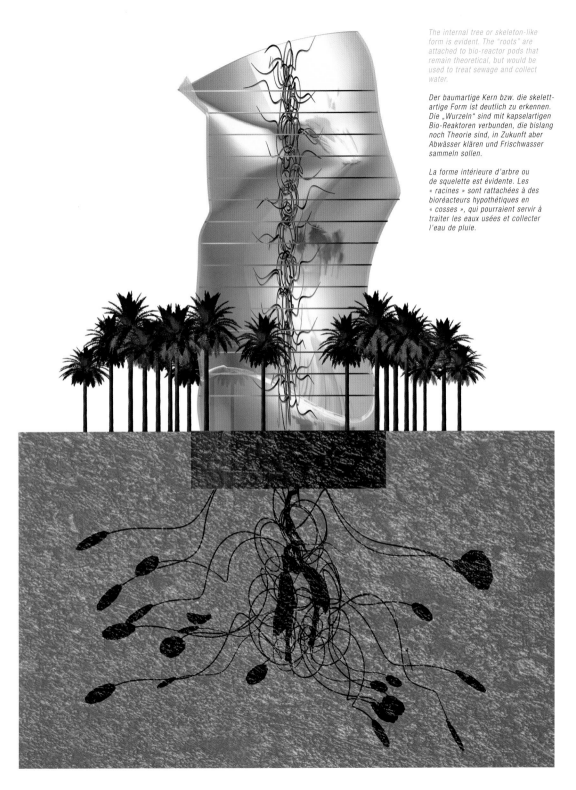

The internal tree or skeleton-like form is evident. The "roots" are attached to bio-reactor pods that remain theoretical, but would be used to treat sewage and collect water.

Der baumartige Kern bzw. die skelettartige Form ist deutlich zu erkennen. Die „Wurzeln" sind mit kapselartigen Bio-Reaktoren verbunden, die bislang noch Theorie sind, in Zukunft aber Abwässer klären und Frischwasser sammeln sollen.

La forme intérieure d'arbre ou de squelette est évidente. Les « racines » sont rattachées à des bioréacteurs hypothétiques en « cosses », qui pourraient servir à traiter les eaux usées et collecter l'eau de pluie.

ECOSISTEMA URBANO

Ecosistema Urbano Arquitectos
Estanislao Figueras 6
Madrid 28008
Spain

Tel: +34 91 559 16 01
E-mail: info@ecosistemaurbano.com
Web: www.ecosistemaurbano.com

ECOSISTEMA URBANO was created in 2000 by two partners: Belinda Tato, born in Madrid in 1971, who studied at the ETSA of Madrid (1999) and the Bartlett School of Architecture, London (1996); and Jose Luis Vallejo, born in Bilbao in 1971, who also studied at the ETSAM (1999) and Bartlett School (1996). Diego Garcia-Setien, born in Madrid in 1974, graduated from the Istituto Universitario di Architettura di Venezia (1997) and the ETSAM (2000) and worked with Tato and Vallejo on the Ecoboulevard project. Ecosistema Urbano has received more than 25 awards since the creation of their firm, in national and international architecture design competitions. In 2007 they were nominated for the European Union Prize for Contemporary Architecture Mies van der Rohe Award for "Emerging European Architects" and they were honored with an *AR* Award for emerging architecture. They received the Silver Award (Holcim Foundation Awards 2008 Europe) for their temporary urban extension in a former landfill in, Maribor, Slovenia. Currently the team is involved in research projects concerning the future of city design that they call "eco-techno-logical cities," financed by the Spanish Ministry of Industry. They are working on several urban proposals for different Spanish municipalities (see the Ecoboulevard of Vallecas in Madrid, 2006, published here) and one of their projects represented Madrid at Shanghai Expo '10.

ECOSISTEMA URBANO wurde 2000 von zwei Partnern gegründet: Belinda Tato, 1971 in Madrid geboren, Studium an der ETSAM in Madrid (1999) und der Bartlett School of Architecture, London (1996), und José Luis Vallejo, 1971 in Bilbao geboren, ebenfalls Studium an der ETSAM (1999) und der Bartlett School (1996). Diego Garcia-Setien, 1974 in Madrid geboren, Abschlüsse am Istituto Universitario di Architettura di Venezia (1997) und der ETSAM (2000), arbeitete mit Tato und Vallejo am Ecoboulevard in Vallecas. Seit Gründung des Büros wurde Ecosistema Urbano mit über 25 Preisen in nationalen und internationalen Entwurfswettbewerben ausgezeichnet. 2007 wurden die Partner für den Mies-van-der-Rohe-Preis für zeitgenössische Architektur der Europäischen Union als „aufstrebende europäische Architekten" nominiert und erhielten einen *AR* Award for Emerging Architecture der britischen Zeitschrift *Architectural Review*. Für ihr temporäres Stadterweiterungsprojekt auf einer ehemaligen Deponie in Maribor, Slowenien, wurden sie mit dem Silver Award (Europapreis 2008 der Holcim Foundation) ausgezeichnet. Zurzeit entwickeln sie Zukunftsperspektiven für die Stadtplanung und arbeiten an einer von ihnen als „öko-techno-logisch" bezeichneten Stadt, Untersuchungen, die vom spanischen Ministerium für Industrie finanziert werden. Das Team arbeitet an einer Reihe von Stadtplanungsentwürfen für verschiedene spanische Gemeinden (u. a. Ecoboulevard in Vallecas, Madrid, 2006, hier vorgestellt). Ein Projekt des Büros vertrat Madrid auf der Expo '10 in Shanghai.

L'agence **ECOSISTEMA URBANO** a été créée en 2000 par deux associés : Belinda Tato, née à Madrid en 1971, qui a étudié à l'ETSA de Madrid (1999) et à l'École Bartlett d'Architecture de Londres (1996), et José Luis Vallejo, né à Bilbao en 1971, qui a également étudié à l'ETSA (1999) et à l'École Bartlett (1996). Diego Garcia-Setien, né à Madrid en 1974, diplômé de l'Institut universitaire d'architecture de Venise (1997) et de l'ETSA de Madrid (2000), a travaillé avec Tato et Vallejo au projet de l'Écoboulevard de Vallecas. Ecosistema Urbano a obtenu plus de 25 distinctions à des concours d'architecture nationaux ou internationaux depuis la création de leur agence. En 2007, ils ont été nominés pour le Prix d'architecture contemporaine de l'Union Européenne-Mies van der Rohe dans la catégorie « Jeunes architectes européens » et ont reçu un *AR* Award pour l'architecture émergeante. En 2008, l'European Holcim Awards (organisé par la Holcim Foundation) leur a décerné un Silver Award pour l'extension urbaine temporaire dans une ancienne déchetterie (Maribor, Slovénie). Actuellement, ils se consacrent à des projets de recherche sur le futur des villes qu'ils appellent les « cités éco-techno-logiques », financées par le ministère espagnol de l'Industrie. Ils travaillent sur plusieurs projets pour diverses villes espagnoles, tels que l'Écoboulevard de Vallecas à Madrid (2006) publié ici, et ont représentés l'Espagne à Expo '10 à Shanghai.

ECOBOULEVARD OF VALLECAS

Madrid, Spain, 2006

Site area: 500 x 45 m
Client: Empresa Municipal de Vivienda y Suelo de Madrid. Cost: €2.6 million

According to the architects: "The proposal for the Ecoboulevard of Vallecas can be defined as an operation of urban recycling that consists of the installation of three socially revitalizing air trees placed in the existing urban pattern, the densification of trees within their existing concourse, the reduction and asymmetric disposition of the traffic routes…" The "air trees," powered with photovoltaic cells, are considered "temporary prostheses," to be dismantled, "leaving remaining spaces that resemble forest clearings." The architects were selected through a competition with a social and environmental program intended to improve daily life in the area. The "air trees" occupy space that should eventually be populated with mature real trees and are intended as gathering places. The "air trees" contain a system that uses water vapor with power generated by the photovoltaic cells to create a space that is "8°C to 10°C cooler than the rest of the street in summer."

Die Architekten erklären: „Der Entwurf für den Ecoboulevard in Vallecas lässt sich als urbane Recyclingoperation definieren, bei der drei sozial stimulierende ‚Luftbäume' in ein bestehendes urbanes Raster integriert werden, sowie als Steigerung der Baumdichte in ihrer unmittelbaren Umgebung und zugleich als Reduzierung und asymmetrische Verschiebung der Verkehrswege …" Die mit Solarzellen betriebenen „Luftbäume" sind als „temporäre Prothesen" gedacht, die letzendlich wieder abgebaut werden und „Räume entstehen lassen, die an Waldlichtungen erinnern". Den Zuschlag erhielten die Architekten im Rahmen eines sozial und umweltpolitisch orientierten Wettbewerbs, dessen Ziel es war, den Alltag im Stadtviertel zu verbessern. Die „Luftbäume" besetzen Flächen, auf denen später große Bäume gepflanzt werden sollen, und dienen als Treffpunkte. Die Bäume sind mit Solarzellen zur Stromerzeugung und einem Wasserzerstäubungssystem ausgestattet. So entsteht ein Ort, der „im Sommer 8 bis 10 °C kühler ist als der übrige Teil der Straße".

« La proposition de l'Écoboulevard de Vallecas peut se définir comme une opération de recyclage urbain qui consiste en l'installation de trois "arbres d'air" insérés dans le tissu urbain, censés dynamiser les relations sociales. Ils s'accompagnent d'une densification des plantations d'arbres existantes, ainsi que d'une réduction et d'une implantation en asymétrie des axes de circulation… », expliquent les architectes. Ces « arbres d'air », alimentés par des cellules photovoltaïques, sont considérés comme des « prothèses temporaires » prévues pour être ultérieurement démantelées « en laissant les espaces subsistants ressembler à des clairières en forêt ». Les architectes ont été retenus, après concours, sur un programme social et environnemental destiné à améliorer la vie quotidienne du quartier. Les « arbres d'air » occupent un espace qui devrait sans doute être davantage planté d'arbres venus à maturité, et deviendra un lieu public agréable. Ils contiennent un système de diffusion de vapeur d'eau dont l'énergie est fournie par des cellules photovoltaïques pour créer un volume dont la température est de « 8 à 10 °C plus basse que le reste de la rue en été ».

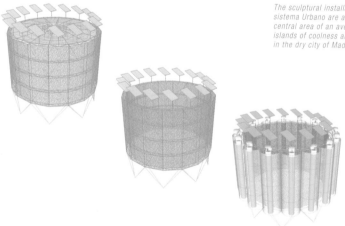

The sculptural installations of Ecosistema Urbano are arrayed in the central area of an avenue, providing islands of coolness and greenery in the dry city of Madrid.

Die skulpturalen Installationen von Ecosistema Urbano sind auf der Mittelachse einer Allee angeordnet und schaffen kühle, grüne Inseln inmitten der Trockenheit von Madrid.

Les installations sculpturales d'Ecosistema Urbano se répartissent le long de la zone centrale du boulevard. Ils constituent des îlots de fraîcheur et de verdure dans l'air sec de Madrid.

The round volumes of the pavilions house nothing but vegetation and serve no "real" purpose in the usual sense of architecture. They might thus be compared to ecological sculptures.

In den runden Baukörpern der Pavillons sind ausschließlich Pflanzen untergebracht, sie dienen keinem „wirklichen" Zweck im üblichen architektonischen Sinn. Man könnte sie also als ökologische Skulpturen verstehen.

Les volumes circulaires des pavillons n'abritent que de la végétation mais ne répondent à aucun objectif concret en termes d'architecture. On pourrait les comparer à des sculptures écologiques.

Another pavilion borrows its formal vocabulary from industrial architecture, but like the others is lifted off the ground, making it function like a tree or perhaps a wind chimney.

Ein weiterer Pavillon orientiert sich formal an industrieller Architektur, ist jedoch wie die übrigen über dem Boden aufgeständert und „funktioniert" am ehesten wie ein Baum oder Windturm.

Un autre pavillon emprunte son vocabulaire à l'architecture industrielle. Comme les autres, il est surélevé par rapport au sol, et opère comme un arbre, ou une cheminée à vent.

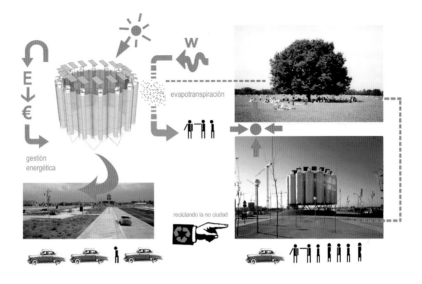

evapotranspiración

gestión energética

reciclando la no ciudad

FEARON HAY

Fearon Hay Architects Ltd.
PO Box 90-311
Victoria Street West
Auckland 1142
New Zealand

Tel: +64 9 309 0128
Fax: +64 9 309 0827
E-mail: enquiry@fearonhay.com
Web: www.fearonhay.com

JEFFREY FEARON was born in 1972 in Auckland. He received his B.Arch degree from the University of Queensland (1990–95). **TIM HAY** was born in 1973, also in Auckland, and received a B.Arch degree from Auckland University (1993–97). They established Fearon Hay Architects in 1998. They describe their own practice and its largely residential work as follows: "Fearon Hay projects include commissions in diverse environments—coastal, urban, rural, lakeside, and alpine. Works are located in both North and South Islands of New Zealand." Their projects include: the Coromandel Beach House (Coromandel Peninsula, 2000); Kellands Commercial Office Building (Auckland, 2001); Parnell House (Auckland, 2002); Darling Point Apartment (Sydney, 2002); Shark Alley Retreat (Great Barrier Island, Auckland, 2002–03, published here); Lake Wakatipu House (Queenstown, 2003); reworking Sargent House (1973) to Dunn House (Auckland, 2005); Clooney Restaurant (Auckland, 2006); Northland Beach House (Rawhiti, 2007); Yates-Allison House (Tutukaka Coast, 2007); Sandhills Road House (Great Barrier Island, Auckland, 2007); Closeburg Station Guest House (Queenstown, 2008); Wintergarden at The Northern Club (Auckland, 2008); and Tribeca Loft (New York, New York, USA, 2008), all in New Zealand and Australia unless stated otherwise.

JEFFREY FEARON wurde 1972 in Auckland geboren. Er schloss sein Studium an der Universität von Queensland (1990–95) mit einem B.Arch. ab. **TIM HAY** wurde 1973 ebenfalls in Auckland geboren und absolvierte seinen B.Arch. an der Universität von Auckland (1993–97). 1998 gründeten die beiden ihr Büro Fearon Hay Architects. Sie beschreiben ihre Firma und deren überwiegendes Engagement im Wohnungsbau wie folgt: „Zu den Projekten von Fearon Hay zählen Aufträge in den verschiedensten Kontexten – an der Küste, in der Stadt, auf dem Land, an Seen und in den Bergen. Die Projekte liegen auf der Nord- ebenso wie auf der Südinsel Neuseelands." Zu ihren Arbeiten zählen: das Haus am Coromandel Beach (Coromandel-Halbinsel, 2000), Kellands Commercial Office Building (Auckland, 2001), Haus Parnell (Auckland, 2002), Darling Point Apartment (Sydney, 2002), Shark Alley Retreat (Great-Barrier-Insel, Auckland, 2002–03, hier vorgestellt), das Haus am Wakatipu-See (Queenstown, 2003), Umbau des Hauses Sargent (1973) zum Haus Dunn (Auckland, 2005), das Restaurant Clooney (Auckland, 2006), das Haus am Northland Beach (Rawhiti, 2007), Haus Yates-Allison (Tutukaka Coast, 2007), Haus Sandhills Road (Great-Barrier-Insel, Auckland, 2007), Gästehaus Closeburg Station (Queenstown, 2008), Wintergarden in The Northern Club (Auckland, 2008) sowie ein Loft in Tribeca (New York, USA, 2008), alle in Neuseeland und Australien, sofern nicht anders vermerkt.

JEFFREY FEARON, né en 1972 à Auckland, est B. Arch de l'université du Queensland (1990–95). **TIM HAY**, né en 1973, également à Auckland, est B. Arch de l'université d'Auckland (1993–97). Ils ont créé Fearon Hay Architects en 1998. Ils présentent ainsi leur agence et leurs interventions, essentiellement dans le domaine résidentiel : « Les projets de Fearon Hay comprennent des commandes pour divers types d'environnement : côtier, urbain, rural, lacustre et montagneux. Leurs réalisations sont situées aussi bien dans l'île Nord que dans l'île Sud de la Nouvelle-Zélande. » Parmi leurs réalisations : la maison Coromandel Beach (Coromandel Peninsula, 2000) ; l'immeuble de bureaux Kellands (Auckland, 2001) ; la maison Parnell (Auckland, 2002) ; l'appartement de Darling Point (Sydney, 2002) ; le chalet de Shark Alley (Great Barrier Island, Auckland, 2002–03, publié ici) ; la maison de Lake Wakatipu (Queenstown, 2003) ; la transformation de la maison Sargent (1973) en la maison Dunn (Auckland, 2005) ; le restaurant Clooney (Auckland, 2006) ; la maison de Northland Beach (Rawhiti, 2007) ; la maison Yates-Allison (Tutukaka Coast, 2007) ; la maison de Sandhills Road (Great Barrier Island, Auckland, 2007) ; la maison d'hôtes de Closeburg Station (Queenstown, 2008) ; le Wintergarden situé dans The Northern Club (Auckland, 2008) et un loft à Tribeca (New York, États-Unis, 2008), toutes en Nouvelle-Zélande et en Australie, sauf exception.

SHARK ALLEY RETREAT

Great Barrier Island, Auckland, New Zealand, 2002–03

Floor area: 250 m². Client: not disclosed. Cost: €400 000

As the topographic site plan above and the photos to the right show, the Shark Alley Retreat is located on a rough, steeply sloped site on the water's edge.

Wie der topografische Geländeplan (oben) und die Fotos rechts zeigen, liegt das Shark Alley Retreat auf einem kargen, steil abfallenden Grundstück direkt am Ufer.

Comme le montrent le plan topographique du site ci-contre et les photos à droite, cette résidence est implantée sur un terrain en pente et vierge, au bord de l'océan.

Great Barrier Island is located 90 kilometers to the northeast of central Auckland in the outer Hauraki Gulf. It is the fourth-largest island of New Zealand's main chain of islands and has a population of about 850 people. The architects describe this house as a "comfortable shelter from a potentially hostile exposure." The hilly, 6.5-hectare site is set at the southern end of Medlands Bay on the east coast of Great Barrier Island. Their strategy was to "set an outdoor courtyard into the side of the hill and use the resulting retaining terraces to nest the overall composition." An open veranda around the courtyard provides the main living areas. Sliding glass doors and sliding aluminum shutters provide a combination of openness and protection from the prevailing sea winds. Given its exposed and rather remote location, the architects had to take into account issues related to the house's environment. Tim Hay explains: "Sustainability and respect for the site were drivers for the house at Shark Alley. The house is completely off the grid and has no connections to utilities. Power is generated by a solar array hidden in the surrounding bush. Sewage is treated by an on-site bio-cycle system and water is harvested from the roof and stored in tanks."

Die Great-Barrier-Insel liegt 90 km nordöstlich von Auckland im äußeren Hauraki-Golf. Sie ist die viertgrößte Hauptinsel Neuseelands und hat 850 Bewohner. Die Architekten beschreiben das Haus als „behaglichen Zufluchtsort in einer potenziell exponierten und feindlichen Lage". Das 6,5 ha große hügelige Grundstück liegt am südlichen Ende der Medlands-Bucht an der Ostküste der Great-Barrier-Insel. Die Strategie der Architekten war es, „den Hof in der Senke des Hügels zu positionieren und die Terrassen ringsum zu nutzen, um die Gesamtkomposition einzurahmen". Die Hauptwohnbereiche liegen an einer offenen Veranda, die den Hof umgibt. Durch verschiebbare Glastüren und Fensterläden aus Aluminium ergibt sich eine Mischung aus Offenheit und Schutz vor den vorherrschenden Seewinden. Angesichts der exponierten und vergleichsweise entlegenen Lage musste sich das Haus zwingend mit seiner Umwelt auseinandersetzen. Tim Hays erklärt: „Nachhaltigkeit und respektvoller Umgang mit dem Grundstück waren Impulse für das Haus in Shark Alley. Es liegt vollkommen jenseits jeglicher Infrastruktur und hat keinerlei Anschluss an die Energieversorgung. Strom wird durch eine Solaranlage erzeugt, die in der umgebenden Buschlandschaft verschwindet. Abwässer fließen vor Ort in einen biologischen Aufbereitungskreislauf; Wasser wird auf dem Dach gesammelt und in Tanks gespeichert."

Great Barrier Island se trouve à 90 km au nord-est d'Auckland dans le golfe d'Hauraki. Peuplée de 850 habitants, c'est la quatrième plus grande île de la chaîne d'îles de la Nouvelle-Zélande. Les architectes décrivent cette résidence comme « un abri confortable face à une exposition potentiellement hostile ». Le terrain vallonné de 6,5 ha est situé à l'extrémité sud de Medlands Bay sur la côte est de l'île. La stratégie adoptée était « d'implanter une cour extérieure dans le flanc de la colline et d'utiliser les terrasses de soutènement qui en résultent pour intégrer la composition globale ». Une véranda ouverte tout autour de la cour constitue en fait les espaces de vie principaux. Des portes en verre et des volets d'aluminium tous coulissants offrent une combinaison d'ouverture et de protection par rapport aux vents dominants venus de la mer. Étant donnée sa position exposée et assez isolée, la maison a dû prendre en compte son propre environnement. Tim Hay explique : « La durabilité et le respect du site nous ont guidés dans la conception de cette maison. Entièrement en dehors de la trame urbanistique, elle n'est reliée à aucun réseau. L'électricité provient d'un dispositif solaire dissimulé dans le bush environnant. Les eaux usées sont traitées par un système à cycle biologique et l'eau de pluie est récupérée par les toits et conservée dans un réservoir. »

*The house is exceedingly simple
in its lines and plan. Its modernism
is undeniable, as is its openness
to the natural environment.*

*Linienführung und Grundriss des
Hauses sind ausgesprochen schlicht.
Der Einfluss der Moderne ist ebenso
wenig zu leugnen wie die Offenheit
zum landschaftlichen Umfeld.*

*La maison est d'apparence et
de plan extrêmement simples.
Son modernisme est indéniable,
de même que son ouverture sur
l'environnement naturel.*

Given the climate, the house boasts
the capacity to be exceptionally open
to the outdoors, making the distinction between inside and outside
sometimes difficult to discern.

Dank des Klimas kann sich das
Haus außergewöhnlich stark nach
außen öffnen, wodurch die Grenzen
zwischen Innen- und Außenraum mit-
unter zu verschwimmen scheinen.

Étant donné le climat, la maison peut
se permettre de s'ouvrir largement
sur la nature, ce qui rend parfois
la distinction entre l'intérieur et
l'extérieur difficilement perceptible.

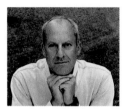

FOSTER + PARTNERS

Foster + Partners / Riverside / 22 Hester Road
London SW11 4AN / UK
Tel: +44 20 77 38 04 55 / Fax: +44 20 77 38 11 07
E-mail: enquiries@fosterandpartners.com / Web: www.fosterandpartners.com

Born in Manchester in 1935, **NORMAN FOSTER** studied Architecture and City Planning at Manchester University (1961). He was awarded a Henry Fellowship to Yale University, where he received his M.Arch degree and met Richard Rogers, with whom he created Team 4. He received the RIBA Gold Medal for Architecture (1983) and was knighted in 1990. The American Institute of Architects granted them their Gold Medal for Architecture in 1994. Sir Norman Foster has notably built the IBM Pilot Head Office (Cosham, UK, 1970–71); the Sainsbury Centre for Visual Arts and Crescent Wing, University of East Anglia (Norwich, UK, 1976–77; 1989–91); the Hong Kong and Shanghai Banking Corporation Headquarters (Hong Kong, 1981–86); London's third airport, Stansted (1987–91); the Faculty of Law at the University of Cambridge (Cambridge, UK, 1993–95); and the Commerzbank Headquarters, Frankfurt (Germany, 1994–97). Recent projects include the airport at Chek Lap Kok (Hong Kong, 1995–98); the new German Parliament, Reichstag (Berlin, Germany, 1995–99); Millennium Bridge (London, 1996–2000); the British Museum Redevelopment (London, 1997–2000); Greater London Authority (1998–2002); Petronas University of Technology (Seri Iskandar, Malaysia, 1999–2004, published here); Millau Viaduct (Millau, France, 1993–2005); 126 Philip Street (Sydney, Australia, 1997–2005); Wembley Stadium (London, 1996–2006); and Beijing Airport (China, 2003–08). Current work includes the Aldar Central Market Towers (Abu Dhabi, UAE, 2006–10); and the 78-story 200 Greenwich Street Tower (World Trade Center, New York, 2006–12).

NORMAN FOSTER wurde 1935 in Manchester geboren, wo er später bis 1961 Architektur und Stadtplanung studierte. Ein Henry Fellowship ermöglichte ihm das Studium in Yale, wo er seinen M.Arch. absolvierte und Richard Rogers begegnete, mit dem er das Büro Team 4 gründete. Er wurde mit der RIBA-Goldmedaille für Architektur ausgezeichnet (1983) und 1990 in den Adelsstand erhoben. 1994 verlieh ihm das American Institute of Architects die Goldmedaille für Architektur. Zu Sir Norman Fosters besonders hervorzuhebenden Bauten zählen: der IBM-Hauptsitz in Cosham (Cosham, Großbritannien, 1970–71), das Sainsbury Centre for Visual Arts und der Crescent Wing, Universität von East Anglia (Norwich, Großbritannien, 1976–77, 1989–91), der Hauptsitz der Hong Kong and Shanghai Banking Corporation (Hongkong, 1981–86), Londons dritter Flughafen Stansted (1987–91), die Fakultät für Rechtswissenschaften der Universität Cambridge (Großbritannien, 1993–95) sowie der Hauptsitz der Commerzbank, Frankfurt am Main (1994–97). Jüngere Projekte sind u. a. der Flughafen Chek Lap Kok (Hongkong, 1995–98), der Umbau des Reichstagsgebäudes (Berlin, 1995–99), die Millennium Bridge (London, 1996–2000), der Umbau des British Museum (London, 1997–2000), die Greater London Authority (1998–2002), die Technische Universität Petronas (Seri Iskandar, Malaysia, 1999–2004, hier vorgestellt), das Viadukt von Millau (Frankreich, 1993–2005), 126 Philip Street (Sydney, Australien, 1997–2005), das neue Wembley-Stadion (London, 1996–2006) und der Flughafen Peking (China, 2003–08). Aktuelle Projekte sind u. a. die Aldar Central Market Towers (Abu Dhabi, VAE, 2006–10) sowie das 78-stöckige Hochhaus 200 Greenwich Street (World Trade Center, New York, 2006–12).

Né à Manchester en 1935, **NORMAN FOSTER** a étudié l'architecture et l'urbanisme à l'université de Manchester (1961). Il a bénéficié d'une Henry Fellowship pour l'université Yale, où il a passé son M. Arch et rencontré Richard Rogers avec lequel il a créé l'agence Team 4. Il a reçu la médaille d'or de l'Institut royal des architectes anglais (RIBA) en 1983, et a été anobli en 1990. L'Institut américain des architectes lui a accordé sa médaille d'or en 1994. Sir Norman Foster a construit en particulier : le siège pilote d'IBM (Cosham, G.-B., 1970–71) ; le Sainsbury Centre for Visual Arts et le Crescent Wing, université de East Anglia (Norwich, G.-B., 1976–77 ; 1989–91) ; le siège de la Hong Kong and Shanghai Banking Corporation (Hong Kong, 1981–86) ; Stansted, troisième aéroport de Londres (1987–91) ; la faculté de droit de l'université de Cambridge (Cambridge, G.-B., 1993–95) et le siège de la Commerzbank à Francfort (Allemagne, 1994–97). Parmi ses récentes commandes : l'aéroport de Chek Lap Kok (Hong Kong, 1995–98) ; le nouveau Parlement allemand, le Reichstag (Berlin, 1995–99) ; le Millenium Bridge (Londres, 1996–2000) ; les nouveaux aménagements du British Museum (Londres, 1997–2000) ; l'immeuble de la Greater London Authority (1998–2002) ; la Petronas University of Technology (Seri Iskandar, Malaisie, 1998–2004, publié ici) ; le viaduc de Millau (Millau, France, 1993–2005) ; l'immeuble du 126 Philip Street (Sydney, Australie, 1997–2005) ; le Wembley Stadium (Londres, 1996–2006) et l'aéroport de Pékin (Chine, 2003–08). Actuellement, son agence travaille, entre autres, sur les projets des tours du Aldar Central Market (Abu Dhabi, EAU, 2006–10) et la tour de 78 niveaux du 200 Greenwich Street (World Trade Center, New York, 2006–12).

PETRONAS UNIVERSITY OF TECHNOLOGY

Seri Iskandar, Malaysia, 1999–2004

Site area: 450 ha. Gross floor area: 240 000 m². Client: Universiti Teknologi Petronas
Cost: not disclosed. Collaboration: GDP Architects

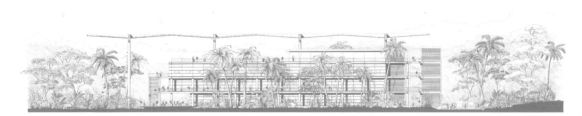

The large canopies of the university and its curving patterns demonstrate its respect for nature and capacity to function efficiently even in periods of very heavy rain.

Die geschwungenen, monumentalen Baldachindächer der Universität zeugen vom Respekt für die Natur und gewährleisten selbst in der Regenzeit effiziente Funktionalität.

Les vastes auvents incurvés de l'université traduisent une volonté de respecter la nature et de fonctionner efficacement même en période de fortes pluies.

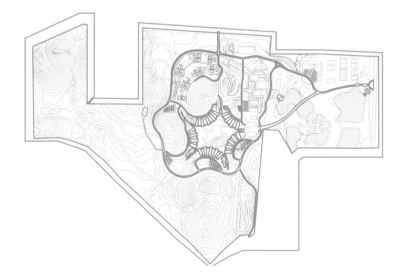

This project includes teaching facilities for 6000 students studying civil, mechanical, chemical, and electrical engineering. Funded in large part by the Malaysian oil company Petronas, the campus is located in the jungle, 300 kilometers north of Kuala Lumpur. A curved roof held up by tall, thin columns marks the pedestrian routes within the complex, acknowledging the frequent heavy rains. Four-story buildings placed under this canopy contain labs, lecture halls, and other communal facilities. The entrance to the campus is singled out by a large drum-shaped resource center containing a library and a multipurpose theater with a capacity for 3000 people. The master plan for the campus takes into account the likelihood of future expansion. A winner of the 2007 Aga Khan Award for Architecture, this project was described by the jury in glowing terms: "A soaring, crescent-form roof supported by steel columns winds around the edge of the site, covering pedestrian routes and providing a defined, shaded zone for social interaction and circulation. To preserve the natural topography, the core academic buildings are wrapped around the base of a series of knolls; viewed from a distance, the university's canopy elevation echoes the tree canopy of the densely forested site. This is an exemplary use of a performance-based approach to architectural design that goes beyond the diagram. The design has been carried through to completion with meticulous detail, rigor, and persistence, and engendered a transfer of knowledge, process, and technology between Foster + Partners and the Malaysian firm GDP Architects, which has in turn led to their collaboration on other projects."

Das Projekt umfasst Unterrichtsräume für 6000 Studenten in den Studiengängen Bauingenieurwesen, Maschinenbau, Verfahrenstechnik und Elektrotechnik. Der zum Großteil von der malaysischen Ölfirma Petronas finanzierte Campus liegt im Dschungel, 300 km nördlich von Kuala Lumpur. Ein von schlanken, hohen Säulen getragenes geschwungenes Baldachindach schützt die Fußgängerwege des Komplexes, was aufgrund der häufigen Regenfälle erforderlich ist. Die unter dem Dach gelegenen vierstöckigen Gebäude bieten Raum für Labors, Vorlesungssäle und andere Gemeinschaftseinrichtungen. Der Eingang zum Campus wird von einem großen Rundbau markiert, in dem sich die Bibliothek und ein Mehrzwecktheater mit 3000 Plätzen befinden. Der Masterplan für den Campus berücksichtigt vorhersehbare Erweiterungen. Das Projekt, 2007 mit dem Aga-Khan-Preis für Architektur ausgezeichnet, wird von der Jury überschwänglich gelobt: „Ein hoch aufragendes, halbmondförmiges, von Stahlsäulen getragenes Dach schmiegt sich an die Grundstücksgrenze, schützt die Fußgängerwege und definiert eine schattenspendende Zone als Ort für soziale Interaktion und Verkehrsfläche. Um die natürliche Topografie zu erhalten, gruppieren sich die akademischen Hauptgebäude um mehrere kleinere Hügel. Aus der Ferne betrachtet wirkt der Aufriss der Dachlandschaft wie ein Echo des Laubdachs des dicht bewaldeten Geländes. Hier kommt ein zweckorientierter architektonischer Entwurfsansatz, der über das Schematische hinausgeht, auf vorbildlichste Weise zum Tragen. Der Bau wurde vom Entwurf bis zu seiner Fertigstellung sorgfältig, strikt, konsequent und bis ins Detail umgesetzt. Der Wissens-, Prozess- und Techniktransfer zwischen Foster + Partners und dem malaysischen Büro GDP Architects führte zu Kooperationen bei weiteren Projekten."

Financé en grande partie par la compagnie pétrolière malaisienne Petronas, ce campus pour 6000 étudiants en ingénierie civile, mécanique, chimique et électrique, est situé dans la jungle, à 300 km au nord de Kuala Lumpur. Les circulations piétonnières à l'intérieur du complexe sont abritées des pluies fréquentes par un auvent incurvé reposant sur de fines colonnes. Les bâtiments de quatre niveaux également placés sous cette protection réunissent laboratoires, salles de conférences et autres équipements communs. L'entrée principale est signalée par un important centre de ressources en forme de tambour contenant une bibliothèque et un auditorium polyvalent de 3000 places. Le plan directeur prend en compte la possibilité de futures extensions. Ce projet, qui a remporté en 2007 le prix Aga Khan d'architecture, a été présenté par le jury en ces termes flatteurs : « Un toit aux formes arrondies et soutenu par des colonnes de métal épouse les formes du site, protège les espaces de déplacement et crée des zones bien définies pour les interactions sociales et la circulation. Afin de préserver la topographie naturelle du lieu, les bâtiments académiques se déroulent au pied d'une série de petites collines et, vus à distance, les auvents de l'université font écho à la canopée de la forêt environnante. C'est un usage exemplaire d'une approche du design architectural qui va au-delà du plan. La conception a été menée jusqu'à l'achèvement avec un soin méticuleux des détails, une grande rigueur et le sens de la persistance. Ce projet a permis un transfert de connaissances, de processus et de technologies entre Foster + Partners et l'agence Malaisienne GDP qui a conduit à leur collaboration sur d'autres projets. »

The soaring spaces and genuine lightness of the architecture give it an originality that responds intelligently to the climatic conditions of Malaysia.

Die hohen Räume und die große Leichtigkeit der Architektur verleihen dem Bau eine Originalität, die intelligent auf die klimatischen Bedingungen in Malaysia eingeht.

Les énormes espaces couverts et la légèreté de l'architecture confèrent une originalité qui répond avec intelligence aux conditions climatiques de la Malaisie.

PETER GLUCK

Peter Gluck and Partners, Architects
423 West 127th Street
New York, NY 10027
USA

Tel: +1 212 690 4950
Fax: +1 212 690 4961
E-mail: info@gluckpartners.com
Web: www.gluckpartners.com

PETER GLUCK received both his B.Arch (1962) and M.Arch (1965) degrees from Yale University. He founded his present firm in New York in 1972. He has been the chairman of AR/CS Architectural Construction Services, a firm that integrates architectural design and construction, since 1992. He is also a cofounder of Aspen GK (1997), a development partnership intended to build "well-designed high-quality housing." After Little Ajax Affordable Housing (Aspen, Colorado, 2005–06, published here), other projects include the East Harlem School (New York, New York, 2008); House on the Bluff (Winnetka, Illinois, 2008); Olive Bridge Tower (Olive Bridge, New York, 2008); Legal Outreach Afterschool Program (New York, New York, 2009); Manes Tuscany Project (Tuscany, Italy, 2009); Bolton Landing / Terraced Family Retreat (Lake George, New York, 2009); Center for Discovery (Harris, New York, 2008–10); an athletic facility for Roosevelt Island (Bronx, New York, 2010); and Mink Building (New York, New York, 2008–14), all in the USA unless stated otherwise.

PETER GLUCK schloss sein Studium in Yale mit einem B.Arch. (1962) und schließlich einem M.Arch. (1965) ab. Sein Büro gründete er 1972 in New York. Seit 1992 ist er Vorsitzender von AR/CS Architectural Construction Services, einem integrierten Architektur- und Bauunternehmen. Darüber hinaus ist er Mitbegründer von Aspen GK (1997) einem Bauunternehmen, das „anspruchsvoll entworfene, qualitativ hochwertige Wohnbauten" realisiert. Neben dem Projekt Little Ajax Affordable Housing (Aspen, Colorado, 2005–06, hier vorgestellt) zählen zu seinen Projekten auch eine Schule in East Harlem (New York, 2008), das House on the Bluff (Winnetka, Illinois, 2008), das Tower House in Olive Bridge (New York, 2008), das Legal Outreach Afterschool Program (New York, 2009), das Projekt Manes in der Toskana (2009), die Familienferienhäuser Bolton Landing (Lake George, New York, 2009), das Center for Discovery (Harris, New York, 2008–10), eine Leichtathletikeinrichtung auf Roosevelt Island (Bronx, New York, 2010) sowie das Mink Building (New York, 2008–14), alle in den USA, sofern nicht anders angegeben.

PETER GLUCK est B. Arch (1962) et M. Arch (1965) de l'université Yale. Il a créé son agence actuelle à New York en 1972. Il est président des AR/CS Architectural Construction Services, agence intégrant conception architecturale et construction depuis 1992. Il est également cofondateur d'Aspen GK (1997), un partenariat de promotion immobilière qui propose de construire « des logements bien conçus de haute qualité ». Après Little Ajax Affordable Housing (Aspen, Colorado, 2005–06, publié ici), d'autres projets comprennent l'école de East Harlem (New York, 2008) ; House on the Bluff (Winnetka, Illinois, 2008) ; la tour d'Olive Bridge (Olive Bridge, New York, 2008) ; le Legal Outreach Afterschool Program (New York, 2009) ; le projet Manes Tuscany (Toscane, Italie, 2009) ; la maison familiale Bolton, à terrasses (Lake George, New York, 2009) ; le Center for Discovery (Harris, New York, 2008–10) ; des équipements d'athlétisme pour Roosevelt Island (Bronx, New York, 2010) et l'immeuble Mink (New York, 2008–14), tous réalisés aux États-Unis, sauf exception.

LITTLE AJAX AFFORDABLE HOUSING

Aspen, Colorado, USA, 2005–06

Floor area: 2322 m². Client: City of Aspen and private developers. Cost: $4 million
Collaboration: Charlie Kaplan, Jason LaPointe

Located on a site previously deemed difficult to develop because of its steep inclination, this project is set close to the center of Aspen. Peter Gluck explains: "We acted as developer, architect, and contractor, providing housing for 14 working families that previously could not afford to live close to their workplace. An open space parcel was created as part of the planning process, linking together the many public trails that surround the site." The particular geometry of the architecture was a solution to the problems posed by the site, and numerous bridges and lookouts give a sense of continuity and relationship to the location, creating a "physical and visual connection to the mountains." High-performance glass in a floor-to-ceiling configuration and colorful, insulated panels were used. The architect writes: "Using multiple strategies, including a compact design, an efficient centralized mechanical system, and a super-insulated building complemented by the use of green building products like bamboo floors, low VOC paints, recycled content carpets, and laminates that did not require finishing, resulted in a building that complied with and far exceeded the strict sustainability code of the City of Aspen."

Das Projekt liegt auf einem Grundstück, das man seiner Steillage wegen bis dato für problematisch gehalten hatte, und befindet sich unweit des Stadtzentrums von Aspen. Peter Gluck führt aus: „Wir fungierten als Bauunternehmer, Architekt und Baufirma und realisierten Wohnraum für 14 berufstätige Familien, die es sich bisher nicht leisten konnten, in der Nähe ihres Arbeitsplatzes zu wohnen. Im Zuge des Planungsprozesses entstand ein offenes Grundstück, das die zahlreichen öffentlichen Wanderwege, die das Gelände umgeben, verbindet." Das spezifische geometrische Design der Architektur war Antwort auf die Probleme, die sich durch das Grundstück ergaben. Zahlreiche Brücken und Aussichtspunkte vermitteln Kontinuität und stellen Bezüge zum Umfeld her, schaffen eine „physische und visuelle Anbindung an die Berge". Zum Einsatz kamen deckenhohe Fenster mit hochisolierender Verglasung und farbige Dämmpaneele. Der Architekt schreibt: „Dank verschiedener Maßnahmen – einem kompakten Entwurf, einer effizienten zentralisierten Haustechnik und hochdämmender Bauweise – gekoppelt mit grünen Baumaterialien wie Bambusböden, emissionsarmen Farben, Teppichböden mit Recyclinganteil und Laminaten, die keine Versiegelung erfordern, entstand ein Wohnbau, der den strengen Nachhaltigkeitsanforderungen in Aspen mehr als entsprach."

Implanté sur un site jugé longtemps difficile du fait de sa pente, cet ensemble de logements se trouve à proximité du centre d'Aspen. « Nous sommes intervenus en tant que promoteurs, architectes et constructeurs pour réaliser ces appartements pour quatorze familles de travailleurs qui, jusque-là, ne pouvaient se permettre de vivre près de leur lieu de travail. Une parcelle ouverte a été dégagée, qui fait lien entre les nombreux cheminements publics qui entourent le terrain », explique Peter Gluck. La géométrie particulière de l'architecture apporte une solution aux problèmes posés par le site. De nombreuses passerelles et plates-formes d'observation donnent un sentiment de continuité et de relation avec le lieu, créant « une connexion physique et visuelle avec les montagnes ». Un verre à hautes performances est utilisé pour les baies du sol au plafond, ainsi que des panneaux d'isolations de couleur. « Le recours à de multiples stratégies, dont un plan compact, un système de ventilation mécanique centralisé efficace, une isolation renforcée complétée par des matériaux de construction "verts" comme les sols en bambou, les peintures à faible contenu de composants organiques volatiles (VOC), des tapis en matières recyclées et des bois lamifiés qui ne requièrent pas de finitions, a permis de réaliser un immeuble qui répond aux codes très stricts de développement durable de la ville d'Aspen et même au-delà. »

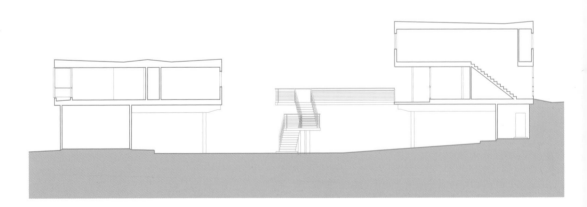

Making housing affordable and environmentally friendly at the same time represents a challenge to any architect in the best of circumstances. Peter Gluck succeeds here in also making these residences attractive.

Selbst unter den besten Voraussetzungen ist es für jeden Architekten eine Herausforderung, Wohnraum zu realisieren, der erschwinglich und umweltfreundlich zugleich ist. Peter Gluck gelingt es hier zudem, die Bauten attraktiv zu gestalten.

Faire un logement abordable et respectueux de l'environnement est un défi pour tout architecte même dans les meilleures circonstances. Peter Gluck a réussi le pari avec ces maisons séduisantes.

Gluck's use of a typology that might well bring to mind a trailer perched on a garage is a testimony to efficiency, but it also results in a cheerful lightness.

Glucks Typologie, die durchaus an einen Wohnwagen denken lässt, der auf einer Garage sitzt, zeugt von Effizienz und verleiht dem Gebäude eine gewisse Leichtigkeit.

L'utilisation par l'architecte d'une typologie qui pourrait évoquer un mobile home perché sur un garage est une solution efficace qui crée également un effet de légèreté.

The houses are at once individual
and separate, but also connected
by stairways and ramps. Interiors
are bright and simple in their
design.

Die Häuser sind zwar individuell
und separat gestaltet, jedoch über
Treppen und Rampen miteinander
verbunden. Das Interieur ist hell
und schlicht gehalten.

Les maisons individuelles sont
séparées, tout en étant reliées
par des escaliers et des rampes.
Les intérieurs sont de conception
simple et lumineuse.

MONIKA GOGL

Architekten Gogl & Partner
Dorfstr. 44
6072 Lans/Tirol
Austria

Tel: +43 512 37 72 13
Fax: +43 512 37 72 13 77
E-mail: office@gogl-architekten.at
Web: www.gogl-architekten.at

MONIKA GOGL was born in 1969 in St. Johann in the Tyrol region of Austria. She received her M.Arch degree under Peter Cook at the Bartlett School of Architecture in London (1996–97), after studying at the University of Innsbruck (1988–95). She created her own office in Linz in 2000. As she describes it, her practice covers "all aspects of design and management," and has included several partnerships, for example with Isabel Hamm for the design of lamps and with Bartel & Gaffal for furniture and interior design. She has lectured in Innsbruck and Linz. Her work includes the Schweiger House (Sistrans, 2005, published here); Obereder House (Kitzbühel, 2006); an office for Dr. Wagner (Salzburg, 2007); head office for Andreas Wieser (Lans, 2007); Strolz House (Fano, Italy, 2008); Hotel Schwarzer Adler (Kitzbühel, 2008); Walde House (Kitzbühel, 2008–10); and the Lanserhof Health Center (Innsbruck, 2009), all in Austria unless stated otherwise.

MONIKA GOGL wurde 1969 in St. Johann in Tirol, Österreich, geboren. Sie schloss ihr Studium bei Peter Cook an der Bartlett School of Architecture in London (1996–97) mit einem M.Arch. ab, nachdem sie zuvor an der Universität Innsbruck studiert hatte (1988–95). 2000 gründete sie ihr eigenes Büro in Linz. Nach eigenen Angaben deckt ihre Praxis „sämtliche Aspekte vom Entwurf bis hin zur Bauleitung" ab und umfasst auch Kooperationen, etwa das gemeinschaftliche Entwerfen von Leuchten mit Isabel Hamm oder von Möbeln und Innenarchitekturprojekten mit Bartel & Gaffal. Monika Gogl hat in Innsbruck und Linz gelehrt. Ihre Projekte sind u. a. Haus Schweiger (Sistrans, 2005, hier vorgestellt), Haus Obereder (Kitzbühel, 2006), Büroräume für Dr. Wagner (Salzburg, 2007), Büroräume für Andreas Wieser (Lans, 2007), Haus Strolz (Fano, Italien, 2008), Hotel Schwarzer Adler (Kitzbühel, 2008), Haus Walde (Kitzbühel, 2008–10) und das Gesundheitszentrum Lanserhof (Innsbruck, 2009), alle in Österreich, sofern nicht anders angegeben.

MONIKA GOGL, née en 1969 à St. Johann dans le Tyrol autrichien, a passé son diplôme de M.Arch sous la direction de Peter Cook à la Bartlett School of Architecture à Londres (1996–97), après avoir étudié à l'université d'Innsbruck (1988–95). Elle a créé son agence à Linz en 2000. Selon sa description, son agence intervient sur « tous les aspects de la conception et de la gestion de chantier », et a participé à de nombreux partenariats comme, par exemple, avec Isabel Hamm pour la conception de lampes, et avec Bartel & Gaffal pour celle de meubles et d'aménagements intérieurs. Elle a enseigné à Innsbruck et Linz. Ses travaux comprennent la maison Schweiger (Sistrans, 2005, publiée ici) ; la maison Obereder (Kitzbühel, 2006) ; le bureau du Dr. Wagner (Salzbourg, 2007) ; le siège d'Andreas Wieser (Lans, 2007) ; la maison Strolz (Fano, Italie, 2008) ; l'hôtel Schwarzer Adler (Kitzbühel, 2008) ; la maison Walde (Kitzbühel, 2008–10) et le Centre de santé de Lanserhof (Innsbruck, 2009), tous réalisés en Autriche sauf exception).

SCHWEIGER HOUSE

Sistrans, Austria, 2005

Floor area: 149 m². Client: Gebhard Schweiger. Cost: not disclosed
Collaboration: Hildegard Platzer-Rieder, Richard Steger

This single-family house was built on a sloped, narrow site to the south of the center of Sistrans. Clad in larch and generously glazed, the long house runs parallel to the southwestern edge of the site, blending "harmoniously and seamlessly into the landscape." Designed to be wheelchair accessible, the house includes an entrance level, living floor, and attic, culminating in a landscaped green roof. Monika Gogl explains the sustainability strategy of the house: "It is a low-energy house, which is to say that it uses less than 0.15 kWh/m² per year. Its design corresponds to the highest possible standards of thermal insulation. The penthouse and roof were built with a prefabricated wood structure that is a sustainable method. As an alternative heat source in the spring and autumn, a masonry heater has been placed in the living area." Finally, the architect underlines the fact that the owner of the house "preserves nature by sitting in his wheelchair, floating over a green vista, with nature at eye level."

Das Einfamilienhaus wurde auf einem abschüssigen schmalen Grundstück südlich des Ortskerns von Sistrans gebaut. Das mit Lärchenholz verblendete und großzügig verglaste Haus liegt parallel zur südwestlichen Grundstücksgrenze und fügt sich „harmonisch und nahtlos in die Landschaft ein". Das barrierefrei angelegte Haus besteht aus einer Zugangsebene und einem Wohn- und Dachgeschoss, das mit einem begrünten Dach abschließt. Monika Gogl erläutert die nachhaltigen Strategien des Hauses: „Es ist ein Niedrigenergiehaus mit einem Verbrauch von unter 0,15 kWh/m² pro Jahr. Der Entwurf entspricht höchsten Dämmstandards. Penthouse und Dach wurden mithilfe eines nachhaltigen Holzfertigbausystems errichtet. Als alternative Heizquelle im Frühjahr und Herbst wurde ein Kachelofen in den Wohnbereich integriert." Schließlich weist die Architektin darauf hin, dass der Bauherr, wenn er „in seinem Rollstuhl über dem grünen Panorama zu schweben scheint und die Natur auf Augenhöhe hat", diese Natur zugleich schützt.

Cette résidence familiale est édifiée sur un étroit terrain en pente au sud du centre de Sistrans. Habillée de bouleau et généreusement vitrée, cette construction tout en longueur se développe en limite sud-ouest du terrain et se fond « harmonieusement et sans rupture avec le paysage ». Conçue pour être accessible en chaise roulante, la maison comprend un niveau d'entrée, un niveau de séjour et un grenier, culminant dans un toit végétalisé paysagé. Monika Gogol explique ainsi la stratégie de durabilité utilisée : « C'est une maison à basse consommation d'énergie, ce qui veut dire qu'elle consomme moins de 0,15 kWh/m² par an. Sa conception répond aux normes d'isolation thermique les plus strictes. Le toit et la *penthouse* font appel à une ossature en bois préfabriquée, méthode durable en soi. Une chaudière en maçonnerie a été installée dans le séjour qui sert de chauffage alternatif au printemps et à l'automne. » L'architecte souligne également que le propriétaire de la maison, handicapé, « a tenu à préserver la nature laquelle est au niveau du regard depuis sa chaise roulante, par cette maison qui flotte au-dessus d'un panorama de verdure. »

The Schweiger House is set in an inclined site as shown by the elevation drawings above and the photos to the right.

Das Haus Schweiger wurde in den Hang hineingebaut, wie die Aufrisse oben und die Fotos rechts zeigen.

La maison Schweiger est implantée sur un terrain incliné, comme le montrent les dessins d'élévations ci-dessus et les photos à droite.

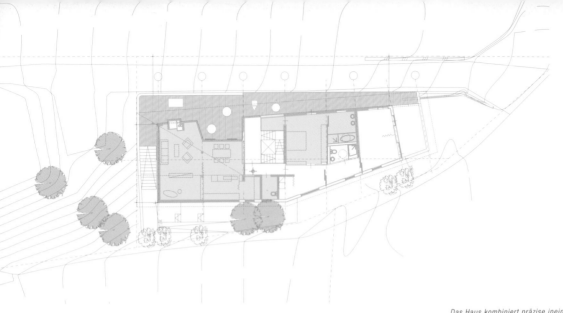

Das Haus kombiniert präzise inein-
andergreifende Innenräume mit
großzügigen Außenbereichen, etwa
den Terrassen.

La maison associe à la fois des
volumes intérieurs enveloppés
et d'amples zones ouvertes dont
ses terrasses.

The house combines carefully
wrapped interior spaces, and ample
open areas, including terraces.

The house lies on a base that includes the garage, and its main façades wrap around in a continuous flow, opening progressively as they rise, forming a fully glazed upper level.

Das Haus ruht auf einem Sockel, in dem sich auch die Garage befindet. Die Hauptfassaden wirken wie eine um das Gebäude herumführende, an den Ecken geknickte Banderole. Mit zunehmender Höhe wird die Fassade offener. Das oberste Geschoss ist vollständig verglast.

La maison repose sur un socle qui contient le garage. Les façades principales sont enveloppées dans un bandeau continu, qui s'ouvre progressivement en s'élevant. Le niveau supérieur est entièrement vitré.

ZAHA HADID

Zaha Hadid Architects
Studio 9 / 10 Bowling Green Lane
London EC1R 0BQ, UK
Tel: +44 20 72 53 51 47 / Fax: +44 20 72 51 83 22
E-mail: mail@zaha-hadid.com / Web: www.zaha-hadid.com

ZAHA HADID studied architecture at the Architectural Association (AA) in London beginning in 1972 and was awarded the Diploma Prize in 1977. She then became a partner of Rem Koolhaas in the Office for Metropolitan Architecture (OMA) and taught at the AA. She has also taught at Harvard, the University of Chicago, in Hamburg and at Columbia University in New York. Well known for her paintings and drawings, she has had a substantial influence, despite having built relatively few projects. She has completed the Vitra Fire Station (Weil am Rhein, Germany, 1990–94); and exhibition designs such as that for "The Great Utopia" (Solomon R. Guggenheim Museum, New York, 1992). Significant competition entries include her design for the Cardiff Bay Opera House (1994–96); the Habitable Bridge (London, 1996); and the Luxembourg Philharmonic Hall (1997). More recently, Zaha Hadid has entered a phase of active construction with such projects as the Bergisel Ski Jump (Innsbruck, Austria, 2001–02); Lois & Richard Rosenthal Center for Contemporary Art (Cincinnati, Ohio, 1999–2003); Phaeno Science Center (Wolfsburg, Germany, 2001–05); and the Central Building of the new BMW Assembly Plant in Leipzig (Germany, 2005). She has completed the MAXXI National Center of Contemporary Arts in Rome (Italy, 2008) and worked on the Guangzhou Opera House (Guangzhou, China, 2006–09); the Sheik Zayed Bridge (Abu Dhabi, UAE, 2005–10); and the E.ON Energy Research Department, RWTH Aachen (Aachen, Germany, 2009–10, published here). In 2004 Zaha Hadid became the first woman to win the coveted Pritzker Prize.

ZAHA HADID studierte ab 1972 an der Architectural Association (AA) in London und erhielt 1977 den Diploma Prize. Anschließend wurde sie Partnerin von Rem Koolhaas im Office for Metropolitan Architecture (OMA) und unterrichtete an der AA. Darüber hinaus lehrte sie in Harvard, an der Universität von Chicago, in Hamburg sowie an der Columbia University in New York. Hadid wurde besonders durch ihr Gemälde und Zeichnungen bekannt. Obwohl nur wenige ihrer Entwürfe realisiert wurden, zählt sie zu den einflussreichsten Vertreterinnen ihrer Zunft. Realisiert wurden u. a. die Feuerwache für Vitra (Weil am Rhein, Deutschland, 1990–94) und Ausstellungs-architekturen wie „The Great Utopia" (Solomon R. Guggenheim Museum, New York, 1992). Zu ihren wichtigsten Wettbewerbsbeiträgen zählen der Entwurf für das Cardiff Bay Opera House (1994–96), die Habitable Bridge in London (1996) und die Philharmonie in Luxemburg (1997). In jüngerer Zeit begann eine Phase des aktiven Bauens für Hadid, etwa mit der Skisprungschanze Bergisel (Innsbruck, Österreich, 2001–02), dem Lois & Richard Rosenthal Center for Contemporary Art (Cincinnati, Ohio, 1999–2003), dem Wissenschaftszentrum Phaeno (Wolfsburg, 2001–05) und dem Zentralgebäude des neuen BMW-Werks in Leipzig (2005). Vor einigen Jahren fertiggestellt wurde das MAXXI, das Nationalmuseum für Kunst des 21. Jahrhunderts in Rom (2008). Anschließend arbeitete Hadid am Opernhaus in Guangzhou (China, 2006–09), an der Scheich-Zajed-Brücke (Abu Dhabi, VAE, 2005–10) sowie dem E.ON Institut für Energieforschung an der RWTH Aachen (2009–10, hier vorgestellt). 2004 wurde Zaha Hadid als erste Frau mit dem begehrten Pritzker-Preis ausgezeichnet.

ZAHA HADID a étudié à l'Architectural Association (AA) de Londres de 1972 à 1977, date à laquelle elle a reçu le Prix du diplôme. Elle devient ensuite partenaire de Rem Koolhaas, à l'Office for Metropolitan Architecture (OMA), et enseigne à l'AA. Elle a également enseigné à Harvard, à l'université de Chicago, à Hambourg et à l'université Columbia de New York. Célèbre pour ses peintures et dessins, elle a exercé une réelle influence, même si elle n'a construit que relativement peu pendant longtemps. Parmi ses réalisations anciennes : un poste d'incendie pour Vitra (Weil am Rhein, Allemagne, 1990–94) et des projets pour des expositions comme « La Grande utopie » au Solomon R. Guggenheim Museum à New York (1992). Elle a participé à de nombreux concours dont les plus importants sont le projet pour l'Opéra de la baie de Cardiff (Pays de Galles, 1994–96) ; la Habitable Bridge (Londres, 1996) et la salle de concerts philharmoniques de Luxembourg (1997). Plus récemment, elle est entrée dans une phase active de grands chantiers, avec des réalisations comme le tremplin de ski de Bergisel (Innsbruck, Autriche, 2001–02) ; le Centre d'art contemporain Lois & Richard Rosenthal (Cincinnati, Ohio, 1999–2003) ; le Centre de la science Phaeno (Wolfsburg, Allemagne, 2001–05) et le bâtiment central de la nouvelle usine BMW de Leipzig (Allemagne, 2005). Il y a quelques années, elle a achevé le Centre national des arts contemporains de Rome MAXXI (2008) et travaille sur les projets de l'Opéra de Guangzhou (Guangzhou, Chine, 2006–09) ; du pont Cheikh Zayed (Abu Dhabi, EAU, 2005–10) et du Centre de recherches d'E.ON, RWTH (Aix-la-Chapelle, Allemagne, 2009–10, publié ici). En 2004, Zaha Hadid a été la première femme à remporter le très convoité Pritzker Prize.

E.ON ENERGY RESEARCH DEPARTMENT

RWTH Aachen, Aachen, Germany, 2009–10

Floor area: 3700 m². Client: Building and Real Estate NRW, Aachen. Cost: €17.4 million
Collaboration: Philipp Vogt, Gernot Finselbach

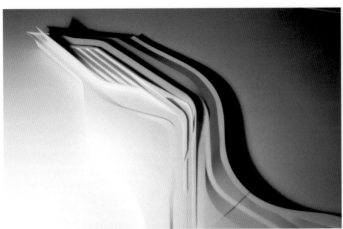 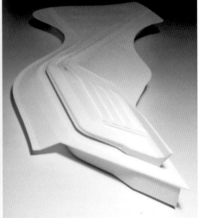

Set between rail tracks and a four-lane road at the RWTH University in Aachen, the E.ON Energy Research Department building makes use of structural and aerodynamic fins and a wind turbine on its roof to "allow for the modulation both of daylight and wind stream over the roof, maximizing the provision of natural light and ventilation to the building interior." Other sustainable features of the building include its orientation, use of thermal mass and minimal volume to surface ratio, and the use of geothermal energy (constant ground temperature of 10°C), wind, and sun (1500 m² of conventional opaque and monocrystalline solar panels). Interior, manually operated sun and glare roller blinds increase the potential protection from solar gain. Careful calculations lead the architects to affirm that the building will produce more energy than it consumes. With this structure, Zaha Hadid shows that her unique design process can be fruitfully adapted to the issue of sustainability—an element that is clearly desired by the client in this instance and also part of the very purpose of energy research. As she says: "Architecture and energy determine and complement one another, the components of the building have more than one function, performing and multi-tasking as hybrid forms."

Das E.ON Institut für Energieforschung an der RWTH Aachen liegt zwischen Gleisanlagen und einer vierspurigen Bundesstraße. Strukturgebende, aerodynamische Grate und eine Windturbine auf dem Dach „erlauben die Modulation von Tageslicht und Windströmen durch das Dach und maximieren die natürliche Belichtung und Belüftung des Gebäudeinneren". Weitere nachhaltige Merkmale sind die Ausrichtung des Baus, die Nutzung der thermischen Masse, ein geringes Volumen-Oberflächen-Verhältnis, die Nutzung von Erdwärme (bei einer konstanten Erdtemperatur von 10 °C), Wind- und Sonnenenergie (mit 1500 m² konventionellen opaken sowie mono-kristallinen Solarmodulen). Im Innern schützen manuell bedienbare Sonnen- und Blendschutzrollos zusätzlich vor potenziellem solarem Wärmegewinn. Nach sorgfältigen Berechnungen geht die Architektin davon aus, dass das Gebäude mehr Energie erzeugen als verbrauchen wird. Mit diesem Bau stellt Zaha Hadid unter Beweis, dass sich ihr unverwechselbarer Entwurfsprozess gewinnbringend an Fragen der Nachhaltigkeit anpassen lässt – was in diesem Fall explizites Anliegen des Auftraggebers war und natürlich Kernthema der Energieforschung überhaupt ist. Die Architektin merkt an: „Architektur und Energie bedingen und ergänzen sich, die einzelnen Komponenten des Baus haben jeweils mehr als eine Funktion und erfüllen als hybride Formen mehrere Aufgaben."

Implanté entre des voies de chemin de fer et une route à quatre voies en limite du terrain de l'école technique supérieure RWTH à Aix-la-Chapelle, l'immeuble du Centre de recherches sur l'énergie d'E.ON utilise des ailettes structurelles et aérodynamiques et une éolienne en toiture pour « permettre la modulation à la fois de l'éclairage naturel et du flux d'air sur le toit, et d'optimiser l'apport d'éclairage et de ventilation naturels à l'intérieur du bâtiment ». Parmi les autres dispositifs durables utilisés figurent l'orientation du bâtiment, la mise à profit de la masse thermique, le rapport minimum entre surfaces et volumes, l'utilisation de la géothermie (la température du sol est en permanence à 10 °C), du vent et du soleil (1500 m² de panneaux solaires conventionnels opaques monocristallins). À l'intérieur, des volets roulants commandés manuellement protègent du gain solaire et de l'éblouissement. Des calculs poussés ont permis aux architectes d'affirmer que l'immeuble produira plus d'énergie qu'il n'en consomme. Par cette réalisation, Zaha Hadid montre que son processus très particulier de conception peut s'adapter avec succès aux enjeux de la durabilité, élément qui fait évidemment partie des souhaits de son client dans ce domaine et aux fonctions de recherche du département. Zaha Hadid a déclaré : « L'architecture et l'énergie se déterminent et se complètent mutuellement, les composantes du bâtiment remplissent plus d'une fonction, ce sont des formes hybrides actives et multitâches. »

Zaha Hadid's design here, as is often the case, is intimately related to its site, and seems almost in the basic models and drawings to be rising directly up out of the earth.

Zaha Hadids Entwurf ist wie so oft eng mit seinem Standort verwoben und scheint in den schlichten Modellen und Zeichnungen fast direkt aus dem Erdboden herauszuwachsen.

Le projet de Zaha Hadid, comme souvent dans son œuvre, est intimement lié au site et, dans les dessins et maquettes, semble même jaillir directement du sol.

Interior spaces are amply lit and flow together much as the exterior forms give a strong impression of continuous movement.

Die Innenräume sind großzügig belichtet und gehen fließend ineinander über. Auch die Formen des Außenbaus bilden ein dynamisches Kontinuum.

Les volumes intérieurs amplement éclairés s'inscrivent dans une configuration de flux, de même que les formes extérieures, ce qui laisse une puissante impression de mouvement continu.

The bands of light shown in the night view (right) underline the strong horizontal lines of the project and indeed its unity. Interior hallways and walkways (below) animate the space and intertwine its volumes.

Die sich in der Nachtansicht abzeichnenden Lichtbänder (rechts) unterstreichen die ausgeprägt horizontale Linienführung des Projekts und betonen seine Einheit. Korridore und Rampen im Innern des Baus (unten) beleben den Raum und verflechten die Volumina miteinander.

Les bandes de lumière qui apparaissent dans cette vue nocturne (à droite) mettent en valeur la forte horizontalité du projet et renforcent son unité. Les halls intérieurs et les passages (ci-dessous) animent l'espace et relient les volumes.

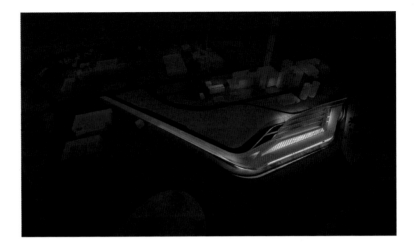

ANNA HERINGER AND EIKE ROSWAG

Anna Heringer
Rottmayrstrasse 24, 83410 Laufen, Germany
E-mail: ah@anna-heringer.com
Web: www.anna-heringer.com

Ziegert I Roswag I Seiler Architekten Ingenieure
Roswag Architekten
Schlesische Straße 26, Aufgang A, 10997 Berlin, Germany
Tel: +49 30 39 80 09 511 / Fax: +49 30 39 80 09 566
E-mail: roswag@zrs-berlin.de / Web: www.zrs-berlin.de

ANNA HERINGER, born 1977 in Rosenheim, Germany, went to Bangladesh for a year as a development aid worker when she was 19. Since then development through architecture has been her passion. She studied at the University of Linz in Austria, where she developed the design for the Handmade School as part of her thesis. In 2011 she was a Loeb Fellow at Harvard Graduate School of Design. Currently she is working on projects in Africa and Asia and gives lectures and workshops worldwide. Her work has won many international awards. **EIKE ROSWAG**, born in 1969 in Gießen, Germany, received his Dipl.-Ing. Architecture degree from the Technical University in Berlin. Natural building materials and earthen construction form the core competencies of his office, under the umbrella of Ziegert I Roswag I Seiler Architekten Ingenieure, located in Berlin. His projects range from a timber-frame fire station in Brandenburg and a white earthen house in the Westend neighborhood of Berlin to school projects in Africa and Pakistan and a historical building renovation in Abu Dhabi. Heringer (design, concept) and Roswag (technical planning) collaborated on the Handmade School published here (Rudrapur, Dinajpur, Bangladesh, 2005), which was honored with the 2007 Aga Khan Award for Architecture.

ANNA HERINGER, 1977 in Rosenheim geboren, ging mit 19 Jahren für ein Jahr zur Unterstützung sozialer Projekte nach Bangladesh. Seitdem ist das Thema Entwicklung durch Architektur ihre Leidenschaft. Sie studierte an der Kunstuniversität Linz, wo auch der Entwurf der Handmade School als Teil ihrer Diplomarbeit entstand, 2011 war sie Loeb Fellow an der Graduate School of Design in Harvard. Derzeit arbeitet sie an Projekten in Afrika und Asien und hält weltweit Vorträge und veranstaltet Workshops. Ihre Arbeiten wurden mehrfach international ausgezeichnet. **EIKE ROSWAG**, 1969 in Gießen geboren, schloss sein Architekturstudium an der TU Berlin als Diplom-Ingenieur ab. Natürliche Baustoffe und der Schwerpunkt Lehmbau bilden die Kernkompetenz seines Büros unter dem Dach von Ziegert I Roswag I Seiler Architekten Ingenieure mit Sitz in Berlin. Die Projekte spannen einen Bogen von einem in Holzbauweise errichteten Gebäude für die Feuerwehr in Brandenburg, einem weißen Lehmhaus im Berliner Westend, über Schulprojekte in Afrika und Pakistan bis hin zu Baudenkmälern auf der Arabischen Halbinsel. Heringer (Entwurf, Konzept) und Roswag (Technische Planung) realisierten gemeinsam die hier vorgestellte Handmade School (Rudrapur, Dinajpur, Bangladesch, 2005), die 2007 mit dem Aga-Khan-Preis für Architektur ausgezeichnet wurde.

À l'âge de 19 ans, **ANNA HERINGER**, né en 1969 à Rosenheim, Allemagne, est partie pendant un an au Bangladesh dans le cadre d'un projet d'aide sociale. Depuis, elle se passionne pour le développement rural au travers de l'architecture. Elle a suivi des études d'architecture à l'université de Linz, et la Handmade School était déjà traité dans son mémoire de fin d'études. En 2011, elle a été professeur invité de la Graduate School of Design à Harvard. Aujourd'hui, elle participe à des réalisations en Afrique et en Asie, et elle donne des conférences et anime des ateliers un peu partout dans le monde. Ses travaux ont reçu de nombreuses distinctions au niveau international. **EIKE ROSWAG**, né en 1969 à Gießen, Allemagne, est Dipl.-Ing. Architect de l'Université Polytechnique de Berlin (1992–2000). Les matériaux de construction naturels et la terre comme matériau de construction sont les spécialités du bureau Ziegert I Roswag I Seiler Architekten Ingenieure, siégeant à Berlin, auquel il est associé. Parmi les projets réalisés : un bâtiment en bois pour les sapeurs-pompiers du Brandebourg, une maison en terre blanche à Berlin Westend, des écoles en Afrique et au Pakistan et des monuments dans la péninsule d'Arabie. Heringer (projet, conception) et Roswag (planification technique) ont collaboré sur le projet de l'école (Handmade School, Rudrapur, Dinajpur, Bangladesh, 2005) publié ici qui a reçu le prix Aga Khan d'architecture en 2007.

HANDMADE SCHOOL

Rudrapur, Dinajpur, Bangladesh, 2005

Floor area: 325 m². Client: Dipshikha/METI, Bangladesh. Cost: €25 000. Collaboration: Anna Heringer and Eike Roswag

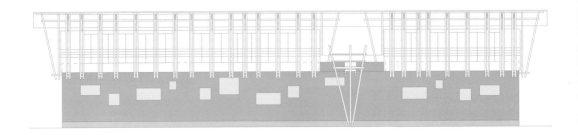

"We believe that architecture is more than simply shelter. It is intimately connected with the creation of identity and self-confidence. And this is the basis of sustainable development," declare Anna Heringer and Eike Roswag. Their school made of earth and bamboo was built for and with the Modern Education and Training Institute (METI) and its NGO mother organization, Dipshikha, in 2005 in Rudrapur in northern Bangladesh. The project was undertaken in cooperation with Shanti Bangladesh and the Papal Children's Mission (PMK). The ground floor of the structure has thick earth walls, while the upper story, where colorful saris are stretched on the ceiling, is made of bamboo. Three classrooms and six organically shaped "caves" are located on the ground floor, and two large, flexible class areas are on the upper floor. Twelve thousand five hundred bamboo strips were used to make the porous façades of the upper level. Made with the assistance of 25 local laborers, the structure makes use of traditional building techniques with "technical improvements." The school is used by 168 children. The jury citation of the 2007 Aga Khan Award for Architecture given to the Handmade School reads: "This joyous and elegant two-story primary school in rural Bangladesh has emerged from a deep understanding of local materials and a heartfelt connection to the local community. Its innovation lies in the adaptation of traditional methods and materials of construction to create light-filled celebratory spaces, as well as informal spaces for children. Earthbound materials, such as loam and straw, are combined with lighter elements like bamboo sticks and nylon lashing to shape a built form that addresses sustainability in construction in an exemplary manner."

„Wir glauben, dass Architektur mehr ist als nur ein Obdach. Sie ist eng verknüpft mit der Bildung von Identität und Selbstbewusstsein. Und sie ist Grundlage einer nachhaltigen Entwicklung", erklären Anna Heringer und Eike Roswag. Ihre Schule aus Bambus und Lehm wurde 2005 für das Modern Education and Training Institute (METI) und dessen NGO-Mutterorganisation Dipshikha in Rudrapur in Nord-Bangladesch erbaut. Das Projekt entstand in Kooperation mit Shanti Bangladesch und dem Päpstlichen Missionswerk der Kinder (PMK). Das Erdgeschoss des Baus hat massive Lehmmauern, während das obere Stockwerk, in dem bunte Saris unter der Decke hängen, aus Bambus gefertigt wurde. Im Erdgeschoss liegen drei Klassenzimmer und sechs organisch geformte „Höhlen", im Obergeschoss befinden sich zwei große flexible Schulräume. Die lichtdurchlässigen Fassaden des Obergeschosses wurden aus 12 500 Bambusstäben gefertigt. Der mithilfe von 25 ortsansässigen Arbeitern errichtete Bau bedient sich regionaler Bautechniken, die „technisch optimiert" wurden. Die Schule wird von 168 Kindern genutzt. In der Begründung der Jury des Aga-Khan-Preises für Architektur, den die Handmade School 2007 erhielt, heißt es: „Die fröhliche und elegante zweistöckige Grundschule im ländlichen Bangladesch entstand aus einem tiefen Verständnis für regionale Materialien und einer zutiefst empfundenen Bindung an die örtliche Gemeinschaft. Ihre Neuheit liegt in der Abwandlung traditioneller Baumethoden und -materialien, um lichterfüllte, festliche und informelle Räume für Kinder zu schaffen. Erdverbundene Materialien wie Lehm und Stroh wurden mit leichteren Materialien wie Bambusstäben und Nylonseilen kombiniert, um einen Raum zu gestalten, der nachhaltiges Bauen exemplarisch umsetzt."

« Nous pensons que l'architecture doit être davantage qu'un simple abri. Elle est intimement liée à la création d'une identité et de la confiance en soi. C'est la base du développement durable », expliquent Anna Heringer et Eike Roswag. Leur école en terre et bambou a été édifiée pour l'Institut moderne d'éducation et de formation (METI) et son organisation non gouvernementale mère, Dipshikha, en 2005 à Rudrapur dans le nord du Bangladesh. Le projet a été initié en coopération avec Shanti Bangladesh et la mission papale pour l'enfance (PMK). Le rez-de-chaussée du bâtiment présente d'épais murs de terre tandis que l'étage, au plafond duquel pendent des saris de couleurs vives, est en bambou. Trois salles de classe et six « cavernes » de forme organique se trouvent au rez-de-chaussée et deux grandes salles d'utilisation souple à l'étage. 12 500 lattes de bambou ont été utilisées pour la façade du niveau supérieur. Mené avec l'aide de 25 paysans locaux, le chantier a fait appel à des techniques traditionnelles « techniquement améliorées ». L'école reçoit 168 enfants. La citation du jury du Prix Aga Khan d'architecture 2007 précisait : « Cette élégante école de deux niveaux dans le Bangladesh rural est le résultat d'une profonde compréhension des matériaux locaux ainsi que d'un rapport sincère avec les populations locales. Son innovation réside dans son adaptation aux méthodes et aux matériaux de constructions traditionnels pour créer d'agréables espaces lumineux ainsi que des espaces informels pour les enfants. Les matériaux issus de la terre, tels que le limon et la paille, sont combinés avec des éléments plus légers tels que les branches de bambou et les cordes de nylon pour réaliser une construction dont la durabilité est exemplaire. »

Originality in architecture may well have to do with first anchoring a structure in local tradition and materials and then making it modern through details in design and construction.

Die Originalität von Architektur hat sicherlich viel damit zu tun, zunächst lokale Traditionen und Materialien zu berücksichtigen und diese erst dann durch gestalterische und bauliche Details modern zu interpretieren.

Souvent en architecture l'originalité tient à l'ancrage du projet dans les traditions et les matériaux locaux. L'apport de la modernité s'affirme alors dans les détails de conception et de construction.

The flow of light and air through the building is obvious in these images. The elegant use of material, despite being simple and locally sourced, does not give away the fact that the building was made on a restricted budget.

Die Bilder veranschaulichen, wie Licht und Luft ungehindert durch das Gebäude strömen. Der ästhetisch höchst reizvolle Umgang mit einfachen Materialien der Region lässt vollkommen vergessen, wie eng der Budgetrahmen war.

Les flots d'air et de lumière qui pénètrent dans l'école sont évidents sur ces images. L'utilisation élégante et intelligente de simples matériaux locaux fait oublier l'étroitesse du budget de ce projet.

HOTSON BAKKER BONIFACE HADEN

Hotson Bakker Boniface Haden architects + urbanistes
406–611 Alexander Street
Vancouver, BC, V6A 1E1
Canada

Tel: +1 604 255 1169
Fax: +1 604 255 1790
E-mail: general@designdialog.ca
Web: www.hbbharc.com

HOTSON BAKKER BONIFACE HADEN has long been involved in what they call "sustainable city-shaping," for example in the progressive adaptive reuse and urbanism of Vancouver's Granville Island. Their Capers building in Vancouver was the first commercial application of geothermal technology in western Canada. In 2007 the firm has completed the campus plan and academic buildings for the new Quest University in Squamish, British Columbia, Canada, where sustainable design "infuses the site planning, the building design, and the curriculum." Further, in contrast with some other approaches to green architecture, HBBH "believes in the importance of making buildings 'visibly green' as a means of fostering public knowledge about key environmental issues, such as greenhouse gas emissions, and the significant role buildings play in global environmental health." Bruce Haden, the partner in charge of the Nk'Mip project published here (Osoyoos, British Columbia, Canada, 2004–06), grew up in Kingston, Ontario, and studied architecture at the University of Waterloo, receiving his M.Arch degree from the University of British Columbia. He has been involved in a number of projects that concern the First Nations peoples, as can be seen in his work with Haida Gwaii and bands in the Northwest Territories.

Das Büro **HOTSON BAKKER BONIFACE HADEN** engagiert sich schon lange für „nachhaltige Stadtgestaltung", etwa mit Projekten wie der fortschrittlichen, flexiblen Umnutzung und Stadtplanung der zu Vancouver gehörenden Granville-Insel. Das Capers Building in Vancouver war das erste kommerzielle Bauprojekt in Westkanada mit Erdwärmetechnik. 2007 stellte das Team Lehrgebäude für die neue Quest University in Squamish, British Columbia, Kanada, fertig, wo nachhaltiges Design „die Planung des Geländes, den baulichen Entwurf und den Lehrplan" beeinflusst. Im Gegensatz zu anderen Ansätzen ist HBBH „überzeugt, dass es entscheidend ist, Bauten ‚sichtbar grün' zu gestalten, um der Öffentlichkeit Schlüsselfragen des Umweltschutzes zu vermitteln, etwa Wissen über Treibhausgase und die bedeutende Rolle, die Bauten für die Gesundheit unseres Planeten spielen". Bruce Haden, verantwortlich für das hier vorgestellte Nk'Mip-Projekt (Osoyoos, British Columbia, Kanada, 2004–06), wuchs in Kingston, Ontario, auf, studierte Architektur an der Universität Waterloo und erwarb seinen M.Arch. an der Universität von British Columbia. Er war an zahlreichen Projekten für heimische Indianerstämme beteiligt, zu denen auch seine Arbeit mit Haida Gwaii und verschiedenen Stammesgruppierungen in den Northwest Territories gehört.

L'agence **HOTSON BAKKER BONIFACE HADEN** s'est longtemps intéressée à ce qu'elle appelle « la mise en forme durable des villes », par exemple dans la démarche de réutilisation progressive adaptée pour l'urbanisme de Granville Island à Vancouver. Son immeuble Capers Building à Vancouver est la première application des technologies géothermiques dans l'ouest du Canada. Elle a réalisé en 2007 le plan du campus ainsi que les bâtiments universitaires de la nouvelle université Quest à Squamish, Colombie britannique, Canada, pour laquelle la conception durable « touche l'ensemble de la planification, la conception des bâtiments et le cours des études ». De plus, à la différence de certaines approches de l'architecture verte, HBBH « croit en l'importance de constructions visiblement "vertes" pour promouvoir la prise de conscience par le public d'enjeux environnementaux clés, comme les conséquences des gaz à effet de serre, et le rôle significatif du bâti dans la santé globale de l'environnement ». Bruce Haden, associé en charge du projet Nk'Mip publié ici (Osoyoos, Colombie britannique, Canada, 2004–06), a grandi à Kingston, Ontario, et a étudié l'architecture à l'université de Waterloo. Il est M. Arch de l'université de Colombie britannique. Il a travaillé sur un certain nombre de projets concernant les tribus indiennes, comme le montre son travail dans les Haida Gwaii et pour les tribus des territoires du Nord-Ouest.

NK'MIP DESERT CULTURAL CENTRE

Osoyoos, British Columbia, Canada, 2004–06

Floor area: 1115 m². Client: Osoyoos Indian Band. Cost: $2.9 million
Project Architect: Brady Dunlop

Hotson Bakker Boniface Haden was hired by the Osoyoos Indian Band to master plan the Nk'Mip Desert Cultural Centre's 81-hectare site, part of a new resort that includes a winery, an 18-hole golf course with clubhouse, and tourist accommodations. The site is located at the far northern end of the American deserts that extend southward to the Sonoran Desert in Mexico. In an unusual climate for Canada, summer temperatures can rise as high as 40°C and fall to -18°C in winter. The program of the center includes indoor and outdoor exhibition spaces, a theater, gift shop, administrative offices, rattlesnake research facilities, and 50 kilometers of hiking trails. The green features of the project include its main rammed-earth wall, its orientation and choice of site, radiant heating and cooling based on ceiling and floor slabs, a habitable green roof, water-use management, and support for endangered-species research. Bluestain pine was used for the cladding because an infestation of pine beetles in British Columbia led to an excess of this type of tree. The center's earthen wall—80 meters long, 5.5 meters high, and 60 centimeters thick—is the largest rammed-earth wall in North America. Made from local soil mixed with concrete, it retains warmth in winter and cools the building in summer.

Die Gruppe der Osoyoos-Indianer beauftragte Hotson Bakker Boniface Haden mit der Erstellung des Masterplans für das 81 ha große Gelände des Nk'Mip Desert Cultural Centre, das Teil eines neuen Erholungsgebiets ist und zu dem auch ein Weingut, ein 18-Loch-Golfplatz mit Klubhaus und Touristenunterkünfte gehören. Das Gelände markiert das nördlichste Ende der amerikanischen Wüstengegenden, die sich nach Süden bis zur Sonora-Wüste in Mexiko ziehen. In einem für Kanada unge-wöhnlichen Klima können die Temperaturen hier auf 40 °C steigen und im Winter auf bis zu −18 °C fallen. Das Programm des Zentrums umfasst Ausstellungsbereiche im Innen- und Außenraum, ein Theater, einen Souvenirladen, Verwaltungsbüros, eine Klapperschlangen-Forschungsstation und insgesamt 50 km Wanderwege. Grüne Merkmale des Projekts sind u. a. die große Hauptmauer aus Stampflehm einschließlich ihrer Standortwahl und Ausrichtung sowie eine in Decken- und Bodenpaneele integrierte Strahlungsheizung und -kühlung, ein begehbares begrüntes Dach, Wassersparsysteme und schließlich das Engagement für die Erforschung bedrohter Arten. Für die Holzverkleidung wählte man Küstenkiefer, da eine Käferepidemie in British Columbia zu Bauholzüberschuss geführt hatte. Die Mauer des Zentrums – 80 m lang, 5,5 m hoch und 60 cm stark – ist die größte Stampflehmmauer Nordamerikas. Die aus einer Mischung aus regionaler Erde und Beton gefertigte Mauer dient im Winter als Wärmespeicher und kühlt das Gebäude im Sommer.

L'agence Hotson Bakker Boniface Haden a été engagée par les Indiens Osoyoos pour réaliser le plan directeur du Centre du patrimoine du désert de Nk'Mip, site de 81 ha qui fait partie de nouvelles installations touristiques comprenant un chai, un golf de 18 trous avec *club-house* et des hébergements pour visiteurs. Le lieu se trouve à l'extrémité nord des grandes étendues désertiques américaines qui partent du désert de Sonora au Mexique. Inhabituelles pour le Canada, les températures d'été peuvent s'élever jusqu'à 40 °C et descendre jusqu'à -18 °C en hiver. Le programme du centre comprend des espaces d'expositions couverts et en plein air, un auditorium, une boutique de cadeaux, des bureaux administratifs, un centre de recherche sur les serpents à sonnettes et 50 km de pistes de randonnée. Les aspects durables du projet comprennent le mur principal en béton de terre, l'orientation et le choix de l'emplacement, le chauffage et le rafraîchissement radiant par les sols et les plafonds, un toit végétalisé habitable, la gestion de l'eau et le soutien à la recherche sur les espèces en voie de disparition. On a utilisé un bardage en pin Bluestain très abondant, car le pin local est infesté de parasites. Le mur de terre du bâtiment du Centre – 80 m de long, 5,5 m de haut et 60 cm d'épaisseur – est le plus grand mur en béton de terre jamais monté en Amérique du Nord. Réalisé en terre locale mélangée à du béton, il retient la chaleur en hiver et conserve la fraîcheur en été.

The basic structure is inserted into the hillside and fronted by the strong rammed-earth wall.

Das schlichte Gebäude wurde in den Abhang hineingebaut und liegt hinter einer mächtigen Stampflehmmauer.

La structure de base est insérée dans le flanc de la colline et comme bloquée par un puissant mur de terre.

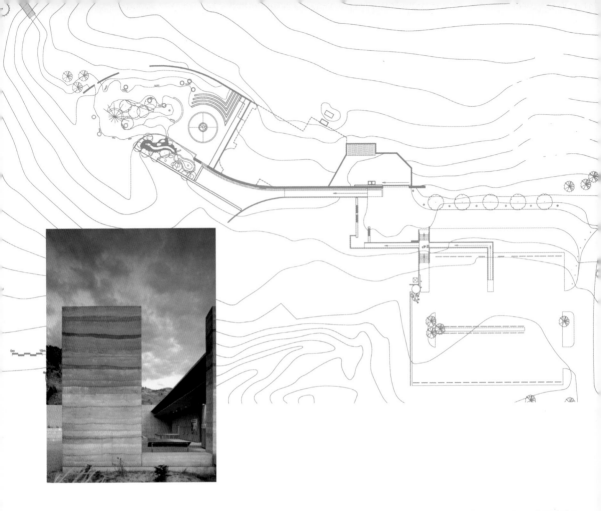

The layered effect of the rammed-earth wall makes it blend into its natural setting, as the site plan with its topographic lines (above) shows from a different perspective. Right, a nod to Okanagan heritage...

Dank ihres Schichteffekts verschmilzt die Stampflehmmauer geradezu mit ihrem Umfeld, wie auch der topografische Geländeplan (oben) aus einer anderen Perspektive deutlich macht. Rechts indianische Artefakte aus dem Okanagan Valley...

L'effet de stratification du mur de terre l'intègre encore mieux dans son cadre naturel, comme le plan du site et les courbes de niveaux (ci-dessus) le montrent sous une perspective différente. À droite, témoignage de la tradition indienne de la vallée de l'Okanagan...

The modern volumes of the center lie behind its long, distinct wall, as seen in the plan below.

Die modernen Baukörper des Centers liegen hinter der lang gestreckten, deutlich sichtbaren Mauer, wie auch der Grundriss unten zeigt.

Comme le montre le plan ci-dessous, les volumes modernes qui composent le centre sont protégés par le long mur de terre.

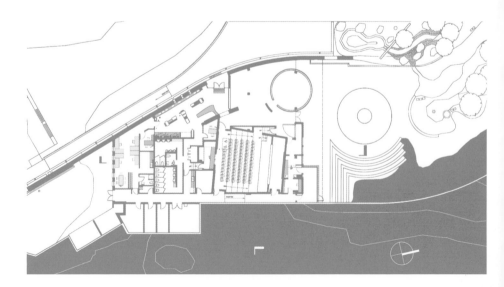

A sense of earthy solidity pervades the architecture and makes it contextual without any sense of pastiche.

Die Architektur ist von erdiger Bodenständigkeit und dabei kontextuell, ohne je den Eindruck eines Pastiche zu vermitteln.

Cette architecture qui diffuse un sentiment de grande solidité matérielle joue le contexte sans tomber pour autant dans le pastiche.

CHRIS JACOBS

Chris Jacobs
United Future / 8500 Steller Drive, Building 5
Culver City, CA 90232 / USA
Tel: +1 310 280 7778 / E-mail: chris@unitedfuture.com
Web: www.unitedfuture.com

CHRIS JACOBS is the cofounder and Executive Creative Director of United Future, a design firm founded in 2005. The goal of the company "is to create cross-cultural, cross-platform solutions that unite people and business processes through the use of transparent-technology ideologies." He worked previously as a Creative Director with Equus (Singapore, 2002) and Lemon Asia (Hong Kong). Jacobs has also worked as an independent consultant for companies such as SAP, Time Warner and Universal Music. He attended the Art College Center of Design (1991–95) and is thus not an architect. He explains: "I've always had a love of architecture, and have designed a few homes while working in the field professionally. My true loves are industrial design and graphic design, with an emphasis on interface design and usability for Internet applications. I always felt that a good designer can design anything, from a shower curtain ring to a movie poster to an automobile. I've always pushed myself to be multidisciplined in a multitude of fields, including typography, digital illustration, 3D, interface usability, etc., etc. Because of my love of industrial design, I forced myself to learn Rhino3D. When I was tasked to design a Vertical Farm [published here], I worked around the clock and designed it in one sitting (using Rhino3D), with the idea that this structure had to be stackable and modular. I then had it remodeled in 3D Studio Max by Dean Fowler with further detail design assistance by Rolf Mohr, an architect we work with on occasion."

CHRIS JACOBS ist Mitbegründer und leitender Creative Director von United Future, einem 2005 gegründeten Designbüro. Ziel der Agentur ist es, „kultur- und grundsatzübergreifende Lösungen zu finden, die Menschen und Geschäftsprozesse durch eine transparente technische Weltanschauung verbinden". Zuvor war er als Creative Director für Equus (Singapur, 2002) und Lemon Asia (Hongkong) tätig. Darüber hinaus war Jacobs als freier Berater für Firmen wie SAP, Time Warner und Universal Music aktiv. Er studierte am Art College Center of Design (1991–95) und ist somit kein akademisch ausgebildeter Architekt. Er erklärt: „Ich hatte schon immer eine Leidenschaft für Architektur und habe im Lauf meiner beruflichen Tätigkeit in diesem Bereich auch einige Häuser entworfen. Doch meine wahre Leidenschaft ist das Produkt- und Grafikdesign, mit einem Schwerpunkt auf Interfacedesign und dessen Umsetzung für Internetanwendungen. Ich war schon immer der Meinung, dass ein guter Designer alles gestalten kann, von Ringen für Duschvorhänge über Kinoplakate bis hin zu Autos. Ich habe mich immer bemüht, multidisziplinär in einer ganzen Bandbreite von Bereichen arbeiten zu können, etwa in der Typografie, der digitalen Illustration, in 3D, benutzerfreundlichen Interfaces etc. etc. Wegen meiner Leidenschaft für Produktdesign war ich gezwungen, mir Rhino3D zu erschließen. Als ich den Auftrag erhielt, einen vertikalen Bauernhof [hier vorgestellt] zu entwerfen, arbeitete ich rund um die Uhr und entwarf das Projekt (mit Rhino3D) in einem Zug. Die Idee war, dass die Konstruktion stapelbar und modular sein sollte. Schließlich musste der Entwurf von Dean Fowler mit 3D Studio Max neu modelliert werden, weitere Unterstützung beim Entwurf von Details kam von Rolf Mohr, einem Architekten, mit dem wir gelegentlich zusammenarbeiten."

CHRIS JACOBS est cofondateur et directeur de création de United Future, une agence de design créée en 2005. L'objectif de cette société est de « trouver des solutions trans-cultures, trans-plates-formes qui réunissent des personnes et des processus économiques à travers l'utilisation d'idéologies de technologies transparentes ». Il a été précédemment directeur de création d'Equus (Singapour, 2002) et de Lemon Asia (Hong Kong). Jacobs a également été consultant indépendant pour des entreprises comme SAP, Time Warner et Universal Music. Il a étudié au Art College Center of Design (1991–95) et n'est donc pas un architecte qualifié. Il explique ainsi : « J'ai toujours éprouvé un grand amour pour l'architecture et j'ai dessiné quelques maisons pendant que je travaillais professionnellement dans ce secteur. J'aime surtout le design industriel et le design graphique, avec un accent sur la conception d'interfaces et leur utilisation dans les applications Internet. J'ai toujours pensé qu'un bon designer pouvait tout concevoir, d'un anneau de rideau de douche à une affiche de film ou une automobile. Je me suis toujours efforcé d'être multidisciplinaire dans une multitude de domaines, dont la typographie, l'illustration numérique, la 3D, la convivialité des interfaces, etc. Dans cette passion pour le design industriel, je me suis forcé à apprendre le logiciel Rhino3D. Lorsque l'on m'a demandé de concevoir une Ferme verticale [publiée ici], j'ai travaillé 24/24 h et je l'ai conçue en une fois (avec Rhino3D), sur l'idée que cette structure devait être modulaire et empilable. Puis je l'ai fait retravailler en 3D Studio Max par Dean Fowler avec l'assistance en conception de détail de Rolf Mohr, un architecte avec lequel nous travaillons occasionnellement. »

VERTICAL FARM

Harlem, New York, New York, USA, 2007

Floor area: not disclosed. Client: Chris Jacobs. Cost: $200 million.
Collaboration: Rolf Mohr

The concept behind this research project is that of bringing an actual farming space to the core of inner cities, from Los Angeles to New York, where Chris Jacobs imagines installing it in Harlem. Jacobs says: "Close your eyes; now imagine 30 stories of contemporary architecture designed to show off the real green with floor-to-ceiling windows, specialized equipment—solar panels everywhere. Put it next to a freeway; make it a 24-hour operation glowing brightly from the inside. A beacon of green technology. Would this technologically advanced 'greenscraper' spawn a new type of Agro-tourism?" Despite dreaming of such a project on a very large scale, Jacobs admits that "a two-story hydroponic structure atop a multistory affordable housing project might be the most pragmatic way to start." Chris Jacobs has thought through the potential for such a structure in the United States, where venture capital or philanthropic foundations might be persuaded to participate in the cost, with the goal of bringing jobs and fresh produce to America's underprivileged inner cities.

Das Konzept dieses Forschungsprojekts war es, eine reale Landwirtschaftsfläche in das Zentrum von Großstädten zu integrieren – von Los Angeles oder New York, wo Chris Jacobs sie an einen fiktiven Standort in Harlem verlegte. Jacobs führt es aus: „Schließ deine Augen und stell dir ein 30-stöckiges zeitgenössisches Gebäude vor, das gebaut wurde, um echtes Grün zu präsentieren, mit geschosshohen Fenstern, spezieller technischer Ausstattung – überall Solarmodule. Stell es dir direkt neben einer Stadtautobahn vor, lass es als 24-Stunden-Fabrik hell von innen leuchten. Ein Leuchtfeuer grüner Technologie. Könnte dieser technisch anspruchsvolle ‚Greenscraper' zu einer neuen Art von Agro-Tourismus führen?" Trotz seiner Träume von einem Projekt in monumentaler Größenordnung räumt Jacobs ein, dass „eine zweistöckige Hydrokultur-Konstruktion auf einem mehrstöckigen Gebäude mit subventionierten Sozialbauwohnungen zu Anfang wohl der pragmatischere Weg wäre". Chris Jacobs hat die Chancen für ein solches Bauwerk in den USA sehr wohl durchdacht: Möglicherweise ließen sich Risikokapitalgeber und karitative Stiftungen überzeugen, Kosten zu übernehmen, um neue Arbeitsplätze zu schaffen und frisches Obst und Gemüse in die unterprivilegierten Innenstädte Amerikas zu bringen.

Le concept de ce projet de recherche est d'installer de vrais espaces agricoles au cœur des villes, de Los Angeles à New York où Jacobs imagine son implantation à Harlem. « Fermez les yeux et imaginez trente étages d'architecture contemporaine conçus pour montrer cette verdure authentique à travers des baies toute hauteur, des équipements spécialisés, y compris des panneaux solaires dans tous les sens. Placez-le tout près d'une autoroute, faites qu'on le voit de jour comme de nuit, brillamment éclairé de l'intérieur. Un concentré spectaculaire de technologie verte ! Ce "gratte-vert" de haute technologie ne pourrait-il pas lancer un nouveau type d'agrotourisme ? » Tout en rêvant à ce projet à très grande échelle, Jacobs admet qu'« une structure hydroponique de deux niveaux au sommet d'un immeuble de logements accessibles à tous pourrait être un point de départ plus pragmatique ». Il a réfléchi au potentiel d'une structure de ce type aux États-Unis, où les investisseurs et les fondations philanthropiques pourraient être convaincus de participer au coût de l'opération dans le but de créer des emplois et de fournir des produits frais aux habitants défavorisés des centres des villes.

Chris Jacobs addresses the question of just how agriculture might well enter the urban environment in a coherent way, assisted by an intelligent use of architecture.

Chris Jacobs setzt sich mit der Frage auseinander, wie sich Landwirtschaft dank intelligenter Architektur schlüssig in ein urbanes Umfeld integrieren lässt.

Chris Jacobs traite le problème de l'introduction éventuelle de l'agriculture dans un cadre urbain de manière cohérente, aidé par une mise en œuvre intelligente de l'architecture.

KEMPE THILL

Atelier Kempe Thill Architects and Planners
Van Nelleweg 8065, Building 8
3044 BC Rotterdam
The Netherlands

Tel: +31 10 750 37 07
Fax: +31 10 750 36 97
E-mail: info@atelierkempethill.com
Web: www.atelierkempethill.com

ANDRÉ KEMPE was born in 1968 in Freiberg, in former East Germany. He attended the Technical University in Dresden (1990–96) and undertook Urban Studies thereafter in Paris (1993–94) and in Tokyo (1994). He worked in the offices of Frits van Dongen (Amsterdam, 1996–97) and Karelse van der Meer (Rotterdam, 1997–2000), before cofounding Atelier Kempe Thill in Rotterdam (2000). **OLIVER THILL** was born in 1971 in Karl-Marx-Stadt (today Chemnitz), in former East Germany. He also attended the Technical University in Dresden (1990–96) before undertaking similar Urban Studies in Paris and Tokyo. He worked in the office of Frits van Dongen (1996–97) and DKV (Rotterdam, 1997–2000), before joining Kempe in the creation of their firm in 2000. Kempe Thill is specialized in public projects, housing, and urban planning. They seek to create "architecture that is neutral and inexpensive, as well as enjoyable and innovative." Their projects include the Hedge Building (Rostock, Germany, 2003, published here); a museum in Veenhuizen (2005–08); a housing estate (Zwolle, 2005–08); the Railwayline Building (Rotterdam, 2007–); Eco Housing (Tienen, Belgium, 2007–); the Confucius Tower (Amsterdam, 2008–); and the Drug Addict's Hotel (Amsterdam, 2008–12), all in the Netherlands unless stated otherwise.

ANDRÉ KEMPE wurde 1968 in Freiberg in Sachsen, geboren. Er besuchte die Technische Universität Dresden (1990–96) und studierte Städtebau in Paris (1993–94) und Tokio (1994). Er arbeitete für Frits van Dongen (Amsterdam, 1996–97) und Karelse van der Meer (Rotterdam, 1997–2000), bevor er in Rotterdam das Atelier Kempe Thill mitbegründete (2000). **OLIVER THILL** wurde 1971 in Karl-Marx-Stadt (heute Chemnitz) geboren. Auch er besuchte die Technische Universität Dresden (1990–96), bevor er sich ähnlichen Studien wie Kempe in Paris und Tokio widmete. Er war ebenfalls für Frits van Dongen tätig (1996–97) sowie für DKV (Rotterdam, 1997–2000), bevor er mit André Kempe 2000 das gemeinsame Büro gründete. Kempe Thill ist auf öffentliche Bauten, Wohnungsbau und Stadtplanung spezialisiert. Ihr Ziel ist es, „Architektur zu gestalten, die sowohl neutral und erschwinglich als auch angenehm und innovativ ist". Zu ihren Projekten zählen u. a. der niederländische Pavillon für die Internationale Gartenbauausstellung in Rostock, das Hedge Building (2003, hier vorgestellt), ein Museum in Veenhuizen (2005–08), ein Sozialbauprojekt in Zwolle (2005–08), die Umnutzung von Gleisunterbauten (Rotterdam, 2007–), ein Ökohausprojekt (Tienen, Belgien, 2007–), der Confucius-Turm (Amsterdam, 2008–) sowie eine Unterkunft für Drogenabhängige (Amsterdam, 2008–12), alle in den Niederlanden, sofern nicht anders vermerkt.

ANDRÉ KEMPE, né en 1968 à Freiberg, dans l'ex-Allemagne de l'Est, a étudié à l'université polytechnique de Dresde (1990–96) et effectué des études d'urbanisme à Paris (1993–94) et Tokyo (1994). Il a travaillé dans les agences de Frits van Dongen (Amsterdam, 1996–97) et de Karelse van der Meer (Rotterdam, 1997–2000), avant de fonder l'Atelier Kempe Thill à Rotterdam (2000). **OLIVER THILL**, né en 1971 à Karl-Marx-Stadt (aujourd'hui Chemnitz), ex-Allemagne de l'Est, a également étudié à l'université polytechnique de Dresde (1990–96) et effectué les mêmes études d'urbanisme à Paris et Tokyo. Il a travaillé dans les agences de Frits van Dongen (1996–97) et DKV (Rotterdam, 1997–2000), avant de rejoindre Kempe pour créer ensemble leur agence en 2000. Kempe Thill est spécialisée dans les projets publics, le logement et l'urbanisme. Elle cherche à créer une « architecture neutre et inexpressive, mais en même temps novatrice et agréable à vivre ». Parmi leurs réalisations : le Hedge Building (Rostock, Allemagne, 2003, publié ici) ; un musée à Veenhuizen (Pays-Bas, 2005–08) ; un ensemble de logements (Pays-Bas, Zwolle, 2005–08) ; l'immeuble de la gare (Rotterdam, 2007–) ; des logements écologiques (Tirlemont, Belgique, 2007–) ; la tour Confucius (Amsterdam, 2008–) et l'hôtel Drug Addict's (Amsterdam, 2008–12), toutes réalisées aux Pays-Bas sauf exception.

HEDGE BUILDING

Rostock, Germany, 2003

Floor area: 200 m². Client: IBC Hillegom/NL. Cost: €400 000.
Collaboration: André Kempe, Cornelia Sailer, Ruud Smeelen, Oliver Thill, Takashi Nakamura.
Landscape Architect: Niek Roozen, Weesp, NL

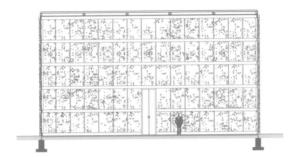

This building served as the Dutch Pavilion at the IGA international garden exhibition in Rostock, Germany, and is now used as a cultural building by the city of Rostock. As the architects write: "The project demonstrates the logic and rationality of Dutch agriculture and unearths surprisingly romantic qualities within its limited conditions." The so-called smart screen, an ivy hedge grown in Dutch greenhouses in sections 1.2 x 1.8 meters in size, can be assembled in sections. Described by the architects as a pergola, the structure is outfitted precisely to allow these smart screens to be used as 10-meter-high green walls. A screen made of translucent plastic covers the interior. The architects insist on the "neutral" aspect of the design, which allows it to be used for different functions. They also insist on the ambiguity thus created between interior and exterior. "The result is a game played between inside and outside," they say. "The light from above makes the space feel like an interior, while the light entering through the hedges gives the space the character of an exterior space. What's more, the gentle sway of the leaves and their shadows enhances the perception of the space."

Der als niederländischer Pavillon auf der Internationalen Gartenbauausstellung (IGA) in Rostock realisierte Bau dient inzwischen als städtische Kultureinrichtung. Die Architekten schreiben: „Das Projekt veranschaulicht die Logik und Rationalität der niederländischen Landwirtschaft und entfaltet im Rahmen seiner begrenzten Möglichkeiten erstaunlich romantische Qualitäten." Der „smart screen", eine in niederländischen Gewächshäusern in 1,2 x 1,8 m großen Segmenten gezogene Efeuhecke lässt sich aus Einzelteilen montieren. Die von den Architekten als Pergola bezeichnete Konstruktion ermöglicht es, diese „smart screens" zu 10 m hohen grünen Mauern aufzurichten. Eine transparente Kunststoffdecke schützt den Raum. Besonders wichtig ist den Architekten die „Neutralität" des Entwurfs, der eine Nutzung für unterschiedlichste Zwecke erlaubt. Darüber hinaus betonen sie die Mehrdeutigkeit von Innen- und Außenraum: „Auf diese Weise ergibt sich ein Spiel zwischen Innen- und Außenraum. Durch die Belichtung von oben wirkt der Raum wie ein Innenraum, dabei verleiht das Licht, das seitlich durch die Hecken fällt, dem Inneren etwas von einem Außenraum. Hinzu kommt, dass das zarte Rascheln der Blätter und ihr Schattenspiel das Raumempfinden verstärkt."

Ce bâtiment a été le pavillon néerlandais pour l'exposition internationale de jardins IGA à Rostock en Allemagne où il sert maintenant de centre culturel. Comme le précise l'architecte : « Ce projet démontre la logique et la rationalité de l'agriculture néerlandaise et révèle des qualités étonnamment romantiques dans ses conditions de vie limitée. » L'ainsi nommé « écran intelligent », composé de haies de lierre venant de serres néerlandaises par section de 1,2 x 1,8 m, a été assemblé. Cette structure, présentée par les architectes comme une pergola, a été montée avec précision pour créer des murs verts de 10 m de haut. Un écran en plastique translucide vert recouvre l'intérieur. Les architectes insistent sur l'aspect « neutre » de cette installation, ce qui lui permet de remplir différentes fonctions et de créer une ambiguïté entre l'intérieur et l'extérieur. « C'est finalement un jeu entre l'intérieur et l'extérieur, disent-ils, la lumière tombant du haut donne l'impression que l'on se trouve à l'intérieur, tandis que celle qui pénètre par les haies donne à l'espace le caractère de salon extérieur. De plus, le léger balancement des feuilles et de leurs ombres accroît la perception de cet espace. »

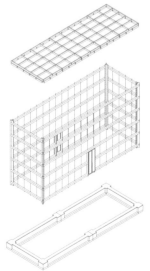

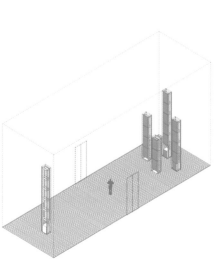

The Hedge Building is almost more of a cage than it is a building, with its high walls filled out with an ivy screen. Here vegetation and architecture are united.

Das Hedge Building ist mit seinen hohen Wänden, in denen Efeurank-gitter angebracht sind, fast mehr Käfig als Gebäude. Hier finden Vegetation und Architektur wirklich zueinander.

Le Hedge Building est autant une cage qu'un bâtiment. Ses hautes parois sont recouvertes de lierre : union de l'architecture et de la végétation.

KIERANTIMBERLAKE

KieranTimberlake
420 North 20th Street
Philadelphia, PA 19130, USA
Tel: +1 215 922 6600 / Fax: +1 215 922 4680
E-mail: kta@kierantimberlake.com / Web: www.kierantimberlake.com

Founded in Philadelphia in 1984 by Stephen Kieran and James Timberlake, **KIERANTIMBERLAKE** comprises a staff of 60. Kieran graduated from Yale University and got his M.Arch from the University of Pennsylvania. Timberlake graduated from the University of Detroit before receiving his M.Arch from the University of Pennsylvania. The firm's projects include programming, planning, and design of all types of new structures and their interiors; and the renovation, reuse, and conservation of existing structures. KieranTimberlake has received over 80 design awards, including the 2008 Architecture Firm Award from the American Institute of Architects. In 2003 the firm developed SmartWrapTM: The Building Envelope of the Future, a mass customizable, high-performance building façade that was initially exhibited at the Smithsonian Institution, Cooper-Hewitt National Design Museum. Structures completed in 2007 include the Sculpture Building Gallery, Yale University (New Haven, Connecticut); and the Suzanne Roberts Theatre, Philadelphia Theatre Company (Philadelphia, Pennsylvania). Buildings by KieranTimberlake completed in 2008 include the Sidwell Friends Middle School (Washington, D.C., 2005–06, published here); and the Multifaith Center and Houghton Memorial Chapel Restoration, Wellesley College (Wellesley, Massachusetts). Further projects are the Northwest Campus Student Housing, University of California (Los Angeles, California); the Center City Building, University of North Carolina at Charlotte (Charlotte, North Carolina); and the Morse and Stiles Colleges, Yale University (New Haven, Connecticut), all in the USA.

KIERANTIMBERLAKE wurde 1984 von Stephen Kieran und James Timberlake in Philadelphia gegründet und hat 60 Mitarbeiter. Kieran schloss sein Studium in Yale ab und erwarb seinen M.Arch. an der University of Pennsylvania. Timberlake machte seinen Abschluss an der University of Detroit und absolvierte seinen M.Arch. ebenfalls an der University of Pennsylvania. Das Büro befasst sich mit Programmentwicklung, Planung und Gestaltung von Neubauten aller Art und deren Innenraumgestaltung sowie der Sanierung, Umnutzung und Erhaltung von Altbauten. KieranTimberlake erhielt über 80 Designpreise, darunter den Architecture Firm Award 2008 des American Institute of Architects. 2003 entwickelte das Büro SmartWrapTM, die Gebäudehülle der Zukunft, eine technisch ausgeklügelte Gebäudefassade, die maßgeschneidert, aber in Massenfertigung hergestellt werden kann und erstmals im Cooper-Hewitt National Design Museum der Smithsonian Institution präsentiert wurde. Zu den 2007 realisierten Bauten zählen die Sculpture Building Gallery an der Yale University (New Haven, Connecticut) und das Suzanne Roberts Theatre für die Philadelphia Theatre Company (Philadelphia, Pennsylvania). 2008 wurden folgende Bauten bezugsfertig: die Sidwell Friends Middle School (Washington D. C., 2005–06, hier vorgestellt) sowie das Multifaith Center und die Sanierung der Houghton Memorial Chapel am Wellesley College (Wellesley, Massachusetts). Weitere Projekte sind ein Studentenwohnheim für den Northwest-Campus der University of California (Los Angeles), das Center City Building der University of North Carolina (Charlotte, North Carolina) sowie das Morse und das Stiles College, Yale University (New Haven, Connecticut), alle in den USA.

Fondée à Philadelphie en 1984 par Stephen Kieran et James Timberlake, l'agence **KIERANTIMBERLAKE** emploie 60 collaborateurs. Kieran est diplômé de Yale et M. Arch de l'université de Pennsylvanie. Timberlake, diplômé de l'université de Detroit, est également M. Arch de l'université de Pennsylvanie. L'agence se consacre à la programmation, l'urbanisme et la conception de tous types de constructions et à leurs aménagements intérieurs ainsi qu'à la rénovation, la réutilisation et la restauration de bâtiments existants. KieranTimberlake a reçu plus de 80 prix, dont celui de l'agence 2008 de l'Institut américain des architectes. En 2003, l'agence a créé SmartWrapTM, « L'enveloppe du bâtiment du futur », façade préfabriquée personnalisable à hautes performances qui a été présentée pour la première fois au Cooper-Hewitt National Design Museum à Washington. Parmi leurs réalisations : la Sculpture Building Gallery de l'université Yale (New Haven, Connecticut) et le théâtre Suzanne Roberts de la Philadelphia Theatre Company (Philadelphie, Pennsylvanie). Parmi leurs projets achevés très récemment : le collège de Sidwell Friends (Washington, D. C., 2005–06, publié ici) et la restauration du Centre œcuménique et du Houghton Memorial Chapel du Wellesley College (Wellesley, Massachusetts). D'autres projets sont des logements pour étudiants du Northwest Campus, université de Californie (Los Angeles, Californie) ; le Center City Building de l'université de Caroline du Nord (Charlotte, Caroline du Nord) et les Morse et Stiles Colleges, université Yale (New Haven, Connecticut), tous au États-Unis.

SIDWELL FRIENDS MIDDLE SCHOOL

Washington, D.C., USA, 2005–06

Floor area: 3623 m² (addition); 3112 m² (renovation). Client: Sidwell Friends School. Cost: $21.5 million.
Collaboration: Andropogon Associates (Landscape), CVM Engineers (Structural Engineers),
Bruce E. Brooks & Associates (Mechanical Engineers)

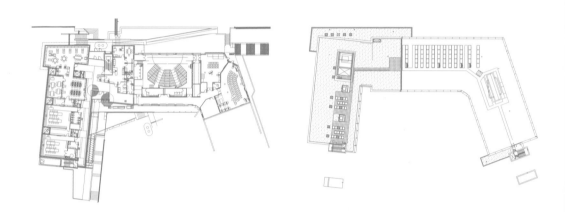

The architects have developed a master plan for this Quaker independent school that places a strong emphasis on environmental responsibility. A new building adds 3623 square meters to the existing facility. The building was awarded a LEED Platinum rating, the highest level of certification attainable from the USGBC, and it is the first school of its type in the United States to receive such a rating. Exterior sunscreens, and classrooms that place an emphasis on natural lighting, are part of the environmental strategy. Occupancy sensors and automatic dimmers reduce electricity consumption. Exterior walls of the addition and the third floor of the existing building are clad in recycled wood from red cedar fermentation barrels. Operable windows encourage the use of natural ventilation. Solar chimneys are designed for mechanically assisted natural ventilation to minimize the need for artificial cooling. A "wetland" zone integrated into the landscaping recycles building wastewater for future gray-water use, thus reducing water consumption from municipal sources by 94%. A "vegetated roof" collects rainwater, and photovoltaic panels generate 5% of electrical requirements.

Für diese freie Quäkerschule entwickelten die Architekten einen Masterplan, der besonderen Wert auf ökologische Verantwortung legt. Ein Neubau erweitert die bestehende Schuleinrichtung um 3623 m². Das Gebäude wurde als erste Schule in den Vereinigten Staaten mit einer LEED-Platinmedaille ausgezeichnet, der höchsten Zertifizierungsstufe des USGBC. Teil des ökologischen Konzepts sind Sonnenschutzvorrichtungen an der Außenfassade und den Klassenräumen, die besonders auf natürliche Belichtung hin ausgelegt sind. Infrarotsensoren und automatische Dimmer reduzieren den Stromverbrauch. Die Außenmauern des Anbaus und der dritte Stock des Altbaus wurden mit Holz von recycelten Fässern aus Riesenlebensbäumen verblendet. Fenster, die sich öffnen lassen, fördern die natürliche Belüftung. Zusätzlich wurden Solarkamine installiert, um die mechanische natürliche Belüftung zu unterstützen und den Bedarf an künstlicher Kühlung zu minimieren. Ein in das Gelände integriertes „Feuchtgebiet" soll Brauchwasser aus den Gebäuden aufbereiten, um das Grauwasser nutzen zu können, wodurch sich der Wasserbedarf aus städtischen Quellen um 94 % senken lässt. Ein begrüntes Dach sammelt Regenwasser, Solarzellen generieren 5 % des Strombedarfs.

Les architectes ont conçu pour cette école quaker un plan qui met un fort accent sur la responsabilité environnementale. Le nouveau bâtiment de 3623 m² complète des installations existantes. Il a reçu la certification LEED Platine, le plus haut niveau accordé par l'USGBC, et est la première école de ce type aux États-Unis à le recevoir. Les écrans extérieurs et les salles de classe qui bénéficient fortement de l'éclairage naturel relèvent de la stratégie environnementale retenue. Des capteurs d'occupation des locaux et des rhéostats automatiques réduisent la consommation d'électricité. Les murs extérieurs du nouveau bâtiment et le troisième niveau des constructions existantes sont habillés de bois recyclé venant de barriques de fermentation en cèdre rouge. Des fenêtres ouvrables encouragent le recours à la ventilation naturelle. Des cheminées solaires facilitent mécaniquement les flux d'air pour réduire les besoins en climatisation. Une zone de lagunage a été intégrée dans les aménagements paysagers pour recycler les eaux usées, ce qui réduit la consommation de l'eau du réseau municipal de 94 %. Un toit végétalisé recueille l'eau de pluie et des panneaux photovoltaïques produisent 5 % de l'électricité consommée.

The addition to this prestigious school by the architects provides a large, efficient volume with a clear emphasis on environmental concerns.

Der Anbau an die renommierte Schule ist ein großer, effizienter Baukörper, der dabei ausdrücklich ökologische Belange berücksichtigt.

L'extension de cette prestigieuse école est un vaste volume efficacement conçu qui met clairement l'accent sur ses ambitions écologiques.

Rooftop planters allow young students to be educated not only about plants but also about environmental concerns and ways to address them.

Pflanzkübel auf dem Dach erlauben nicht nur, die Schüler an Pflanzen heranzuführen, sondern ebenso an Umweltfragen und Möglichkeiten, wie man diesen gerecht werden kann.

Les jardinières du toit permettent aux élèves d'être sensibilisés non seulement à la culture des plantes mais aussi aux préoccupations environne-mentales et aux façons d'y répondre.

The bright, open classrooms seem very much in harmony with banks of solar arrays seen to the right.

Die hellen offenen Klassenzimmer harmonieren hervorragend mit den aufgereihten Solarmodulen auf dem Dach (rechts).

Les salles de cours largement ouvertes paraissent en harmonie avec les installations de panneaux solaires (à droite).

RAFAEL DE LA-HOZ

Rafael de La-Hoz Arquitectos
Paseo de la Castellana, 82–2ºA / 28046 Madrid / Spain
Tel: +34 91 745 35 00 / Fax: +34 91 561 78 03
E-mail: estudio@rafaeldelahoz.com / Web: www.rafaeldelahoz.com

Born in Córdoba in 1955, **RAFAEL DE LA-HOZ** studied Architecture at the ETSA in Madrid and got his M.Arch degree from the city's Polytechnic University (1981). His built work includes "Encina Real," 60 housing units in Encinar de los Reyes (2002); the headquarters of Vodafone (Madrid, 2002); the "Parque Norte" (Madrid, 2001) and "Bilma" Business Parks (Madrid, 2003); the main offices of Endesa (Madrid, 2003); special planning for the high speed train at Vigo Airport (Vigo, 2004); the headquarters of the Chamber of Commerce in Madrid (2004); the Master Plan for Vilamoura (Algarve, Portugal, 2004); the Pentax offices (Madrid, 2004); the BMW Dealership (Madrid, 2005); the main offices of the Madrid legal firm Uría & Menéndez (2005); the municipal meeting facilities of the district of Retiro (Madrid, 2004); the auditorium of the Spanish Olympic Committee (Madrid, 2005); the sustainable office building "Pórtico" (Madrid, 2005); offices of the Madrid legal firm Garrigues (2004–06); District C of Telefónica (Madrid, 2002–07, published here); and "Rafael del Pino" Foundation offices (Madrid, 2001–08). As well as winning the competition for Chamartín Island Tower (Madrid, 2008–11), his work includes the Hércules Towers in "Los Barrios" (Cádiz, 2005–09); lecture rooms for the University of Córdoba (2005–09); a sports complex in a former bus station (Granada, 2006–09); "El Paraíso" Foundation (Córdoba, 2007–09); Gran Via 48 (Madrid, 2007–09); building for the Juvenile Court (Madrid, 2007–10); AMA Headquarters (Madrid, 2007–10); Repsol Headquarters (Madrid, 2008–10); Residential Complex and Hotels (Warsaw, Poland, 2007–11); extension for the Vilamoura Marina (Algarve, Portugal, 2008–11); and a building for the Criminal Court (Madrid, 2008–11).

RAFAEL DE LA-HOZ wurde 1955 in Córdoba geboren. Er studierte zunächst Architektur an der ETSAM in Madrid und erwarb einen M.Arch. an der Polytechnischen Hochschule von Madrid (1981). Realisierte Bauten sind u. a. „Encina Real", 60 Wohneinheiten in Encinar de los Reyes (2002), die Verwaltungszentrale für Vodafone (Madrid, 2002), die Gewerbegebiete „Parque Norte" (Madrid, 2001) und „Bilma" (Madrid, 2003), die Verwaltungszentrale für Endesa (Madrid, 2003), Spezialplanungen für den Hochgeschwindigkeitszug am Flughafen Vigo (Vigo, 2004), die Hauptniederlassung der Handelskammer in Madrid (2004), der Masterplan für Vilamoura (Algarve, Portugal, 2004), ein Bürogebäude für Pentax (Madrid, 2004), die BMW-Niederlassung (Madrid, 2005), das Hauptbüro der Anwaltskanzlei Uría & Menéndez (Madrid, 2005), das Stadtratsgebäude für den Madrider Bezirk Retiro (Madrid, 2004), der Versammlungssaal des spanischen Olympischen Komitees (Madrid, 2005), das umweltfreundliche Bürogebäude „Pórtico" (Madrid, 2005), Büros für die Madrider Anwaltskanzlei Garrigues (2004–06), der Distrito C für Telefónica (Madrid, 2002–07, hier vorgestellt) sowie Büros für die Stiftung Rafael del Pino (Madrid, 2001–08). Weitere Projekte sind neben einem gewonnenen Wettbewerb für das Hochhaus Isla Chamartín (Madrid, 2008–11) das Hércules-Hochhaus in „Los Barrios" (Cádiz, 2005–09), Hörsäle für die Universität Córdoba (2005–09), ein Sportkomplex im ehemaligen Busbahnhof (Granada, 2006–09), die Stiftung El Paraíso (Córdoba, 2007–09), das Gebäude Gran Vía 48 (Madrid, 2007–09), ein Neubau für das Jugendgericht (Madrid, 2007–10), die AMA-Hauptverwaltung (Madrid, 2007–10), die neue Hauptniederlassung für Repsol (Madrid, 2008–10), ein Wohnbaukomplex mit Hotels in Warschau (2007–11), der Erweiterungsplan für den Jachthafen in Vilamoura (Algarve, Portugal, 2008–11) und ein Neubau für das Strafgericht in Madrid (2008–11).

Né à Cordoue en 1955, **RAFAEL DE LA-HOZ** a étudié l'architecture à l'ETSA à Madrid et a obtenu son M. Arch de l'Université polytechnique de la même ville (1981). Parmi ses réalisations : « Encina Real », 60 logements à Encinar de los Reyes (2002) ; le siège de Vodafone (Madrid, 2002) ; les parcs d'affaires « Parque Norte » (Madrid, 2001) et « Bilma » (Madrid, 2003) ; les bureaux d'Endesa (Madrid, 2003) ; la planification du TGV à l'aéroport de Vigo (2004) ; le siège de la Chambre de commerce de Madrid (2004) ; le plan directeur de Vilamoura (Algarve, Portugal, 2004) ; les bureaux de Pentax (Madrid, 2004) ; la concession principale BMW (Madrid, 2005) ; le siège du cabinet juridique madrilène Uría & Menéndez (2005) ; des installations municipales dans le quartier du Retiro (Madrid, 2004) ; l'auditorium du Comité olympique espagnol (Madrid, 2005) ; un immeuble « vert », le Pórtico (Madrid, 2005) ; les bureaux du cabinet juridique madrilène Garrigues (2004–06) ; les bureaux « District C » de Telefónica (Madrid, 2002–07, publié ici) et les bureaux de la Fondation Rafael del Pino (Madrid, 2001–08). D'autres projets sont la tour de l'île de Chamartín (Madrid, 2008–11), ses travaux comprennent les tours Hércules à « Los Barrios » (Cádiz, 2005–09) ; un bâtiment de salles de conférences pour l'université de Cordoue (2005–09) ; un complexe sportif dans l'ancienne gare routière (Grenade, 2006–09) ; la Fondation « El Paraíso » (Cordoue, 2007–09) ; l'immeuble Gran Via 48 (Madrid, 2007–09) ; le nouveau bâtiment du tribunal pour enfants (Madrid, 2007–10) ; le siège d'AMA (Madrid, 2007–10) ; le nouveau siège de Repsol (Madrid, 2008–10) ; un complexe résidentiel et hôtelier (Varsovie, Pologne, 2007–11) ; l'extension de la marina de Vilamoura (Algarve, Portugal, 2008–11) et un nouveau bâtiment pour la Cour criminelle de Madrid (2008–11).

TELEFÓNICA DISTRICT C

Las Tablas, Madrid, Spain, 2002–07

*Floor area: 390 000 m². Client: Telefónica de España SA. Cost: €490 million.
Collaboration: Hugo Berenguer, Francisco Arévalo, Siegfried Bürger*

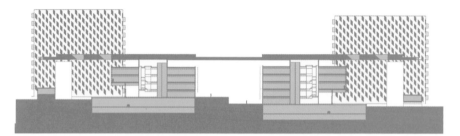

The District C buildings are very large in scale, a fact that belies their landscaping and division into distinct volumes, which are nonetheless joined together by the large canopy roofs.

Die Bauten des Distrito C sind ungewöhnlich groß, ein Eindruck, der durch die landschaftliche Gestaltung und die Aufteilung des Komplexes in einzelne, durch monumentale Baldachindächer miteinander verbundene Baukörper abgeschwächt wird.

Les bâtiments du District C sont de très vastes dimensions, que font presque oublier les aménagements paysagers et leur division en volumes séparés mais néanmoins reliés par d'immenses auvents.

As part of its corporate strategy, the Telefónica Group, the largest company in Spain, decided to build a new headquarters in order to bring together all of its companies and divisions, which were previously spread in different locations in Madrid. The selected site measures 19 hectares, has its own subway station, and is intended for up to 12 000 employees. The program required at least ten buildings measuring between 3 and 11 stories, with each floor offering at least 2500 square meters of space. The architect chose to make glass the predominant visible material, and to base the composition on a square grid, with a linking landscape. Very large, high roof canopies cover large parts of the complex. According to the architect: "None of the buildings actually imposes its identity on the rest; instead, each building submits its volume to the whole, just as all the buildings are protected under the same canopy that unifies them and brings them together." Clear glass with a strict pattern of silk-screen dots that make it appear opaque from the interior, while users can still see out with little impression that the glass is even tinted, is used with different degrees of opacity throughout the complex in 4 x 2 meter panes. With glass fins set at right angles to the façades, angular shadows play across the surface of the buildings in patterns dictated by the movements of the sun. Indeed, the strong sun of Madrid is an essential element in the sustainability strategy of the architect. Rafael de La-Hoz writes: "Finally and fundamentally, the roof is photovoltaic, constituting the largest horizontal surface for collecting solar energy in Europe. The solar panels that cover 26 000 square meters of the top of the canopy, transform solar thermal energy into electricity, at the rate of 4 389 000 kWh/year, which represents a reduction of 2000 tons of CO_2 emitted into the atmosphere. The roof's shadow, cast over the façades, cloisters and entrances, unifies and protects."

Aus firmenpolitischen Gründen beschloss die Telefónica-Gruppe, das größte Unternehmen Spaniens, einen neuen Hauptsitz zu bauen, in dem alle Unterfirmen und Abteilungen zusammengelegt werden sollten, die bis dato über verschiedene Standorte in Madrid verstreut waren. Das ausgewählte Grundstück hat eine Größe von 19 ha, eine eigene U-Bahnstation und wird 12 000 Angestellten Platz bieten. Das Programm erforderte mindestens zehn drei- bis elfstöckige Gebäude mit je 2500 m² Geschossfläche. Der Architekt entschied sich für Glas als dominierendes sichtbares Baumaterial und gestaltete den Entwurf auf Grundlage eines quadratischen Rasters, in das er landschaftliche Elemente integrierte. Monumentale hohe Baldachindächer überspannen weite Teile des Komplexes. Rafael de La-Hoz erklärt: „Keiner der Einzelbauten stellt mit seinem Profil die übrigen Gebäude in den Schatten, vielmehr trägt jedes Gebäude mit seinem Volumen zum Ganzen bei, ebenso werden die Gebäude von einem Baldachindach geschützt, das sie eint und zusammenführt." Im gesamten Komplex wurden 4 x 2 m große Klarglastafeln mit einem strengen Muster aus Siebdruckpunkten eingesetzt, das das Glas von innen opak und dennoch kaum getönt erscheinen lässt, wobei der Opazitätsgrad variiert. Lotrecht zur Fassade stehende Glaselemente lassen je nach Sonnenstand scharfkantige Schatten über die Fassaden spielen. Das intensive Sonnenlicht in Madrid ist ein wesentliches Element in der nachhaltigen Strategie des Architekten; er schreibt: „Von entscheidender Bedeutung ist schließlich das Fotovoltaikdach, insgesamt die größte horizontale Fläche zur Erzeugung von Solarenergie in ganz Europa. Die Solarmodule, die 26 000 m² Dachfläche bedecken, erzeugen durch Sonnenenergie 4 389 000 kWh Strom pro Jahr, was einer Reduzierung der CO_2-Emissionen in die Atmosphäre um 2000 t gleichkommt. Der auf die Fassaden, ‚Kreuzgänge' und Eingänge fallende Schatten des Dachs wirkt einend und schützend zugleich."

Dans le cadre de sa stratégie institutionnelle, le groupe Telefónica, la plus grande entreprise espagnole, a décidé d'édifier un nouveau siège afin de rassembler ses multiples sociétés et divisions dispersées dans Madrid. Le site de 19 ha a sa propre station de métro et a été conçu pour accueillir 12 000 employés. Le programme portait sur au moins dix immeubles de trois à onze niveaux, chaque niveau offrant 2500 m² chacun de surface au minimum. L'architecte a décidé de faire du verre le matériau dominant et d'appuyer sa composition sur une trame carrée et des aménagements paysagers qui unifient l'ensemble. D'importants auvents de grande hauteur recouvrent une vaste partie du complexe. Selon l'architecte : « Aucun immeuble n'impose son identité par rapport aux autres. Au contraire, chacun est soumis aux volumes de l'ensemble, de même que tous sont protégés par un même auvent qui les regroupe et les unifie. » Les panneaux de verre clair de 4 x 2 m sont sérigraphiés de pastilles qui les font sembler opaques, depuis l'extérieur, mais restent translucides et légèrement teintées, depuis l'intérieur. Leur degré d'opacité varie selon l'exposition au soleil. Des ailettes de verre verticales perpendiculaires aux façades créent des jeux d'ombres anguleux sur les façades selon la course du soleil. Particulièrement fort à Madrid, celui-ci est un élément essentiel de la stratégie de durabilité adoptée par l'architecte. Rafael de La-Hoz explique : « Très important, le toit photovoltaïque est la plus grande surface horizontale de captation de l'énergie solaire mise en œuvre en Europe. Les panneaux solaires, qui couvrent 26 000 m² de l'auvent, transforment l'énergie thermique en électricité au taux de 4 389 000 kWh par an, soit une diminution de 2000 tonnes de rejets de CO_2 dans l'atmosphère. L'ombre de la toiture se projette sur les façades, les patios et les entrées. Elle unifie et protège. »

The glass fins that protrude at right angles to a number of the façades reduce solar gain and also create varied patterns on the building according to the movement of the sun.

Glasgrate, die lotrecht aus den Fassaden einzelner Bauten herausragen, reduzieren den Wärmegewinn und lassen zudem je nach Sonnenstand unterschiedlichste Muster über die Fassaden spielen.

Les ailettes de verre qui se projettent perpendiculairement d'un certain nombre de façades réduisent le gain solaire et créent des effets visuels variés selon la course du soleil.

MICHAEL B. LEHRER

Lehrer Architects
2140 Hyperion Avenue
Los Angeles, CA 90027
USA

Tel: + 1 323 664 4747
Fax: + 1 323 664 3566
E-mail: architect@lehrerarchitects.com
Web: www.lehrerarchitects.com

MICHAEL B. LEHRER received a B.A. degree from the College of Environmental Design, UC Berkeley, in 1975. He received his M.Arch degree at the Harvard GSD in 1978. Michael B. Lehrer worked as a Senior Project Architect in the office of Frank O. Gehry (1984–85), and created his own firm, Lehrer Architects, in 1985. He is an Adjunct Associate Professor of Architecture at the University of Southern California, School of Architecture, and President of the American Institute of Architects Los Angeles. His work includes the Water + Life Museum and Campus (Hemet, 2001–06, published here); his own office in Los Angeles (2006), a converted warehouse that won an AIA National Honor Award; Registrar Recorder Clerk, County of Los Angeles (Los Angeles, 2008); Westwood United Methodist Church Master Plan (Los Angeles, 2009); Canyon Residence (Santa Monica, 2009); Westside Jewish Community Center Natatorium (Los Angeles, 2009); and Lofts on Croft Court (West Hollywood, 2010), all in California, USA.

MICHAEL B. LEHRER schloss sein Studium am College of Environmental Design in Berkeley 1975 mit einem B.A. ab. Seinen M.Arch. erhielt er 1978 an der Harvard Graduate School of Design. Michael B. Lehrer war als leitender Projektarchitekt bei Frank O. Gehry (1984–85) und gründete 1985 sein eigenes Büro, Lehrer Architects. Er ist außerordentlicher Professor für Architektur an der Universität von Southern California und Präsident des American Institute of Architects Los Angeles. Zu seinen Projekten zählen der Water + Life Museum and Campus (Hemet, 2001–06, hier vorgestellt), seine eigenen Büroräume in Los Angeles (2006), ein umgebautes Lagerhaus, ausgezeichnet mit dem AIA National Honor Award, das Amtsgebäude des Registrar Recorder Clerk für Los Angeles (Los Angeles, 2008), der Masterplan für die Westwood United Methodist Church (Los Angeles, 2009), die Canyon Residence (Santa Monica, 2009), die Schwimmhalle des Gemeindezentrums der Westside Jewish Community (Los Angeles, 2009) sowie Lofts am Croft Court (West Hollywood, 2010), alle in Kalifornien.

MICHAEL B. LEHRER est B.A. du College of Environmental Design d'UC Berkeley (1975) et a passé son M. Arch à la Harvard GSD en 1978. Il a travaillé comme architecte de projet senior chez Frank O. Gehry (1984–85) et crée son agence, Lehrer Architects, en 1985. Il est professeur adjoint d'architecture à l'École d'architecture de l'université de Californie du Sud, et président de l'Institut américain des architectes à Los Angeles. Parmi ses réalisations : le Water + Life Museum and Campus (Hemet, 2001–06, publié ici) ; ses propres bureaux à Los Angeles (2006), la conversion d'un entrepôt qui a remporté un Prix d'honneur national de l'AIA ; le siège du Registrar Recorder Clerk du comté de Los Angeles (Los Angeles, 2008) ; le plan directeur de l'église méthodiste unifiée de Westwood (Los Angeles, 2009) ; la résidence Canyon (Santa Monica, 2009) ; le Westside Jewish Community Center Natatorium (Los Angeles, 2009) et les Lofts sur Croft Court (West Hollywood, 2010), toutes en Californie, États-Unis.

WATER + LIFE MUSEUM AND CAMPUS

Hemet, California, USA, 2001–06

*Floor area: 6340 m². Client: The Center for Water Education and Western Center for Archeology and Paleontology.
Cost: $40 million. Collaboration: Mark Gangi, AIA, Lehrer + Gangi Design + Build*

Built on a 6.9-hectare site near Diamond Valley Lake, the program for this project required the design of "an engaging museum campus that celebrates the link between southern California's water infrastructure and the evolution of life. Phase 1 of the campus includes two museums," laboratories, classrooms, administrative offices, support facilities, gift shop, café, and interpretive/educational landscape." The program further stipulated that the architecture should be a "living example of sustainability and conservation." The design with five 12-meter-high steel towers was inspired by architecture created for the Los Angeles Metropolitan Water District, such as Gordon B. Kaufman's pump buildings at the Parker Dam near Lake Havasu. The complex was the first museum to receive a LEED Platinum rating, the highest bestowed by the USGBC. Abundant natural light is used, and a 540-kilowatt, 3000-panel photovoltaic installation provides the complex with almost half of its total power needs. Heat-blocking glass and a network of electronic sensing devices and timers optimize energy consumption, while heating and cooling are run through a sophisticated mechanical system of radiant flooring and forced-air units.

Das Programm für dieses Projekt, das unweit des Diamond Valley Lake auf einem 6,9 ha großen Gelände liegt, erforderte den Entwurf „eines lebendigen Museumscampus, der sich mit der Wasserversorgung Südkaliforniens ebenso wie mit der Evolutionsgeschichte auseinandersetzt. Die erste Bauphase des Campus umfasst zwei Museen, Labors, Lehrräume, Verwaltungsbüros, technische Einrichtungen, einen Museumsshop, ein Café sowie eine suggestive Landschaftsgestaltung". Darüber hinaus forderte das Programm eine Architektur als „lebendiges Beispiel für Nachhaltigkeit und Naturschutz". Der Entwurf mit seinen fünf 12 m hohen Stahltürmen wurde von Bauten des Los Angeles Metropolitan Water District inspiriert, etwa den Pumpenhäusern von Gordon B. Kaufman am Parker-Staudamm in der Nähe des Lake Havasu. Der Komplex wurde als erstes Museum mit einer LEED-Platinmedaille ausgezeichnet, der höchsten vom US Green Building Council verliehenen Auszeichnung. Das außerordentlich helle Licht wird für natürliche Belichtung genutzt, 3000 Solarmodule mit einer Leistung von je 540 kW versorgen den Komplex mit nahezu 50 % seines Energiebedarfs. Wärmeschutzverglasung und ein Netzwerk elektronischer Sensoren optimieren den Stromverbrauch. Heizung und Kühlung erfolgen über ein ausgeklügeltes System aus Fußbodenheizung und Luftschächten.

Réalisé sur un terrain de 6,9 ha près du lac de Diamond Valley, ce projet répond à un programme précis de création d'« un musée séduisant qui célèbre le lien entre les infrastructures hydrauliques californiennes et l'évolution de la vie. La Phase 1 du campus comprend deux musées, des laboratoires, des salles de cours, des bureaux administratifs, des installations techniques, une boutique, un café et un environnement paysager aménagé pour l'interprétation et l'éducation ». Il stipulait également que l'architecture devait être « un exemple vivant de durabilité et de préservation ». La conception des cinq tours d'acier de 12 m de haut s'inspire des réalisations architecturales du Los Angeles Metropolitan Water District, et en particulier des bâtiments des pompes de Gordon B. Kaufman pour le barrage Parker près du lac Havasu. Le complexe a été le premier musée à recevoir la certification LEED Platine, le plus haut niveau accordé par l'US Green Building Council. L'éclairage naturel est privilégié et une installation de 3000 panneaux photovoltaïques de 540 kW fournit près de la moitié de la consommation électrique du complexe. Des verres thermiques et un réseau de capteurs électroniques et de minuteries optimisent la consommation d'électricité tandis que le chauffage et le refroidissement sont fournis par un système mécanique sophistiqué de sols radiants et d'unités à air pulsé.

This complex makes it clear that green design can go hand in hand with crisp, modern forms.

Dieser Komplex macht deutlich, dass grünes Design Hand in Hand gehen kann mit klarer, moderner Formgebung.

Ce complexe montre clairement qu'une conception écologique peut aller de pair avec des formes modernes.

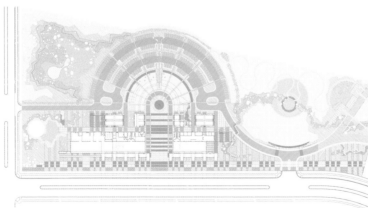

The vertical blocks of the building, divided into two groups of five, form a strong horizontal continuity that was inspired by California dam design.

Die vertikalen Blöcke, die in zwei Fünfergruppen angeordnet sind, bilden ein ausdrucksstarkes horizontales Kontinuum, das vom kalifornischen Staudammbau inspiriert wurde.

Les blocs verticaux, divisés en deux groupes de cinq, présentent une forte continuité horizontale inspirée des barrages californiens.

The complex is defined by repetitive volumes, alternating between light and more opaque, heavier elements.

Der Komplex ist von sich wiederholenden Volumina und einem Wechsel heller und dunkler, schwererer Elemente geprägt.

Le complexe est défini par des masses répétées, alternant des éléments légers et d'autres plus lourds et plus opaques.

Vast surfaces covered by photovoltaic cells are visible in the image above, which also emphasizes the industrial origin of the architectural vocabulary.

Das Bild oben zeigt weitläufige Solarmodulfelder, was die industriellen Wurzeln der architektonischen Formensprache zusätzlich betont.

Les importantes étendues de panneaux solaires photovoltaïques visibles ci-dessus expriment également l'origine industrielle du ton architectural employé.

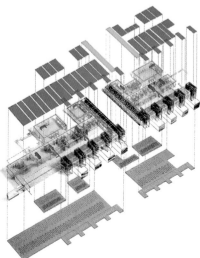

MORPHOSIS

Morphosis
2041 Colorado Avenue
Santa Monica, CA 90404
USA

Tel: +1 310 453 2247
Fax: +1 310 829 3270
E-mail: studio@morphosis.net
Web: www.morphosis.net

MORPHOSIS Principal Thom Mayne, born in Connecticut in 1944, received his B.Arch in 1968 from the University of Southern California, Los Angeles, and his M.Arch degree from Harvard in 1978. He created Morphosis in 1979 with Michael Rotondi, who later left to create his own firm, RoTo. He has taught at UCLA, Harvard, Yale, and SCI-Arc, of which he was a founding Board Member. Thom Mayne was the winner of the 2005 Pritzker Prize. Some of the main buildings by Morphosis are the Lawrence House (Hermosa Beach, California, 1981); Kate Mantilini Restaurant (Beverly Hills, California, 1986); Cedar's Sinai Comprehensive Cancer Care Center (Beverly Hills, California, 1987); Crawford Residence (Montecito, 1987–92); Yuzen Vintage Car Museum (project, West Hollywood, 1992); Blades Residence (Santa Barbara, California, 1992–97); and International Elementary School (Long Beach, California, 1997–99). Further work includes the University of Cincinnati Student Recreation Center (Cincinnati, Ohio, 1999–2005); the NOAA Satellite Operation Facility in Suitland (Maryland, 2001–05); the San Francisco Federal Building (San Francisco, California, 2003–07, published here); a proposal for the 2012 Olympics in New York City made prior to the selection of London; and the Phare Tower (Paris, France, 2006–12). They are also participating in Brad Pitt's "Make It Right" initiative in New Orleans with their "Floating Prototype House," and are working on the Museum of Nature and Science (Dallas, Texas) and the Alexandria Bay Port of Entry (Alexandria Bay, New York), all in the USA unless stated otherwise.

Thom Mayne, Direktor von **MORPHOSIS**, wurde 1944 in Connecticut geboren. 1968 erlangte er den Abschluss eines B.Arch. an der University of Southern California, Los Angeles (UCLA), und 1978 seinen M.Arch. in Harvard. 1979 gründete er mit Michael Rotondi das Büro Morphosis. Rotondi machte sich jedoch später mit seiner eigenen Firma RoTo selbstständig. Mayne lehrte an der UCLA, in Harvard, Yale und am Southern California Institute of Architecture (SCI-Arc), zu dessen Gründungsmitgliedern er zählt. 2005 wurde Mayne mit dem Pritzker-Preis ausgezeichnet. Zu den wichtigsten Bauten von Morphosis zählen das Lawrence House (Hermosa Beach, Kalifornien, 1981), das Kate Mantilini Restaurant (Beverly Hills, Kalifornien, 1986), die Cedar's-Sinai-Krebsklinik (Beverly Hills, Kalifornien, 1987), die Crawford Residence (Montecito, Kalifornien, 1987–92), das Yuzen-Oldtimermuseum (Projekt, West Hollywood, Kalifornien, 1992), die Blades Residence (Santa Barbara, Kalifornien, 1992–97) sowie die International Elementary School (Long Beach, Kalifornien, 1997–99). Weitere Arbeiten sind das Freizeitzentrum für Studenten der University of Cincinnati (Cincinnati, Ohio, 1999–2005), das NOAA-Satellitenzentrum in Suitland (Maryland, 2001–05), das San Francisco Federal Building (San Francisco, Kalifornien, 2003–07, hier vorgestellt), ein Entwurf für die Olympischen Spiele 2012 in New York (vor der Entscheidung für London aus Austragungsort entstanden) sowie das Hochhaus Phare (Paris, 2006–12). Darüber hinaus ist das Büro mit seinem „Floating Prototype House" an Brad Pitts Initiative „Make It Right" in New Orleans beteiligt und arbeitet an einem Museum für Naturkunde (Dallas, Texas) sowie am Hafen Alexandria Bay (Alexandria Bay, New York).

Le dirigeant de **MORPHOSIS**, Thom Mayne, né dans le Connecticut en 1944, est B. Arch de USC, Los Angeles (1968) et M. Arch de Harvard (1978). Il fonde l'agence en 1979 avec Michael Rotondi qui la quitte pour créer par la suite sa propre structure, RoTo. Il a enseigné à UCLA, Harvard, Yale, et SCI-Arc dont il est un des fondateurs. Thom Mayne a reçu le Prix Pritzker en 2005. Parmi ses principales réalisations : la maison Lawrence (Hermosa Beach, Californie,1981) ; le restaurant Kate Mantilini (Beverly Hills, Californie, 1986) ; le Cedar's Sinai Comprehensive Cancer Care Center (Beverly Hills, Californie, 1987) ; la résidence Crawford (Montecito, Californie, 1987–92) ; le Yuzen Vintage Car Museum (projet, West Hollywood, 1992) ; la résidence Blades (Santa Barbara, Californie, 1992–97) ; et l'International Elementary School de Long Beach (Californie, 1997–99). D'autres travaux comprennent le Student Recreation Center de l'université de Cincinnati (Ohio, 1999–2005) ; le NOAA Satellite Operation Facility (Suitland, Maryland, 2001–05) ; le San Francisco Federal Building (San Francisco, 2003–07, publié ici) ; il a soumis une proposition pour la candidature de New York aux Jeux olympiques 2012 (faite avant la sélection de Londres) et mis au point le projet de la tour Phare (Paris La-Défense, 2006–12). Morphosis participe à l'initiative de Brad Pitt « Make It Right » à la Nouvelle-Orléans à travers sa proposition de « maison flottante prototype » et travaille sur les projets du musée de la nature et de la science (Dallas, Texas) et de l'entrée du port d'Alexandria Bay (Alexandria Bay, New York), tous aux États-Unis sauf exception.

SAN FRANCISCO FEDERAL BUILDING

San Francisco, California, USA, 2003–07

Floor area: 41 806 m². Client: US General Services Administration (GSA). Cost: $144 million.
Collaboration: Tim Christ (Project Manager), Brandon Weiling (Project Architect)

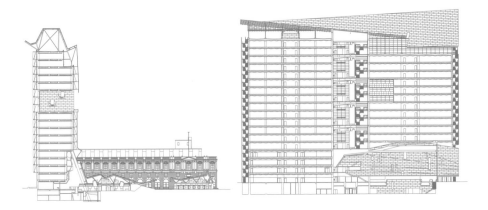

Morphosis worked in this instance with the GSA, which seeks "to reduce consumption of natural resources, minimize waste, and create a healthy and productive work environment for all tenants who occupy federal workspace." Eighteen stories high (73 m) and intended for 1500 employees, the Federal Building is occupied by a number of US government offices, including the Departments of Defense, Labor, and Agriculture. The methods employed to render the building sustainable are numerous. Computer systems open and close windows, vents, and sunscreens according to temperature conditions. The thermal mass of exposed concrete columns is used to cool or warm the building. The GSA attempts to use no more than 55 000 Btu of energy/square foot/year in its buildings. The San Francisco Federal Building surpasses the GSA's target as well as California's restrictive Title 24 Energy Code. The naturally ventilated floors have an average energy consumption of less than 25 000 Btu/square foot/year. Natural light illuminates 85% of the structure's interior, resulting in a further reduction in electricity consumption. The GSA mandated that 75% of materials used during construction be recycled. Currently, the project is recycling 87% of its waste material. In 2007 Morphosis won the first international Zumtobel Group Award for Sustainability and Humanity in the Built Environment for the Federal Building. Thom Mayne states: "Our primary interest was to produce a performance-driven building that would fundamentally transform its urban surroundings, the nature of the workplace, and the experiences of the people who use it, while making intelligent use of natural resources. For me, this project represents the epitome of an optimistic architecture…"

Bei diesem Projekt arbeitete Morphosis mit der amerikanischen Regierungsagentur General Service Administration (GSA) zusammen, die sich dafür einsetzt, „den Verbrauch natürlicher Ressourcen zu reduzieren, Abfall zu minimieren und ein gesundes, produktives Umfeld für all jene zu schaffen, die in Arbeitsräumen der Bundesverwaltung tätig sind". Das Federal Building, 18 Stockwerke hoch (73 m) und für 1500 Angestellte vorgesehen, wird von verschiedenen Bundesbehörden wie den Ämtern für Verteidigung, Arbeit und Landwirtschaft genutzt. Verschiedenste Methoden kamen zum Einsatz, um das Gebäude umweltfreundlich zu gestalten. Computersysteme öffnen und schließen Fenster, Lüftungsschächte und Sonnenblenden je nach Temperatur. Die thermische Masse der frei liegenden Betonsäulen wird genutzt, um das Gebäude zu kühlen oder zu erwärmen. Die GSA strebt an, in ihren Gebäuden nicht mehr als 55 000 Btu (British thermal units) jährlich pro 0,09 m² zu verbrauchen. Das Federal Building in San Francisco unterschreitet diese Grenze ebenso wie die strengen Vorgaben in Kalifornien, den „Title 24 Energy Code". Die natürlich belüfteten Etagen haben einen durchschnittlichen Energieverbauch von jährlich unter 25 000 Btu pro 0,09 m². 85 % des Innenraums werden mit Tageslicht versorgt, was zu einer weiteren Reduzierung des Stromverbrauchs führt. Die GSA forderte, dass die verwendeten Baumaterialien zu 75 % recyclingfähig sein müssten. Derzeit werden 87 % der Abfälle recycelt. 2007 gewann Morphosis mit seinem Federal Building den ersten Internationalen Zumtobel Group Award for Sustainability and Humanity in the Built Environment (Preis der Zumtobel-Gruppe für Nachhaltigkeit und Menschlichkeit in der gebauten Umwelt). Thom Mayne erklärt: „Unser primäres Ziel war es, ein leistungsorientiertes Gebäude zu gestalten, das sein urbanes Umfeld fundamental verändern würde, ebenso wie die Art des Arbeitsplatzes und die Erfahrung derjenigen, die dort arbeiten. Zugleich sollten natürliche Ressourcen auf intelligente Weise zum Einsatz kommen. Für mich ist dieses Projekt der Inbegriff einer optimistischen Architektur…"

Morphosis a étroitement collaboré avec son client, l'Administration générale des services fédéraux, qui cherche « à diminuer la consommation des ressources naturelles, réduire les déchets et créer un environnement de travail sain et productif pour les utilisateurs des lieux de travail fédéraux ». Prévu pour 1500 employés, ce Federal Building de 18 niveaux (73 m de haut) est occupé par divers bureaux et agences fédérales dont ceux de la Défense, du Travail et de l'Agriculture. Les méthodes pour rendre cet immeuble durable sont multiples. Des systèmes informatiques ouvrent et ferment les fenêtres et orientent des ailettes et des écrans de protection solaire selon la température. La masse thermique des colonnes de béton que l'on voit sert à réchauffer ou rafraîchir l'immeuble. Le GSA tente d'imposer une consommation maximum de 1908 kW/m² par an dans ses locaux. L'immeuble de San Francisco affiche une consommation inférieure à cet objectif fédéral et à celui du Titre 24 du Code de l'énergie californien. Les niveaux bénéficiant d'une ventilation naturelle peuvent se targuer d'une consommation de moins de 867 kW/m² par an. 85 % de l'intérieur du bâtiment reçoit la lumière naturelle, ce qui contribue à la réduction de la consommation d'électricité. Le GSA a également exigé que 75 % des matériaux utilisés pendant la construction soient recyclables. Actuellement, l'immeuble recycle 87 % de ses déchets. En 2007, Morphosis a remporté le premier prix international de durabilité et « d'humanité dans l'environnement bâti » du groupe Zumtobel. Thom Mayne a déclaré : « Notre objectif fondamental était de produire un immeuble axé sur la performance qui transforme fondamentalement son environnement urbain, la nature du poste de travail et l'expérience quotidienne de ceux qui y vivent, tout en pratiquant une utilisation intelligente des ressources. Pour moi, ce projet représente l'épitomé d'une architecture optimiste… »

As is often the case, the building designed by Morphosis has an unusual, one might say enigmatic, mechanical appearance, a green machine in this instance.

Wie so oft bei Morphosis mutet der Entwurf ungewöhnlich, fast rätselhaft und an eine technische Apparatur erinnernd an, wie eine – in diesem Fall grüne – Maschine.

Comme souvent le cas, le bâtiment conçu par Morphosis présente un aspect étonnant, mécanique, presque énigmatique, celui d'une « machine » écologique.

The architects excel at creating unexpected volumes and spaces, including the large urban window (left).

Die Architekten verstehen es hervorragend, überraschende Volumina und Räume zu gestalten, etwa das riesige Fenster mit Blick auf die urbane Landschaft (links).

L'architecte excelle dans la création de volumes et d'espaces surprenants, comme cette énorme fenêtre sur la ville (à gauche).

ALBERTO MOZÓ

OWA
Alberto Mozó
Parque Industrial Los Libertadores
Blanco 15 I-1 / Galpon #1
Colina, Santiago
Chile

Tel: +56 2 366 0384
E-mail: www.alberto@mozo.cl
Web: www.owa.cl

ALBERTO MOZÓ was born in 1963 in New York and emigrated with his family to Santiago, Chile, at the age of seven. After completing college in Santiago, he graduated in 1991 from the Pontificia Universidad Católica de Chile. His first architectural projects involved the creation of interior spaces and the design of furniture for bars. He was thus in the midst of the creation of meeting places for the young generation emerging after Chile's transition to democracy. Simultaneously he worked on the restoration of old houses in Santiago. In 2002 he received an award from the Province Council of Andalucia (Spain) for the rehabilitation of old houses situated in the Ibero-American historic districts. His work includes the Schkolnick Photo Studio (Sur Providencia, Santiago, 1999); Yankovic House (Aculeo, Santiago, 2002); Rivadeneira House (Tunquén, Valparaiso, 2004); and the BIP Computer Office and Shop (Providencia, Santiago, 2007, published here), all in Chile.

ALBERTO MOZÓ wurde 1963 in New York geboren und zog im Alter von sieben Jahren nach Santiago, Chile. Nachdem er dort das College absolviert hatte, schloss er 1991 sein Studium an der Pontificia Universidad Católica de Chile ab. Seine ersten architektonischen Projekte waren die Gestaltung von Innenräumen und der Entwurf von Möbeln für Bars. Auf diese Weise war er unmittelbar an der Gestaltung von Treffpunkten für die junge Generation nach Chiles Demokratisierung beteiligt. Gleichzeitig arbeitete er an der Sanierung von Altbauten in Santiago. 2002 wurde er von der Provinzverwaltung in Andalusien für die Renovierung von Altbauten in ibero-amerikanischen Altstädten mit einem Preis ausgezeichnet. Zu seinen Projekten zählen das Fotoatelier Schkolnick (Sur Providencia, Santiago, 1999), die Casa Yankovic (Aculeo, Santiago, 2002), die Casa Rivadeneira (Tunquén, Valparaiso, 2004) sowie die Büro- und Ladenräume der Computerfirma BIP (Providencia, Santiago, 2007, hier vorgestellt), alle in Chile.

ALBERTO MOZÓ, né en 1963 à New York, s'est installé avec sa famille à Santiago, Chili, quand il avait sept ans. Il est diplômé en architecture de la Pontifica Universidad Católica du Chili (1991). Ses premières commandes ont porté sur la création d'espaces intérieurs et de mobilier pour des bars. Il se trouvait ainsi au centre des lieux de rencontre de cette nouvelle génération apparue après le retour à la démocratie du Chili. Simultanément, il restaurait des maisons anciennes à Santiago. En 2002, il a reçu un prix du Conseil de la province d'Andalousie (Espagne) pour la réhabilitation de vieilles demeures dans les quartiers historiques de villes ibéro-américaines. Ses réalisations comprennent le studio photo Schkolnick (Sur Providencia, Santiago, 1999) ; la maison Yankovic (Aculeo, Santiago, 2002) ; la maison Rivadeneira (Tunquén, Valparaiso, 2004) et les bureaux et boutique de BIP Computer (Providencia, Santiago, 2007, publiés ici), toutes au Chili.

BIP COMPUTER OFFICE AND SHOP

Providencia, Santiago, Chile, 2007

Floor area: 569 m². Client: Nicolas Moens de Hase. Cost: $450 000.
Collaboration: Francisca Cifuentes, Mauricio Leal

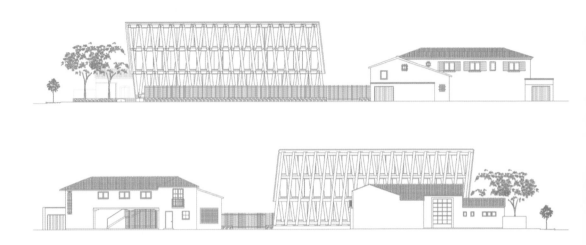

The BIP Computer Office was built between two restored old houses and is three stories high. The architect notes that local zoning regulations allow a building of 12 stories in this particular location, yet he decided to make a lower, essentially rectangular and laminated wood structure that is easily dismountable. Wood beams 9 x 34.2 centimeters in size were chosen for reasons of efficiency as it is a standard dimension used in Chile. Mozó explains: "It is important to mention that the wood utilized is an incentive for reforestation, since it is a type of wood that comes from a renewable forest. Wood is the construction material that produces the lowest carbon emissions, a significant factor with respect to global warming." The architect further states that the BIP Building is the combined result of his "vision of the next building generation," which is environmentally friendly, easy to build, transitory, and economically viable.

Das Bürogebäude für die Computerfirma BIP wurde zwischen zwei sanierten zweistöckigen Altbauten errichtet und hat drei Stockwerke. Der Architekt weist darauf hin, dass die örtlichen Bebauungspläne sogar bis zu zwölf Etagen zugelassen hätten. Dennoch entschied man sich für eine bedeutend niedrigere, im Grunde rechteckige Konstruktion aus laminiertem Holz, die sich leicht demontieren lässt. Gearbeitet wurde mit 9 x 34,2 cm starken Holzbalken, ein Standardformat in Chile und deshalb besonders kosteneffizient. Mozó erklärt: „Es ist wichtig, darauf hinzuweisen, dass das gewählte Bauholz zugleich ein Anreiz zur Wiederaufforstung ist, da es aus einem nachhaltig bewirtschafteten Waldgebiet stammt. Holz ist das Baumaterial mit den geringsten CO_2-Emissionen, ein signifikanter Faktor im Hinblick auf die Erderwärmung." Darüber hinaus ist das BIP-Gebäude nach Aussage des Architekten Ergebnis seiner „Vision für Gebäude der nächsten Generation" – umweltfreundlich in der Konstruktion, temporär und wirtschaftlich erschwinglich.

L'immeuble de deux étages de BIP Computers a été construit entre deux maisons anciennes restaurées. Les architectes font remarquer que la réglementation de zonage locale encourageait la construction de 12 niveaux et qu'ils ont décidé de faire en sorte que cette structure rectangulaire en bois lamellé soit facilement démontable. Des poutres de bois de 9 x 34,2 cm de section ont été choisies car il s'agit d'une dimension standard utilisée par l'industrie du bois chilienne pour des raisons d'efficacité. Alberto Mozó explique qu'« il est important de mentionner que le bois utilisé encourage la reforestation puisque qu'il provient d'une forêt gérée écologiquement. Le bois est le matériau de construction au plus faible taux d'émissions de carbone, facteur important pour lutter contre le réchauffement global ». Cet immeuble, ajoute-t-il, est le résultat « de sa vision d'une nouvelle génération de constructions » qui sera respectueuse de l'environnement, facile à construire, transitoire et économiquement viable.

Contrary to many buildings, this office and shop is designed to be easily dismounted, a fact that contributes in a fundamental manner to its green credentials.

Anders als viele andere Gebäude wurde dieses Bürohaus mit Ladengeschäft so entworfen, dass es leicht demontiert werden kann, ein Aspekt, der fundamental zu seinem grünen Profil beiträgt.

Contrairement à de nombreuses réalisations, cet ensemble bureaux/magasin a été conçu pour être facilement démontable, ce qui contribue de manière fondamentale à la qualité de son impact environnemental.

Stacked wood stairs and a volume
that makes the building fit into its
environment, where it might have
been as many as 12 stories high,
are part of its respectful design.

Bestandteil des umsichtigen Designs
sind unter anderem eine Treppe aus
gestapelten Holzbohlen und der Baukörper selbst. Er wurde seinem Umfeld angepasst, obwohl er bis zu 12
Geschosse hoch hätte gebaut werden
können.

L'escalier fait de lourdes marches
de bois empilées et le volume adapté
à l'échelle du quartier (alors qu'il
aurait pu compter jusqu'à 12 étages),
font partie intégrante d'une approche
respectueuse de l'environnement.

Wooden beams are repetitive but animated, especially in the diagonal placement of the columns. The interior space is high and bright.

Träger und Stützen aus Holz sind regelmäßig angeordnet und wirken aufgelockert – im Fall der Stützen dank ihrer diagonalen Positionierung. Der Innenraum ist hoch und hell.

La disposition répétitive des poutres et des piliers de bois est animée, dans le cas des colonnes, par leur pose croisée. Le lumineux volume intérieur bénéficie d'une grande hauteur sous plafond.

MANFREDI NICOLETTI

Studio Nicoletti Associati
Via di San Simone 75
00186 Rome
Italy

Tel: +39 06 68 805 903
E-mail: studio.nicoletti@inwind.it
Web: www.manfredinicoletti.com

MANFREDI NICOLETTI, born in Rieti, Italy, in 1930, graduated from Rome's "La Sapienza" University, and earned his M.Arch at MIT (1955), before obtaining his Ph.D. in Urban Design at Rome University. He worked in the offices of Walter Gropius, Minorou Yamasaki, and P. L. Nervi, before opening his own office in Rome, in 1960. He is a Professor at Rome's "La Sapienza" University and Vice President of the International Academy of Architecture. In 2004 Giulia Falconi and Luca Nicoletti joined Studio Nicoletti Associati as partners. His work includes the Palermo Sport Palace (Palermo, Italy, 1995–2001); scientific greenhouse for tropical butterflies, Catania University (Catania, Italy, 1999–2002); G8 Conference Center, Chamber of Deputies' Annex, Palazzo Marini (Rome, Italy, 2000–02); Millennium Park (Abuja, Nigeria, 2003–04); and Astana Kazakhstan State Auditorium (Astana, Kazakhstan, 2003–07). Further work includes the Nigeria National Complex, City Hall, Cultural Center, and Millennium Tower (Abuja, Nigeria, 2006–09); and the Putrajaya Precinct 4 Waterfront Development (Kuala Lumpur, Malaysia, 2008–10, published here).

MANFREDI NICOLETTI, geboren 1930 Rieti, Italien, absolvierte ein Studium an der Universität La Sapienza in Rom und erwarb einen M.Arch. am MIT (1955), bevor er an der Universität Rom in Stadtplanung promovierte. Er arbeitete für Walter Gropius, Minorou Yamasaki und P. L. Nervi und gründete schließlich 1960 sein eigenes Büro in Rom. Nicoletti ist Professor an der dortigen Universität La Sapienza und Vizepräsident der Internationalen Akademie für Architektur. 2004 schlossen sich Giulia Falconi und Luca Nicoletti dem Studio Nicoletti Associati als Partner an. Seine Arbeiten sind u. a. der Sportpalast in Palermo (Italien, 1995–2001), das wissenschaftliche Gewächshaus für tropische Schmetterlinge, Universität Catania (Italien, 1999–2002), das G8-Konferenzzentrum, ein Anbau an die Abgeordnetenkammer, Palazzo Marini (Rom, 2000–02), der Millenniumpark (Abuja, Nigeria, 2003–04) sowie das Staatsauditorium Astana (Astana, Kasachstan, 2003–07). Zu seinen weiteren Projekten zählen der nigerianische Staatskomplex mit Rathaus, Kulturzentrum und Millenniumturm (Abuja, Nigeria, 2006–09) sowie die Ufererschließung des 4. Bezirks von Putrajaya (Kuala Lumpur, Malaysia, 2008–10, hier vorgestellt).

MANFREDI NICOLETTI, né à Rieti, Italie, en 1930, est diplômé de l'université de Rome « La Sapienza », M.Arch du MIT (1955), et docteur en urbanisme de l'université de Rome. Il a travaillé dans les agences de Walter Gropius, Minorou Yamasaki et P. L. Nervi, avant d'ouvrir sa propre agence à Rome en 1960. Il est professeur à « La Sapienza » et vice-président de l'Académie internationale d'architecture. En 2004, Giulia Falconi et Luca Nicoletti se sont associés dans le cadre du Studio Nicoletti Associati. Ses réalisations comprennent le Palais des sports de Palerme (Palerme, 1995–2001) ; une serre pour l'étude des papillons tropicaux à l'université de Catane (1999–2002) ; le Centre de conférences du G8, annexe de la Chambre des députés, Palazzo Marini (Rome, 2000–02) ; le Millennium Park (Abuja, Nigeria, 2003–04) et l'Auditorium national du Kazakhstan (Astana, Kazakhstan, 2003–07). Parmi ses autres projets, on compte le Nigeria National Complex, hôtel de ville, centre culturel et Millennium Tower (Abuja, Nigeria, 2006–09), et le développement résidentiel de la zone en bordure du lac de Putrajaya (Zone 4, Kuala Lumpur, Malaisie, 2008–10, publié ici).

PUTRAJAYA PRECINCT 4 WATERFRONT DEVELOPMENT

Kuala Lumpur, Malaysia, 2008–10

Floor area: 200 000 m². Client: Putrajaya Holdings, Ltd. Cost: €184.166 million.
Associated Architects: Hijjas Kasturi Associates SDN

Nicoletti takes this opportunity in Putrajaya, the administrative capital of Malaysia, as an occasion to introduce a degree of architectural and environmental inventiveness that has not yet been seen much in this new city.

Nicoletti nimmt sein Projekt in Putrajaya, der Verwaltungshauptstadt von Malaysia, zum Anlass, architektonische und ökologische Innovationen einzubringen, die man dort so bislang nicht gesehen hat.

Nicoletti a fait de sa présence à Putrajaya, capitale administrative de la Malaisie, l'occasion d'introduire un niveau d'inventivité architecturale et environnementale assez rare dans cette ville nouvelle.

Putrajaya is the new administrative capital of Malaysia, located just south of Kuala Lumpur and founded in 1995. Manfredi Nicoletti's project was the winner of an international design competition for a waterfront area with an emphasis on allowing the permeability of building blocks of varied heights along a boulevard. The radial pattern adopted allows views to the artificial lake and boulevard and also ensures the interpenetration of architecture and landscape. "Designing an iconic residential development for Putrajaya requires a rethink to what makes Putrajaya unique in the context to the world," says Nicoletti. "The building should have a uniqueness that tells of its place of origin, which is culturally modern, Islamic, and tropical in nature…. This group of buildings is on an artificial lake, so we conceived a complex of elements like a fleet, inspired by the metaphor of eight majestic 'sails,' both light and transparent." The sustainability of the designs is a major element for the architect and the client. A double skin allows efficient sunshading and natural ventilation—the outer skin is not sealed. Balconies, vertical structural elements, and horizontal brise-soleils reduce the need for cooling, and a good number of windows will be operable. Gas or biomass-fired heating and power are envisaged, as are a surface-water heat-pump system, micro wind turbines, and photovoltaic cells. An emphasis is placed on natural lighting and controlled artificial lights to reduce electricity consumption.

Putrajaya ist die neue Verwaltungshauptstadt von Malaysia, die 1995 gegründet wurde und unmittelbar südlich von Kuala Lumpur liegt. Manfredi Nicolettis Projekt war Gewinner eines internationalen Entwurfswettbewerbs für ein am Ufer gelegenes Stadtviertel. Besonderer Wert wurde darauf gelegt, die entlang eines Boulevards errichteten Gebäude von unterschiedlicher Höhe durchlässig wirken zu lassen. Die radiale Anlage der Stadt erschließt Sichtachsen auf einen künstlichen See ebenso wie zum Boulevard und sorgt für eine gegenseitige Durchdringung von Architektur und Landschaft. „Um eine unverwechselbare Wohnbebauung für Putrajaya entwickeln zu können, ist es unerlässlich, noch einmal darüber nachzudenken, was Putrajaya im globalen Kontext so einzigartig macht", erklärt Nicoletti. „Die Bauten sollten Einmaligkeit ausstrahlen, die auf ihren Herkunftsort verweisen, in diesem Fall also kulturell modern, islamisch und tropisch… Die Siedlung befindet sich am Ufer eines künstlichen Sees, und so entwarfen wir einen Komplex aus Elementen, die an eine Schiffsflotte denken lassen, ließen uns von der Metapher acht majestätischer ‚Segel' inspirieren, hell und transparent." Die Nachhaltigkeit des Entwurfs war von entscheidender Bedeutung für Architekten und Auftraggeber. Eine doppelte Gebäudehaut sorgt für effizienten Sonnenschutz und natürliche Belüftung – die äußere Haut ist offen. Balkone, vertikale Strukturelemente und horizontale Sonnenblenden minimieren den Kühlbedarf, viele Fenstern lassen sich öffnen. Geplant sind außerdem eine Gas- bzw. Biomasseheizung und -stromversorgung sowie ein Wärmepumpensystem, Mikrowindkrafträder und Fotovoltaikzellen. Besonderer Wert wurde auf natürliche und auf computergesteuerte künstliche Beleuchtung gelegt, um den Stromverbrauch zu drosseln.

Putrajaya, nouvelle capitale administrative de la Malaisie, a été fondée en 1995, juste au sud de Kuala Lumpur. Le projet de Nicoletti a remporté le concours international organisé pour une zone en bordure de lac partant de l'idée de perméabilité des blocs d'immeubles de hauteurs variées le long d'un boulevard. Le plan radial adopté permet des vues sur le lac artificiel et le boulevard ainsi que l'interpénétration de l'architecture et du paysage. « Concevoir ici un ensemble résidentiel iconique a demandé de repenser ce qui pouvait rendre cette ville unique dans le contexte mondial », explique l'architecte. « L'immeuble doit avoir une originalité qui raconte son lieu d'origine, qui est moderne, islamique et de nature tropicale… Cet ensemble donne sur un lac artificiel, aussi avons-nous conçu ce complexe d'éléments comme une flotte de navires, inspirée de la métaphore de huit majestueuses "voiles", à la fois légères et transparentes. » Le caractère durable est un élément majeur de ce projet, pour l'architecte et son client. Une double peau permet une protection solaire et une ventilation naturelle – la peau extérieure n'est pas étanche. Des balcons, des éléments structurels verticaux et des brise-soleil horizontaux réduisent les besoins en climatisation et bon nombre de fenêtres sont commandées manuellement. Le chauffage et la fourniture d'énergie par gaz ou biomasse sont envisagés ainsi qu'un système de récupération de la chaleur de surface, une installation de micro-éoliennes et des cellules photovoltaïques. L'accent est mis sur l'éclairage naturel et le contrôle des sources lumineuses artificielles afin de réduire la consommation d'électricité.

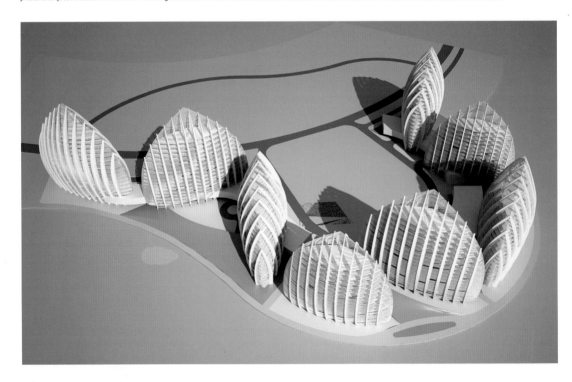

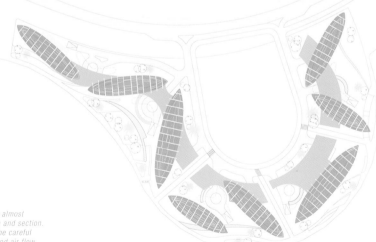

The design assumes an almost
biomorphic form in plan and section.
Drawings above show the careful
attention paid to heat and air flow
throughout the structures.

In Grund- und Aufriss wirken die
Formen des Entwurfs fast biomorph.
Die Zeichnungen oben veranschaulichen, wie präzise Wärme- und Luftströme in den Bauten berücksichtigt
wurden.

Les formes du projet sont quasi
biomorphiques en plan comme
en coupe. Les dessins ci-dessus
montrent le soin porté à la ventilation naturelle qui parcourt les
immeubles.

OFFICE DA

Nader Tehrani – Office dA – NADAAA
1920 Washington Street, #2 / Boston, MA 02118, USA
Tel: + 1 617 442 6232 / Fax: + 1 888 442 1417
E-mail: nada@nadaaa.com / Web: www.nadaaa.com

Nader Tehrani was born in England in 1963 and is of Iranian descent. He received a B.A. in Fine Arts (1985) and a B.Arch (1986) from the Rhode Island School of Design, and an M.Arch in Urban Design from the Harvard GSD in 1991. In 2006 **OFFICE DA** designed the main library for the Rhode Island School of Design in Providence. Office dA recently completed the first LEED-certified, multi-housing building in Boston, the Macallen Building (2005-07), with over 140 environmentally sensitive condominium units (published here). Helios House, the first LEED-rated gas station, was completed in Los Angeles in 2007 (also published here). Tehrani has served as principal-in-charge of various projects on digital fabrication (Helios House, Los Angeles, California, USA, 2006–07; Banq, Boston, Massachusetts, USA, 2008; Model Home Gallery, Seoul, South Korea, 2012), institutional projects of complex programmatic order (Interfaith Spiritual Center at Northeastern University, Boston, Massachusetts, USA, 1994–98; RISD Fleet Library, Providence, Rhode Island, USA, 2006), and residential projects of large and small scale (Tongxian Art Gatehouse, Beijing, China, 2001–03; Macallen Building, Boston, Massachusetts, USA, 2005–07; Dortoir Familial, Ramatuelle, France, 2012). Having won the commissions of three schools of architecture, Tehrani has completed the Hinman Research Building at the Georgia Institute of Technology (Atlanta, Georgia); and is currently working on the Faculty of Architecture, Building and Planning at the University of Melbourne (Australia); and the Daniels Faculty of Architecture, Landscape, and Design at the University of Toronto, Canada.

Nader Tehrani wurde 1963 in England geboren, seine Familie stammt aus dem Iran. Er erwarb einen B.A. in bildender Kunst (1985) sowie einen B.Arch. (1986) an der Rhode Island School of Design und schließlich 1991 einen M.Arch. in Stadtplanung an der Harvard Graduate School of Design (GSD). 2006 entwarf **OFFICE DA** die Hauptbibliothek der Rhode Island School of Design in Providence, Rhode Island. Zudem gewann das Büro den ersten Preis im Villa-Moda-Wettbewerb für einen Baukomplex mit gemischter Nutzung in Kuwait, zu dem Wohnungen, Geschäfte, ein Kino, ein Messeareal und Sporteinrichtungen gehören. Außerdem konnte Office dA den ersten LEED-zertifizierten Wohnkomplex in Boston fertigstellen, das Macallen Building mit über 140 umweltgerechten Eigentumswohnungen (2005–07, hier vorgestellt). Das Helios House, die erste LEED-zertifizierte Tankstelle, wurde 2007 in Los Angeles realisiert (ebenfalls hier vorgestellt). Tehrani hat als verantwortlicher Direktor für verschiedene Projekte im Bereich digitaler Fertigungsverfahren gearbeitet (Helios House, Los Angeles, Kalifornien, USA, 2006–07; Banq, Boston, Massachusetts, USA, 2008; Model Home Gallery, Seoul, Südkorea, 2012), für Projekte in einem institutionellen Kontext mit komplexem Anforderungsprofil (Interfaith Spiritual Center an der Northeastern University, Boston, Massachusetts, USA, 1994–98; RISD Fleet Library, Providence, Rhode Island, USA, 2006) sowie für Wohnprojekte unterschiedlicher Größe (Tongxian Art Gatehouse, Peking, China, 2001–03; Macallen Building, Boston, Massachusetts, USA, 2005–07; Dortoir Familial, Ramatuelle, Frankreich, 2012). Nachdem er die von drei Architekturschulen durchgeführte Ausschreibung gewonnen hatte, beendete Tehrani 2011 die Arbeit für das Hinman Research Building am Georgia Institute of Technology (Atlanta, Georgia, USA); derzeit arbeitet er am Konzept für die Neubauten der Fakultät für Architektur, Bauwesen und Raumordnung der Universität von Melbourne (Australien) sowie der Daniels-Fakultät für Architektur, Raumordnung und Design an der Universität von Toronto, Kanada.

Nader Tehrani est né en Grande-Bretagne, en 1963, de parents iraniens. Il est B.A. en Beaux-Arts (1985), B.Arch (1986) de la Rhode Island School of Design et M.Arch d'urbanisme de l'Harvard GSD (1991). En 2006, **OFFICE DA** a conçu la bibliothèque principale de la Rhode Island School of Design à Providence. L'agence a remporté le concours de la Villa Moda pour un immeuble mixte à Koweït, qui comprend des logements, des commerces, une salle multiplexe, un centre de congrès et des équipements sportifs. Elle a achevé le premier immeuble mixte certifié LEED à Boston, le Macallen Building, qui compte plus de 140 appartements en copropriété (2005–07, publié ici). Helios House, première station-service certifiée LEED, a été achevée en 2007 (Los Angeles, également publiée ici). Tehrani eut en charge plusieurs projets architecturaux de fabrication numérique (Helios House, Los Angeles, Californie, États-Unis, 2006–07 ; Banq, Boston, Massachusetts, États-Unis, 2008 ; Model Home Gallery, Séoul, Corée du Sud, 2012), des projets institutionnels à la programmatique complexe (Interfaith Spiritual Center, Northeastern University, Boston, Massachusetts, États-Unis, 1994-98 ; RISD Fleet Library, Providence, Rhode Island, États-Unis, 2006) et des projets d'immeubles résidentiels de plus ou moins grande envergure (Tongxian Art Gatehouse, Beijing, Chine, 2001–03 ; Macallen Building, Boston, Massachusetts, États-Unis, 2005–07 ; Dortoir familial, Ramatuelle, France, 2012). Ayant remporté les appels d'offre pour trois écoles d'architecture, Tehrani vient de terminer le Hinman Research Building du Georgia Institute of Technology (Atlanta, Géorgie, États-Unis) et finalise actuellement la Faculty of Architecture, Building and Planning de l'Université de Melbourne (Australie) ainsi que la Daniels Faculty of Architecture, Landscape, and Design de l'Université de Toronto, Canada.

HELIOS HOUSE

Los Angeles, California, USA, 2006–07

Floor area: 975 m². Client: BP Corporation of North America
Cost: not disclosed. Architect of Record: Johnston Marklee
Creative and Design Firm: BIG at Ogilvy & Mather

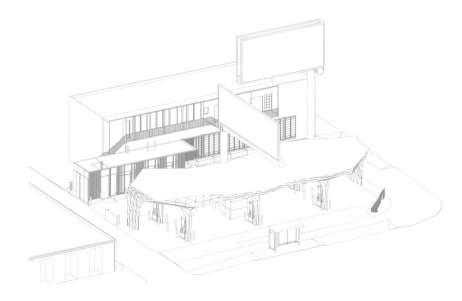

The idea of an ecological design for a gas station might seem contradictory, but the client and the architects have taken it up with energy and originality.

Das Konzept einer ökologisch gestalteten Tankstelle mag zunächst widersprüchlich erscheinen, doch Auftraggeber und Architekten stellten sich der Herausforderung engagiert und mit großer Originalität.

L'idée de conception écologique d'une station-service peut sembler contradictoire en soi, mais le client et les architectes l'ont traitée avec originalité et énergie.

Though its essential function is that of a gas station, Helios House was intended to be a "learning lab," to stimulate dialogue, promote education, and foster discussion on the topic of environmental stewardship. Built to maximize sustainability and energy efficiency, the structure is located at the intersection of Robertson and Olympic Boulevards in the location of a former conventional gas station. Existing billboards and bus stops were maintained "to attract attention to the station's experimental and educational mission." The architects make reference to the rich history of gas station architecture in America, while calling attention to "green" issues. A triangulated prefabricated steel-panel structure makes use of what the architects call "mass-customization" of the building elements. All potentially contaminated runoff water from the site is collected and placed in an underground cistern, filtered, and used to water plants. Ninety solar panels on the canopy roof "provide approximately 15 000 kWh of energy to the station—enough electricity to power two to three typical American homes for a year." Energy-efficient lights are used and the canopy was designed to reflect light, reducing electricity consumption by 16% as compared to conventional stations. Sensors further optimize the use of artificial light through a 24-hour cycle. Recycled materials were used wherever possible, and the project is LEED certified. Energy-related videos are visible for customers.

Trotz der Hauptfunktion als Tankstelle war Helios House als „Lernlabor" gedacht, um Gespräche anzuregen, Wissen zu vermitteln und Diskussionen zum Umgang mit der Umwelt anzustoßen. Die Konstruktion, bei deren Bau auf Maximierung von Nachhaltigkeit und Energieeffizienz geachtet wurde, liegt an der Kreuzung von Robertson und Olympic Boulevard, wo vorher eine konventionelle Tankstelle stand. Bereits vorhandene Werbetafeln und Bushaltestellen wurden übernommen, um „Aufmerksamkeit auf die experimentelle und informative Mission der Tankstelle zu lenken". Die Architekten nehmen Bezug auf die facettenreiche Geschichte der Tankstellenarchitektur in Amerika, jedoch mit der Besonderheit, Aufmerksamkeit auf „grüne" Aspekte zu lenken. Eine in Dreiecke segmentierte Plattenkonstruktion aus vorgefertigten Metallelementen überspannt die gesamte Anlage. Für die Produktion der einzelnen Bausegmente griffen die Architekten auf maßgeschneiderte, aber in Massenfertigung hergestellte Teile zurück. Das gesamte potenziell verunreinigte Ablaufwasser auf dem Grundstück wird in einer unterirdischen Zisterne gesammelt, gefiltert und zur Bewässerung der Bepflanzung genutzt. 90 Solarmodule auf dem Dach „erzeugen rund 15 000 kWh Strom für die Tankstelle – ausreichend Elektrizität, um zwei bis drei durchschnittliche amerikanische Eigenheime pro Jahr zu versorgen". Energiesparleuchten wurden eingesetzt, zudem wurde das Dach lichtreflektierend gestaltet, was den Stromverbrauch im Vergleich zu herkömmlichen Tankstellen um 16 % reduziert. Darüber hinaus optimieren Sensoren den Einsatz künstlicher Beleuchtung rund um die Uhr. Wo möglich, wurden für das LEED-zertifizierte Projekt recycelte Materialien verwendet. Videos zum Thema Energie werden den Kunden gut sichtbar im Außenbereich präsentiert.

Bien que sa fonction essentielle soit d'être une station-service, Helios House avait aussi pour vocation d'être « un laboratoire d'apprentissage » pour stimuler, dialoguer, promouvoir la formation, et susciter le débat sur l'économie des sujets environnementaux. Construite avec la volonté d'optimiser sa durabilité et son efficacité énergétique, cette structure se trouve à l'angle des boulevards Robertson et Olympic à la place d'une ancienne station-service. Les arrêts de bus et les panneaux d'affichage existants ont été conservés « pour attirer l'attention sur la mission expérimentale et éducative de la station ». Les architectes se sont référés à la riche histoire des stations-service aux États-Unis, mais avec une importante nuance : attirer l'attention sur les enjeux écologiques. Une structure triangulée en panneaux d'acier préfabriqués recouvre toute la construction et les fonctions dans un effort de ce que les architectes appellent « une personnalisation massive » des éléments constructifs. Toute l'eau, potentiellement contaminée, collectée par cette structure est collectée et envoyée vers une citerne souterraine, avant d'être filtrée et de servir à arroser les plantes. Les 90 panneaux solaires placés sur le toit « fournissent environ 15 000 kWh d'électricité, suffisamment pour alimenter trois maisons américaines typiques pendant un an ». Des ampoules économiques ont été mises en place, et l'auvent a été dessiné de façon à refléter la lumière et réduire la consommation d'électricité de 16 % par rapport aux stations-service classiques. Des capteurs optimisent en permanence la consommation de l'éclairage artificiel. À chaque fois que c'était possible, des matériaux recyclés ont été utilisés et le projet a reçu une certification LEED. Des vidéos sur le thème de l'énergie informent les clients.

The articulated triangular panel canopy over the pumps morphs into the roof of the gas station itself.

Das dynamisch artikulierte Baldachindach aus dreieckigen Paneelen über den Zapfsäulen geht nahtlos in das Dach der Tankstelle über.

L'auvent des pompes, composé d'un assemblage articulé de triangles, se fond dans la couverture de la station-service.

In the image below, it is clear that the roof is also an arching protective wall, with its triangular forms becoming larger as it reaches the ground.

Im Bild unten ist deutlich zu sehen, wie sich das Dach zu einer geschwungenen Wand entwickelt, deren Dreieckselemente größer werden, je näher sie dem Boden kommen.

Dans l'image ci-dessous, le toit semble se transformer en mur de protection, les triangles s'agrandissant en se rapprochant du sol.

The folded shape of the station is seen in the drawings below, as well as in the images, which demonstrate the flexibility of the concept, bending to each planned use in the program.

Der Falteffekt der Tankstelle zeigt sich besonders gut an den Zeichnungen unten und den Aufnahmen, die die Flexibilität des Konzepts verdeutlichen, das jeder vorgesehenen Nutzung angepasst werden kann.

Les effets de pliage de la station-service sont détaillés dans les dessins ci-dessous. Les photos montrent la souplesse de ce concept qui s'adapte à chaque spécification du programme.

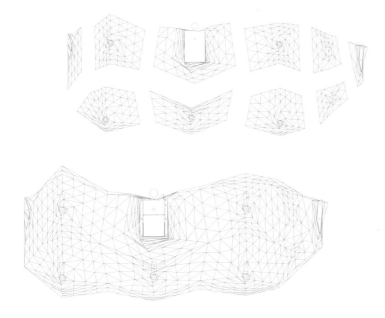

The architects explain, "The bathrooms incorporate farmed wood and uniquely designed tile mosaics, made from 100% recycled glass."

Die Architekten erläutern: „Für die Toiletten wurde mit Plantagenholz und individuell gestalteten Fliesenmosaiken aus 100% recyceltem Glas gearbeitet."

Descriptif des architectes : « Les toilettes sont en bois naturel et mosaïque de céramique spécialement créée en verre 100 % recyclé. »

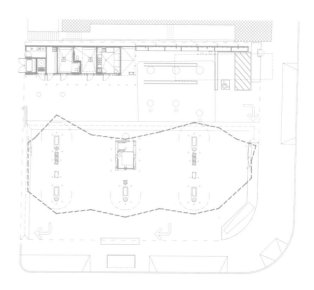

MACALLEN BUILDING

Boston, Massachusetts, USA, 2005–07

Floor area: 18.023 m². Client: Pappas Enterprises, Inc.
Cost: not disclosed. Architect of Record: Burt Hill. Landscaping: Landworks Studio

This condominium building in South Boston was built with a "financially competitive budget." The building responds in its design to a nearby highway with a curtain wall on the western side, while brick is used on the eastern side, because of a more residential context. Bronzed aluminum panels are used on the north and south to "reflect the industrial component" of the neighborhood. A landscaped roof and terraces are part of the scheme. The architects say: The Macallen building was designed from the ground up to take advantage of 'green' building techniques and materials. It is the first LEED Gold certified building of its type in Boston." The large scale of this building and its complex urban site make its role as setting an example for environmentally responsible construction all the more evident. The work of Office dA in this instance also demonstrates that sustainability can go hand in hand with architectural quality.

Das Gebäude mit Eigentumswohnungen in South Boston wurde innerhalb „eines wettbewerbsfähigen Budgetrahmens" realisiert. Der Entwurf reagiert auf den nahe gelegenen Highway mit einer vorgehängten Fassade auf der Westseite des Baus, während die Ostseite mit Backstein verblendet wurde, um ihn in den Kontext des angrenzenden Wohngebiets zu integrieren. Im Norden und Süden wurden bronzierte Aluminiumtafeln verwendet, um „die industrielle Komponente" der Umgebung aufzugreifen. Ein begrüntes Dach und begrünte Terrassen sind Teil des Konzepts. Die Architekten erläutern: „Hinzu kam, dass das Macallen Building von Grund auf daraufhin angelegt wurde, optimal von ‚grünen' Bautechniken und -materialien zu profitieren. Es ist das erste LEED-goldprämierte Gebäude dieser Art in Boston." Die Größe des Gebäudes und seine komplexe urbane Lage lassen umso deutlicher werden, welche Vorbildfunktion die Anlage für umweltbewusstes Bauen hat. Hier beweist die Arbeit von Office dA zudem, dass Nachhaltigkeit und architektonische Qualität durchaus Hand in Hand gehen können.

Cet immeuble d'appartements en copropriété, situé dans le sud de Boston, a été réalisé « dans le cadre d'un budget très compétitif ». Sa conception a pris en compte la présence à l'ouest d'une grande voie de circulation par l'adoption d'un mur-rideau, tandis que la façade est, donnant sur une zone plus résidentielle, est en brique. Les panneaux d'aluminium de couleur bronze sur les façades nord et sud « reflètent l'aspect industriel » du quartier. Un toit paysager et des terrasses font partie du plan. « L'immeuble Macallen a été conçu, dès le départ, pour bénéficier des techniques de construction et des matériaux "verts". C'est le premier immeuble certifié LEED Or de ce type à Boston », précise l'architecte. Les grandes dimensions du bâtiment, la complexité de son contexte en font un exemple particulièrement remarquable de construction respectueuse de l'environnement. Le travail d'Office dA a été ici de démontrer que la durabilité peut aller de pair avec la qualité architecturale.

The varying scales of the building respond to its environment in the South Boston area.

Die unterschiedliche Bauhöhe des Komplexes berücksichtigt die bauliche Umgebung in Süd-Boston.

Les différences d'échelle de l'immeuble répondent à l'environnement du quartier de South Boston.

On the eastern side, brick cladding reflects that of the residential building fabric, "extending the logic of the storefront and pedestrian scale elements on that façade."

An der Ostseite stellt eine Klinkerverblendung Bezüge zum umliegenden Wohngebiet her, während „das Konzept von Ladenschaufenstern und deren auf Fußgänger zugeschnittene Maße in der Gebäudefront aufgegriffen wird."

Côté est, l'habillage en brique reflète celui des immeubles environnants, « étendant la logique de ses composants à l'échelle piétonnière ou à celle des magasins de cette façade ».

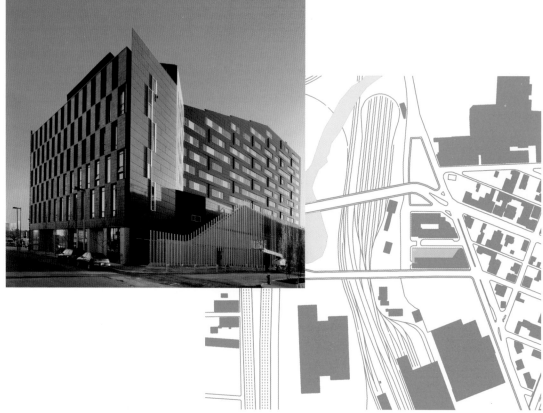

On the north and south façades, bronzed aluminum panels "reflect the industrial neighborhood component and express the structural system organization."

Bronzierte Aluminiumpaneele an den Nord- und Südfassaden „greifen die industrielle Komponente der Gegend auf und veranschaulichen die Organisationsstruktur des Baus."

Sur les façades nord et sud, des panneaux d'aluminium de couleur bronze « reflètent les composants du voisinage industriel et expriment l'organisation structurelle de l'immeuble. »

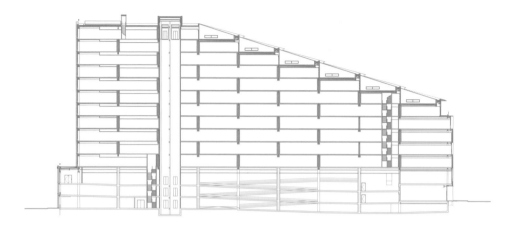

The unusual, varying façade treatments and scale, ramping up where the urban environment encourages it to do so, make this a particularly responsive building.

Die ungewöhnlich abwechslungsreichen Fassaden und Dimensionen – mit Aufstockungen, wo immer es dem urbanen Umfeld entspricht – zeigen, wie gut das Gebäude in sein Umfeld passt und auf dieses antwortet.

Le traitement inhabituel des échelles et des façades, qui s'élèvent vers le ciel lorsque l'environnement urbain les y encourage, en fait un immeuble particulièrement réactif à son cadre.

In these images, façade-cladding
elements emphasize the verticality of
the building as opposed to the more
intimate scale of the other side.

Die Verblendelemente der Fassade
unterstreichen die Vertikalität des
Gebäudes, ganz anders als bei der
geringeren Bauhöhe (gegenüber).

Dans ces images, les éléments
d'habillage de la façade soulignent
la verticalité de l'immeuble par
opposition à l'échelle plus intime
de ses autres composants.

The apartment types are stacked on top of one another, so that plumbing and mechanical shafts can generate maximum structural and environmental efficiency.

Die verschiedenen Wohnungstypen wurden übereinander gestaffelt, sodass Installations- und Versorgungsschächte strukturell und umwelttechnisch optimiert angelegt werden konnten.

Les divers types d'appartement sont empilés et décalés de telle façon que les descentes techniques permettent une efficacité structurelle et environnementale maximum.

The structural system of the building provides for versatility in apartment types ranging from studios, to lofts, to one-, two-, or three-bedroom units, duplexes, triplexes, and garden suites on the terrace.

Das Konstruktionssystem des Gebäudes ermöglicht die Realisierung verschiedenster Wohnungstypen, von 1-Zimmer-Wohnungen bis hin zu Lofts, 3- oder 4-Zimmer-Wohnungen, Maisonette-Wohnungen, Wohnungen über drei Ebenen und Gartenapartments mit Terrasse.

Le système structurel de l'immeuble permet de multiplier les types d'appartements, du studio aux lofts en passant par les 2, 3, 4 pièces, duplex, triplex et studios avec jardins sur les terrasses.

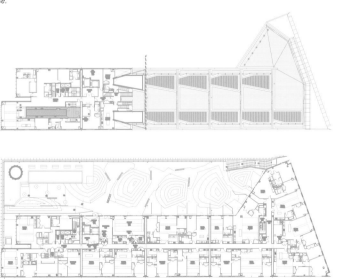

SERGIO PALLERONI

Sergio Palleroni
3134 SE Main Street
Portland, OR 97214
USA

Tel: +1 503 725 8403
E-mail: sergio@basicinitiative.org
Web: www.basicinitiative.org

SERGIO PALLERONI, born in Berkeley, California, in 1955, received his B.Arch degree at the University of Oregon and a SMArchS in Architecture (History, Theory, and Criticism) at MIT. He was Associate Professor of architecture at the University of Washington, Seattle (1993–2004), Research Fellow and Associate Professor at the Center for Sustainable Development, University of Texas, Austin (2004–08); and is currently Professor and Fellow at the Center for Sustainable Processes and Practices, Portland State University. He was Director and cofounder of the Building Sustainable Communities (BaSiC) Initiative, University of Washington, University of Texas, Penn State University, and University of Wisconsin; a member of the United Nations Think Tank on Climate Change (SBCI TTWG); and a member of the Luce Foundation Workshop on Sustainable Development (University of Texas). Through the BaSiC Initiative, Sergio Palleroni has worked with his students to build housing, clinics, and schools in poor communities in the rural United States, Mexico, Africa, and India. He was Co-Principal Investigator with Jen-Hui Tsai for an Urban Development Grant, National Taipei University of Technology (NTUT, Taiwan, 2008–09).

SERGIO PALLERONI, geboren 1955 in Berkeley, Kalifornien, erwarb seinen Grad des B.Arch. an der Universität von Oregon in Eugene und einen Master of Science in Architecture Studies (Geschichte, Theorie und Kritik) am Massachusetts Institute of Technology (MIT). Er war außerordentlicher Professor für Architektur an der Universität von Washington, Seattle (1993–2004), Forschungsmitarbeiter und außerordentlicher Professor am Center for Sustainable Development, Universität von Texas in Austin (2004–08), und ist derzeit Professor und Mitglied am Center for Sustainable Processes and Practices an der Portland State University. Er war Direktor und Mitbegründer der Initiative „Building Sustainable Communities" (BaSiC) der Universitäten Washington und Texas, der Penn State University sowie der Universität von Wisconsin. Palleroni war Mitglied des Think Tank der Vereinten Nationen zum Klimawandel (SBCI TTWG) und des Arbeitskreises Nachhaltige Entwicklung der Luce Foundation (Universität von Texas). Im Rahmen der BaSiC-Initiative arbeitete Palleroni gemeinsam mit seinen Studenten an Wohnungs-, Klinik- und Schulbauprogrammen in finanziell benachteiligten Gemeinden in länd-lichen Regionen der USA, Mexikos, Afrikas und Indiens. Gemeinsam mit Jen-Hui Tsai war er Forschungsleiter für das Stipendium für Stadtentwicklung an der Technischen Nationaluniversität Taipei (Taiwan, 2008–09).

SERGIO PALLERONI, né à Berkeley, Californie, en 1955, est B. Arch de l'université de l'Oregon et M.S. en études sur l'architecture (histoire, théorie, et critique) au MIT. Professeur associé en architecture à l'université de Washington, Seattle (1993–2004), chercheur et professeur associé au Center for Sustainable Development de l'université du Texas, à Austin (2004–08), il est actuellement membre et professeur titulaire du Center for Sustainable Processes and Practices de l'université d'État de Portland. Il a été fondateur et directeur de la Building Sustainable Communities (BaSiC), initiative présente dans diverses universités : université de Washington, université du Texas, université Penn State, université du Wisconsin ; membre du Comité de réflexion des Nations unies sur le changement climatique (SBCI TTWG) et de l'atelier de la Fondation Luce sur le développement durable (Université du Texas). Dans le cadre de la BaSiC Initiative, Sergio Palleroni a travaillé avec ses étudiants sur la construction de logements, de cliniques et d'écoles pour des communautés pauvres rurales aux États-Unis, au Mexique, en Afrique et en Inde. Il a été chercheur principal, avec Jen-Hui Tsai, pour le Fonds de développement urbain de l'Université nationale de technologie de Taipei (NTUT, Taïwan, 2008–09).

ZHONG-XIAO BOULEVARD
URBAN ECOLOGICAL CORRIDOR

Taipei, Taiwan, 2005–07

*Site area: 50 000 m² (urban landscape and rooftops); 140 m² (building). Client: National Taipei University of Technology, Taipei City Government
Cost: not disclosed. Collaboration: Sergio Palleroni, Jen-Hui Tsai, James Adamson*

This project includes a campus garden designed and built by a group of architecture, planning, and engineering students; a "green" pavilion designed by students, built with assistance from the local construction industry, and other initiatives. An entrance to the campus along Zhong-Xiao Boulevard formerly occupied by a long wall is the location for a garden and bioswale.[1] Solar panels used as window shades on campus buildings power the pumps used for the project. Planting was carried out with the assistance of the local community. The so-called Lotus Pavilion is a large room that makes use of passive cooling and low-energy lighting. Rising almost ten meters above the ground, the structure captures passing breezes for cooling and also makes use of solar panels. The partially planted roof serves as insulation. An exterior bamboo rain screen tops the insulation, leaving a gap for air to flow through, thus further reducing solar gain. Students participating in this project went on to install various green devices, including solar panels and mesh screens for vines to grow on around the bioswale. This initiative is exemplary both in terms of student, community, and professional participation, and also in the mixture of different techniques employed, ranging from the expected passive strategies to landscape solutions.   [1] A bioswale is a landscape element designed to remove silt and pollution from surface runoff water. It consists of a drainage course with gently sloped sides filled with vegetation or compost.

Zum Projekt gehören ein Campusgarten, der von einer Gruppe von Architektur-, Stadtplanungs- und Ingenieurstudenten entworfen und gebaut wurde, sowie ein „grüner" Pavillon, der von Studenten geplant und mithilfe ortsansässiger Bauunternehmen und weiterer Initiativen gebaut wurde. Am Eingang des Campusgeländes am Zhong-Xiao-Boulevard stand früher eine lange Mauer. Heute befinden sich hier ein Garten und eine ökologisch angelegte Bodensenke, deren obere Schicht das Sickerwasser filtert.[1] Solarmodule auf den Campusbauten, die auch als Fensterläden dienen, liefern Strom für die Pumpanlagen des Projekts. Die Bepflanzung wurde mit der Hilfe von Anwohnern realisiert. Der sogenannte Lotuspavillon ist ein großer Raum, der passiv gekühlt wird und mit Energiesparlampen ausgestattet ist. Der fast 10 m über dem Boden aufgeständerte Bau fängt den kühlenden Luftzug ein und nutzt zudem Solarmodule. Das teilweise begrünte Dach wirkt dämmend. Ein außen zum Schutz vor Regen angebrachter Wandschirm aus Bambus verstärkt die Isolierung, durch eine Lücke kann Luft ziehen, was den solaren Wärmegewinn minimiert. Die am Projekt beteiligten Studenten installierten außerdem Rankhilfen im Bereich der Bodensenke, etwa Solarmodule und Drahtgitter, an denen Wein emporwachsen kann. Vorbildfunktion hat die Initiative sowohl im Hinblick auf die Einbindung von Studenten, Fachleuten und der Anwohnerschaft als auch durch die Kombination verschiedener Ansätze – von den zu erwartenden Passivstrategien bis hin zur Landschaftsgestaltung.   [1] Eine ökologisch konzipierte Bodensenke ist ein Landschaftselement, um Schlick und Schadstoffe aus Stauwasser zu filtern. Sie besteht aus einem abgesenkten, mit Pflanzen oder Kompost versehenen Dränagelauf.

Ce projet comprend un jardin de campus conçu et réalisé par un groupe d'étudiants en architecture, urbanisme et ingénierie, et un pavillon « vert » dessiné par les étudiants et construit avec l'assistance d'entreprises et autres partenaires locaux. La zone d'entrée du campus donnant sur le Boulevard Zhong-Xiao anciennement masquée par un grand mur est l'emplacement choisi pour le jardin et une zone de biorétention[1]. Des panneaux solaires qui font également fonction d'écrans de protection solaire sur les bâtiments du campus fournissent l'énergie aux pompes utilisées sur place. Les plantations ont été effectuées par les gens du quartier. Le Pavillon du lotus est une vaste pièce qui bénéficie d'un refroidissement passif de l'atmosphère et d'un éclairage à faible consommation. De près de 10 m de haut, il capte les vents utilisés pour la ventilation naturelle et utilise également des panneaux solaires. Le toit en partie planté apporte une isolation thermique. Il est entouré d'un écran en bambou dont les ouvertures laissent circuler l'air et participent à la protection solaire. Les étudiants ont mis en place divers dispositifs dont des panneaux solaires et des écrans en treillis métallique sur lesquels poussent des plantes grimpantes. Cette initiative est exemplaire tant en termes de participation des étudiants, de la communauté et des professionnels locaux que d'association de techniques variées, allant de stratégies passives à des solutions qui relèvent de l'aménagement du paysage.   [1] Une zone de biorétention est un élément de paysage qui réduit le limon et la pollution des eaux d'écoulement de surface. Il consiste en plans de drainage dont les côtés, légèrement inclinés, sont recouverts de plantes ou de compost.

This intervention has turned space that was otherwise unused and uncared for into useful, ecologically productive gardens.

Diese Intervention ist zugleich die Umnutzung einer Fläche, die zuvor brach lag und nicht gepflegt wurde, als ökologisch produktiver Garten.

Cette intervention a permis de transformer des lieux inutilisés et mal entretenus en jardins écologiques productifs.

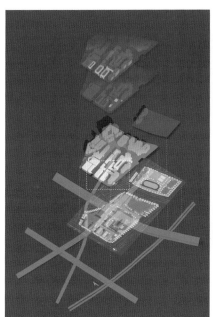

This pavilion is basically one large room, with an open loft over the southern portion. Set on steel stilts, the lightweight metal-stud structure rises to a height of 9.7 meters above the ground to catch available breezes.

Dieser Pavillon ist im Prinzip ein einziger großer Raum mit einem offenen Loftbereich über dem südlichen Abschnitt. Die Leichtbau-Metallskelettkonstruktion erhebt sich 9,7 m hoch über dem Boden, um den verfügbaren Luftzug zu nutzen.

Ce pavillon est en fait une vaste pièce avec atelier ouvert au sud. Posée sur des pilotis d'acier, cette structure métallique légère s'élève jusqu'à une hauteur de 9,7 m au-dessus du sol pour capter la brise.

Student initiatives include a green
roof on top of an existing building,
and channeled water runoff to irrigate
the plants.

Studenteninitiativen legten ein begrüntes Dach auf einem bestehenden
Gebäude und ein Kanalisierungs-
system für das Ablaufwasser zur
Bewässerung der Pflanzen an.

Parmi les initiatives des étudiants
figurent un jardin sur le toit d'un
bâtiment existant et l'utilisation
de l'eau de pluie pour irriguer les
plantes.

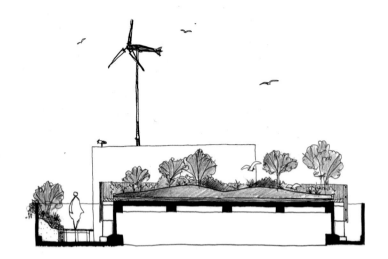

Palleroni's initiatives in an educational environment show that ecologically
driven projects can be woven into an
existing urban environment.

Palleronis Studenteninitiativen
beweisen, dass sich ökologisch moti-
vierte Projekte in ein bestehendes
urbanes Umfeld integrieren lassen.

Les initiatives éducatives de Palleroni
montrent que des projets de nature
écologique peuvent s'intégrer à un
environnement urbain existant.

RENZO PIANO

Renzo Piano Building Workshop
34 rue des Archives / 75004 Paris / France
Tel: +33 1 42 78 00 82 / Fax: +33 1 42 78 01 98

Via Rubens 29 / 16158 Genoa / Italy
Tel: +39 010 61 711 / Fax: +39 010 61 71 350
E-mail: info@rpbw.com / Web: www.rpbw.com

RENZO PIANO was born in 1937 in Genoa, Italy. He studied at the University of Florence and at the Polytechnic Institute (Milan, 1964). He formed his own practice (Studio Piano) in 1965, then associated with Richard Rogers (Piano & Rogers, 1971–78). Piano completed the Centre Pompidou in Paris in 1977. From 1978 to 1980 he worked with Peter Rice (Piano & Rice Associates). He created the Renzo Piano Building Workshop in 1981 in Genoa and Paris. Piano received the RIBA Gold Medal in 1989. His built work includes Menil Collection Museum (Houston, Texas, 1981–86); San Nicola Stadium (Bari, Italy, 1987–90); the 1988–90 extension of the IRCAM (Paris, France); Kansai International Airport Terminal (Osaka, Japan, 1988–94); Cité Internationale de Lyon (Lyon, France, 1985–96); Beyeler Foundation (Riehen, Basel, Switzerland, 1991–97); Jean-Marie Tjibaou Cultural Center (New Caledonia, 1991–98); Mercedes-Benz Design Center (Stuttgart, Germany, 1993–98); reconstruction of a section of Potsdamer Platz (Berlin, Germany, 1992–2000); Parma Auditorium (Italy, 1997–2001); Maison Hermès (Tokyo, Japan, 1998–2001); Rome Auditorium (Italy, 1994–2002); conversion of the Lingotto Factory Complex (Turin, Italy, 1983–2003); Padre Pio Pilgrimage Church (San Giovanni Rotondo, Foggia, Italy, 1991–2004); renovation and expansion of the Morgan Library (New York, New York, 2000–06); New York Times Building (New York, New York, 2005–07); High Museum of Art Expansion (Atlanta, Georgia, 2005–08); renovation and expansion of the California Academy of Sciences (San Francisco, California, 2005–08, published here); and the Art Institute of Chicago Expansion (Chicago, Illinois).

RENZO PIANO wurde 1937 in Genua geboren. Er studierte an der Universität Florenz und der Polytechnischen Hochschule Mailand (1964). Sein Büro Studio Piano gründete er 1965, gefolgt von einer Partnerschaft mit Richard Rogers (Piano & Rogers, 1971–78). Die Arbeiten am Centre Pompidou in Paris konnte Piano 1977 abschließen. Von 1978 bis 1980 arbeitete er mit Peter Rice (Piano & Rice Associates). 1981 gründete er sein Büro Renzo Piano Building Workshop mit Sitz in Genua und Paris. 1989 wurde Piano mit der RIBA-Goldmedaille ausgezeichnet. Zu seinen realisierten Bauten zählen u. a. das Menil Collection Museum (Houston, Texas, 1981–86), das Stadion San Nicola (Bari, Italien, 1987–90), der Erweiterungsbau des IRCAM (Paris, 1988–90), der Flughafenterminal Kansai International (Osaka, Japan, 1988–94), die Cité Internationale de Lyon (Lyon, Frankreich, 1985–96), die Fondation Beyeler (Riehen, Schweiz, 1991–97), das Kulturzentrum Jean-Marie Tjibaou (Neukaledonien, 1991–98), das Mercedes-Benz Design Center (Stuttgart, 1993–98), die Neugestaltung eines Abschnitts des Potsdamer Platzes (Berlin, 1992–2000), das Auditorium in Parma (Italien, 1997–2001), die Maison Hermès (Tokio, 1998–2001), das Auditorium in Rom (1994–2002), die Umgestaltung des Lingotto-Werkskomplexes (Turin, 1983–2003), die Pilgerkirche Padre Pio (San Giovanni Rotondo, Foggia, Italien, 1991–2004), die Renovierung und Erweiterung der Morgan Library (New York, 2000–06), das New York Times Building (New York, 2005–07), die Erweiterung des High Museum of Art (Atlanta, Georgia, 2005–08), die Renovierung und Erweiterung der California Academy of Sciences (San Francisco, 2005–08, hier vorgestellt) sowie die Erweiterung des Art Institute of Chicago.

RENZO PIANO, né en 1937 à Gênes, en Italie, étudie à l'université de Florence et à l'Institut polytechnique de Milan (1964). Il crée son agence, Studio Piano, en 1965, puis s'associe à Richard Rogers (Piano & Rogers, 1971–78). Ils achèvent le Centre Pompidou à Paris en 1977. De 1978 à 1980, il collabore avec Peter Rice (Piano & Rice Associates). Il fonde le Renzo Piano Building Workshop, en 1981, à Gênes et Paris. Il a reçu la médaille d'or du RIBA en 1989. Parmi ses réalisations : le Menil Collection Museum (Houston, Texas, 1981–86) ; le stade San Nicola (Bari, Italie, 1987–90) ; l'extension de l'IRCAM (Paris, 1988–90) ; le terminal de l'aéroport international du Kansai (Osaka, Japon, 1988–94) ; la Cité internationale (Lyon, 1985–96) ; la Fondation Beyeler (Riehen, Bâle, Suisse, 1991–97) ; le centre culturel Jean-Marie Tjibaou (Nouvelle-Calédonie, 1991–98) ; le Mercedes-Benz Design Center (Stuttgart, Allemagne, 1993–98) ; la reconstruction d'une partie de la Potsdamer Platz (Berlin, 1992–2000) ; l'auditorium de Parme (1997–2001) ; la maison Hermès (Tokyo, 1998–2001) ; l'auditorium de Rome (1994–2002) ; la conversion de l'usine du Lingotto (Turin, Italie, 1983–2003) ; l'église de pèlerinage du Padre Pio (San Giovanni Rotondo, Foggia, Italie, 1991–2004) ; la rénovation et l'agrandissement de la Bibliothèque Morgan (New York, 2000–06) ; le New York Times Building (New York, 2005–07) ; l'extension du High Museum of Art (Atlanta, Georgie, 2005–08) ; la rénovation et l'angrandissement de la California Academy of Sciences (San Francisco, 2005–08, publiée ici) ; ainsi que l'extension du Chicago Art Institute (Chicago, Illinois).

RENOVATION AND EXPANSION
OF THE CALIFORNIA ACADEMY OF SCIENCES

San Francisco, California, USA, 2005–08

Site area: 74 322 m². Floor area: 34 374 m². Client: California Academy of Sciences
Cost: $370 million (including exhibition program and costs associated with the Academy's temporary housing)
Collaboration: Gordon H. Chong and Partners Architects, San Francisco

The green roof of the new building of the California Academy of Sciences is its most prominent ecological element, with a skylight visible here.

Das auffälligste ökologische Element des Neubaus der California Academy of Sciences ist das begrünte Dach – hier ein Oberlicht.

Le toit végétalisé du nouveau bâtiment de l'Académie des sciences de Californie est son plus important atout écologique. Ci-dessous, une des verrières.

One of the ten largest natural history museums in the world, the California Academy of Sciences was founded in 1853. The institution declared: "The new CAS will be at the forefront of green building design, showcasing world-class architecture that fully integrates green building features to reflect its mission to protect the natural world." The completed structure has a LEED Platinum rating, reflecting its strategies to conserve energy and to use environmentally friendly building materials. The undulating roof of the structure, with a surface of more than one hectare, is covered with 1.8 million native California plants. Careful study of the plants themselves, but also of the seismic implications of a planted roof, was part of the preparation of this aspect of the design that is open to visitors. It is calculated that the design of the roof reduces temperatures inside the museum by about 6°C. A rainwater collection system is designed to store and reuse about 13 500 cubic meters of water each year, reused for irrigation and gray water. The roof's shape and, indeed, the entire design of the museum were conceived to form a continuum with the surrounding park environment. Intended for schoolchildren and the general public, the academy focuses on education and research on conserving natural environments and habitats.

Die 1853 gegründete California Academy of Sciences zählt zu den weltweit zehn größten Museen für Naturgeschichte. Die Institution ließ verlautbaren: „Die neue CAS wird sich als Pionier grüner Gebäudeplanung erweisen und Weltklasse-Architektur zeigen, die grüne Bautechniken umfassend integriert, um ihrer Mission, die Natur zu schützen, Rechnung zu tragen." Der fertiggestellte Bau wurde mit einer LEED-Platinmedaille ausgezeichnet, eine Würdigung der Energiesparstrategien sowie der Verwendung umweltfreundlicher Baumaterialien. Das geschwungene Dach mit einer Fläche von über einem Hektar wurde mit 1,8 Millionen einheimischen kalifornischen Pflanzen begrünt. Im Zuge der Vorbereitungen für diesen öffentlichen Gebäudeabschnitt setzte man sich intensiv mit den Pflanzen auseinander ebenso wie mit den seismischen Aspekten des begrünten Dachs. Berechnungen zufolge reduziert das Dach die Innentemperatur des Museums um rund 6 °C. Eine Regenwassersammelanlage speichert und nutzt rund 13 500 m³ Wasser pro Jahr, die zur Bewässerung und als Grauwasser zum Einsatz kommen. Die Form des Dachs und im Grunde die gesamte Gestaltung des Museums wurden darauf angelegt, ein Kontinuum mit dem umgebenden Park zu bilden. Die Institution, die sich an Schulkinder und an ein allgemeines Publikum wendet, bietet in erster Linie Bildungsprogramme an und widmet sich der Forschung zum Schutz der Umwelt und Lebensräume.

La California Academy of Sciences, un des dix plus grands musées d'histoire naturelle du monde, a été fondée en 1853. À son lancement, l'institution avait fait savoir que « la nouvelle Académie serait à l'avant-garde des constructions "vertes", grâce à une architecture de niveau international qui intégrerait pleinement les spécificités de la construction écologique, reflétant ainsi sa mission de protection du monde naturel. » Le bâtiment achevé a reçu la certification LEED Platine pour ses stratégies d'économie d'énergie et d'utilisation de matériaux écologiques. La toiture de forme ondulée qui recouvre plus d'1 ha est plantée de 1,8 million de plants de végétaux californiens. L'étude approfondie des plantes, mais aussi les implications du poids d'un toit végétal en cas de séisme, ont déterminé la conception de cette couverture fréquentée par les visiteurs. On a calculé que ce principe de végétalisation permettait de réduire la température à l'intérieur du musée de 6 % environ. Un système de collecte des eaux de pluie récupère, stocke et réutilise environ 13 500 m³ d'eau chaque année pour l'irrigation et autres usages courants. La forme du toit et la conception du musée tout entier forment un continuum avec le parc environnant. Ouverte au grand public et aux enfants des écoles, l'Académie se consacre à l'éducation et à des recherches portant sur la conservation des environnements et des habitats naturels.

Piano's light columns and canopy are almost a signature feature here, giving the building an airiness that might seem to contrast with the earth- and vegetation-covered roof.

Pianos schlanke Stützen und leichte Baldachindächer wirken hier fast wie ein Markenzeichen und verleihen dem Bau eine Luftigkeit, die geradezu als Gegenpol zur Erdmasse und Begrünung des Dachs fungieren.

Les colonnes légères et l'auvent créés par Piano relèvent presque de sa signature. Ils confèrent au bâtiment une légèreté qui semble trancher avec le toit recouvert de terre et de végétation.

Piano has used dome-shaped elements in his architecture—in Turin
at the Lingotto Factory and in the
context of the Columbus International
Exhibition in Genoa. Left, an interior
view of the dome with its walkways
and trees.

Bereits an anderer Stelle hat Piano
Kuppeln in seiner Architektur eingesetzt – beim Lingotto-Werk in Turin
und bei der Internationalen Kolumbus-
Ausstellung in Genua. Links eine
Innenansicht mit Blick auf die Kuppel,
ihre Laufstege und Bäume.

Piano a souvent utilisé des formes
en coupole, comme à Turin (Usine
du Lingotto) ou dans le contexte de
l'Exposition internationale Christophe
Colomb à Gênes. À gauche, vue
intérieure de la coupole, avec ses
coursives et ses arbres.

POLK STANLEY
WILCOX ARCHITECTS

Polk Stanley Wilcox Architects
2222 Cottondale Lane, Suite 100
Little Rock, AR 72202
USA

Tel: +1 501 378 0878
Fax: +1 501 372 7629
E-mail: rrowland@polkstanleywilcox.com
Web: www.polkstanleywilcox.com

REESE ROWLAND was born in Pomona, California. He attended the University of Arkansas School of Architecture (1986–90). He worked with Wittenberg Delony and Davidson Architects (1990–96) before joining **POLK STANLEY** in 1996. He is a principal of the firm, responsible for project conceptual design and development. He was the project designer for the World Headquarters of Heifer International (Little Rock, Arkansas, 2004–06, published here, which was built by Polk Stanley Rowland Curzon Porter, now part of Polk Stanley Wilcox Architects). Born in Little Rock, **JOE STANLEY** also attended the University of Arkansas School of Architecture (1964–69). He is a founding partner and senior principal of the firm. He was the project managing principal for the Heifer Building. Amongst the significant projects of the firm are the Historic Arkansas Museum (Little Rock, 2002); First Tee of Arkansas (Little Rock, 2002); Acxiom River Market Tower (Little Rock, 2004); University of Arkansas Clinton School of Public Service (Little Rock, 2004); University of Arkansas Harmon Avenue Transit Facility (Fayetteville, 2006); Acxiom Corporate Data Center (Little Rock, 2007); and the Arkansas Studies Institute (Little Rock, 2008), all in Arkansas, USA.

REESE ROWLAND wurde in Pomona, Kalifornien, geboren. Er studierte Architektur an der Universität Arkansas (1986–90). Zunächst arbeitete er für Wittenberg Delony and Davidson Architects (1990–96), 1996 schloss er sich **POLK STANLEY** an. Als einer der Partner des Büros ist er für den Konzeptentwurf und die Entwicklung der Projekte zuständig. Er zeichnete für den Projektentwurf der Firmenzentrale von Heifer International verantwortlich (Little Rock, Arkansas, 2004–06, hier vorgestellt), gebaut von Polk Stanley Rowland Curzon Porter, die nun zu Polk Stanley Wilcox Architects gehören. **JOE STANLEY** wurde in Little Rock geboren und studierte ebenfalls Architektur an der Universität Arkansas (1964–69). Er ist Gründungsmitglied und Seniorpartner des Büros und übernahm die Projektleitung für das Heifer Building. Zu den wichtigsten Bauten und Baumaßnahmen des Büros zählen u. a. das Historic Arkansas Museum (Little Rock, 2002), das First Tee of Arkansas (Little Rock, 2002), der Acxiom River Market Tower (Little Rock, 2004), die Clinton School of Public Service an der Universität Arkansas (Little Rock, 2004), der ÖPNV-Knotenpunkt der Universität Arkansas an der Harmon Avenue (Fayetteville, 2006), das Acxiom Corporate Data Center (Little Rock, 2007) sowie das Arkansas Studies Institute (Little Rock, 2008), alle in Arkansas, USA.

REESE ROWLAND, né à Pomona, Californie, a étudié à l'École d'architecture de l'université de l'Arkansas (1986–90). Il a travaillé pour Wittenberg Delony and Davidson Architects (1990–96), avant de rejoindre **POLK STANLEY** en 1996. Il est un des dirigeants de l'agence, responsable des projets de conception et du développement. Il a conçu le projet du siège mondial d'Heifer International (Little Rock, Arkansas, 2004–06, publié ici et construit par Polk Stanley Rowland Curzon Porter, appartient désormais à Polk Stanley Wilcox Architects). Né à Little Rock, **JOE STANLEY** a effectué les mêmes études (1964–69). Il est associé fondateur et principal dirigeant de l'agence, et a dirigé la réalisation de l'immeuble Heifer. Parmi les réalisations les plus importantes de l'agence : l'Historic Arkansas Museum (Little Rock, 2002) ; le First Tee of Arkansas (Little Rock, 2002) ; la River Market Tower Acxiom (Little Rock, 2004) ; la Clinton School of Public Service (Université de l'Arkansas, Little Rock, 2004) ; le centre de transit d'Harmon avenue (Université de l'Arkansas, Fayetteville, 2006) ; le centre informatique d'Acxiom (Little Rock, 2007) ; et l'Arkansas Studies Institute (Little Rock, 2008), toutes en Arkansas, États-Unis.

HEIFER INTERNATIONAL WORLD HEADQUARTERS

Little Rock, Arkansas, USA, 2004–06

Floor area: 9105 m². Client: Heifer International. Cost: $17.9 million
Collaboration: Reese Rowland, David Porter, Joe Stanley

The basic form of the Heifer International Headquarters building is a simple arc. Its lightness and transparency is apparent in these images.

Die Grundform der Heifer International Headquarters ist ein schlichter Bogen. Diese Bilder veranschaulichen ihre Leichtigkeit und Transparenz.

La forme de base du siège de Heifer International est celle d'un simple arc. Sa légèreté et sa transparence sont sensibles dans ces photographies.

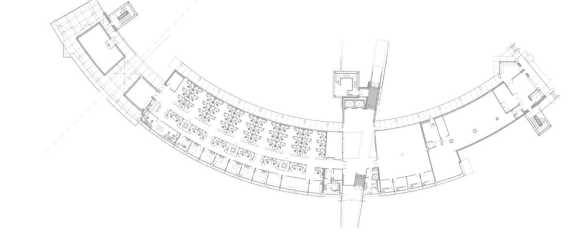

Named one of the top ten green projects in the United States for 2007 (AIA/COTE), and holder of a USGBC LEED Platinum rating for its sustainability and environmental performance, the Heifer Building is located in a former rail-yard site. Built for the world hunger organization Heifer International, the landfill for the site and paving came from the former masonry and bricks of the rail facilities. Located next to the Clinton Library, the two projects form a 25-hectare green zone. Designed to "maximize sunlight and rainwater while conserving energy and avoiding pollutants, the headquarters will see a 55% energy saving over conventional buildings." The narrow design allows for views to the green areas around the building for the 472 employees. Wetland areas and bioswales[1] are used to help with water recycling and natural cooling. The architects explain: "Structural 'tree' columns visually extend wetland trees, representing a symbiotic relationship between man-made and nature." For all of its environmental credentials the building also stands out for its obvious architectural quality—a proof that sustainability need not go hand in hand with unattractive design. The building won an AIA Honor Award (2008). [1] A bioswale is a landscape element designed to remove silt and pollution from surface runoff water. It consists of a drainage course with gently sloped sides filled with vegetation or compost.

Das auf einem ehemaligen Verschiebebahnhof gelegene Heifer Building kam 2007 in die Top Ten der grünsten Projekte der Vereinigten Staaten (AIA/COTE) und wurde vom USGBC mit einer LEED-Platinmedaille für Nachhaltigkeit und Umweltfreundlichkeit gewürdigt. Mauerwerk und Ziegel der ehemaligen Bahnanlagen wurden genutzt, um das Grundstück, auf dem der Neubau für die weltweit im Kampf gegen Hunger engagierte Organisation Heifer International errichtet wurde, aufzufüllen und Wege zu pflastern. Die Firmenzentrale, die so angelegt wurde, dass „Sonnenlicht und Regenwasser optimal genutzt werden, wird im Vergleich zu herkömmlichen Bauten eine 55 %ige Energieersparnis verzeichnen können". Der schmale Grundriss des Baus ermöglicht den 472 Angestellten im gesamten Gebäude Ausblicke auf die grüne Umgebung. Feuchtgebiete und Bodensenken[1] wurden eingesetzt, um die Wasseraufbereitung und natürliche Klimatisierung zu unterstützen. Die Architekten erklären: „Tragende baumähnliche Stützen knüpfen formal an die Bäume in den Feuchtgebieten an und stehen für ein symbiotisches Verhältnis von Natur und Menschenwerk." Abgesehen von seinen Umweltqualitäten zeichnet sich der Bau durch seine offensichtliche architektonische Qualität aus – ein Beweis dafür, dass Nachhaltigkeit keineswegs mit unattraktiver Gestaltung gleichzusetzen ist. Das Gebäude wurde 2008 mit einem Ehrenpreis des AIA ausgezeichnet. [1] Eine ökologisch konzipierte Bodensenke ist ein Landschaftselement, um Schlick und Schadstoffe aus Stauwasser zu filtern. Sie besteht aus einem abgesenkten, mit Pflanzen oder Kompost versehenen Dränagelauf.

Désigné comme l'une des dix premières réalisations « vertes » aux États-Unis en 2007 (AIA/COTE) et détenteur d'une certification LEED Platine de l'USGBC pour sa durabilité et ses performances environnementales, cet immeuble, édifié pour l'organisation internationale contre la faim Heifer International, se trouve sur le terrain d'anciens dépôts ferroviaires. Les terrassements et les pavements proviennent d'anciennes constructions en brique existant sur place. Situé à proximité de la bibliothèque Clinton, ils bénéficient tous deux d'un espace vert de 25 ha. Conçu de façon à « optimiser l'utilisation de la lumière solaire, de l'eau de pluie, et de manière à éviter les polluants, le siège économisera 55 % de l'énergie consommée par un immeuble classique ». La minceur du bâtiment permet d'offrir une vue sur la verdure environnante aux 472 employés ». Des zones humides et des zones de biorétention[1] servent à recycler l'eau et à la climatisation naturelle. Les architectes expliquent que « des colonnes structurelles en "arbre" démultiplient visuellement la présence des arbres des zones humides, tout en créant une relation symbiotique entre ce qui est dû à la main de l'homme et ce qui est naturel ». En dehors de ses performances environnementales, l'immeuble se remarque également pour sa qualité architecturale évidente, et prouve que la durabilité n'est pas toujours synonyme de « peu séduisant ». Il a remporté un Prix d'honneur de l'AIA (2008). [1] Une zone de biorétention est un élément de paysage qui réduit le limon et la pollution des eaux d'écoulement de surface. Il consiste en plans de drainage dont les côtés, légèrement inclinés, sont recouverts de plantes ou de compost.

The building's outer curve is somewhat more closed than the inner one, as can be seen in the image above and that opposite.

Die Außenseite des geschwungenen Baus wirkt geschlossener als seine Innenseite, wie die Bilder oben und auf der rechten Seite zeigen.

La façade extérieure de l'arc est un peu plus fermée que sa façade intérieure, comme on peut le voir sur l'image ci-dessus et à droite.

Set amongst vegetation in the image above, the building seems the
perfect incarnation of the green
office. Below, interior views show the
generous, bright spaces.

*Eingebettet in die Vegetation der
Umgebung, präsentiert sich der Bau
als ideale Inkarnation des grünen
Büros. Die Innenansichten zeigen die
großzügigen, hellen Räumlichkeiten.*

*Photographié au milieu de la
végétation (ci-dessus) l'immeuble
semble une parfaite incarnation de
l'architecture écologique de bureaux.
Ci-dessous, vues intérieures montrant
la lumineuse générosité des volumes.*

RAU

RAU
Office KNSM-Laan 65
1019 LB Amsterdam
The Netherlands

Tel: +31 20 419 02 02
E-mail: info@rau.eu
Web: www.rau.eu

THOMAS RAU, who is German, was born in 1960. He studied Architecture and Engineering at the Technical University of Aachen (1983–89). He created his present firm in 1992 in Amsterdam, after having worked in a number of offices in the same city between 1989 and 1992. The most significant projects of the firm include the City Hall Middelburg (1999–2004); Sprengeloo Technical and Vocational School (Apeldoorn, 2003–06); World Wide Fund For Nature Headquarters (Zeist, 2003–06, published here); Triodos Bank International headquarters (Zeist, 2000–07); faculty building for the University of Groningen (2003–07); De Woonplaats Office (Enschede, 2004–07); Piter Jelles Nijlân Vocational School (Leeuwarden, 2002–08); community college (Leiden, 2003–09); Carré de Soie Offices and Housing (Lyon, France, 2007–10), all in the Netherlands unless otherwise indicated.

Der Deutsche **THOMAS RAU** wurde 1960 geboren. Er studierte Architektur und Bauingenieurwesen an der RWTH Aachen (1983–89). Sein derzeitiges Büro gründete er 1992 in Amsterdam, nachdem er dort von 1989 bis 1992 für verschiedene Büros tätig gewesen war. Zu den wichtigsten Projekten des Büros zählen das Rathaus Middelburg (1999–2004), die Technische und Berufsschule Sprengeloo (Apeldoorn, 2003–06), der World Wide Fund For Nature (Zeist, 2003–06, hier vorgestellt), die internationale Zentrale der Triodos Bank (Zeist, 2000–07), das Fakultätsgebäude der Universität Groningen (2003–07), das Büro De Woonplaats (Enschede, 2004–07), die Piter-Jelles-Nijlân-Berufsschule (Leeuwarden, 2002–08), ein Gemeindekolleg in Leiden (2003–09) sowie der Büro- und Wohnkomplex Carré de Soie (Lyon, Frankreich, 2007–10), alle in den Niederlanden, sofern nicht anders angegeben.

THOMAS RAU, qui est Allemand, est né en 1960. Il a étudié l'architecture et l'ingénierie à l'Université polytechnique d'Aix-la-Chapelle (1983–89). Il a fondé son agence à Amsterdam en 1992, après avoir travaillé dans un certain nombre d'agences de cette ville entre 1989 et 1992. Parmi les principales réalisations de l'agence : le bureau municipal de Middelburg (1999–2004) ; le centre de formation technique et professionnelle Sprengeloo (Apeldoorn, 2003–06) ; le siège du WWF (Zeist, 2003–06, publié ici) ; le siège international de la banque Triodos (Zeist, 2000–07) ; le bâtiment Pôle de recherche et d'enseignement de l'université de Groningue (2003–07) ; les bureaux De Woonplaats (Enschede, 2004–07) ; le lycée professionnel Piter Jelles Nijlân (Leeuwarden, 2002–08) ; un bâtiment scolaire (Leiden, 2003–09) ; un immeuble de bureaux et de logements pour le quartier Carré de Soie (Lyon, France, 2007–10), toutes aux Pays-Bas, sauf exception.

WORLD WIDE FUND FOR NATURE

Zeist, The Netherlands, 2003–06

Floor area: 3800 m². Client: WWF Netherlands. Cost: not disclosed

WWF-Netherlands launched a project to develop a new office on the site of a former agricultural research laboratory in the Schoonoord Nature Reserve in 2003. Its initial aim was to create a carbon-neutral building. Since then, the project has evolved to apply the full set of One Planet Living principles, and is aiming to achieve a sustainable footprint. Ecological "footprinting" is a tool developed by the Global Footprint Network that measures how much land and water is needed to produce resources consumed, and waste absorption. As the architects explain: "In the moisture-balancing mud ceilings, continuous circulation through glass tubes spreads human and mechanical warmth, and—even more importantly—cooling. Through horizontal wooden blinds, a maximum amount of useful light enters. All materials were screened for environmental friendliness as well as child labor. And of course space was made for wildlife: 'bird-friendly roofing tiles' and 'bat basements.'" The former center of the 1954 building was demolished to make way for an "amorphous" central pavilion. A solar power station on the roof provides energy, and all installations run on vegetable oil. The building is energy self-sufficient and emits no CO_2.

2003 initiierte der niederländische WWF ein Projekt zur Entwicklung einer neuen Niederlassung auf dem Gelände eines ehemaligen landwirtschaftlichen Forschungslabors im Naturschutzgebiet Schoonoord. Anfängliches Ziel war es, ein CO_2-emmissionsfreies Gebäude zu bauen. Seither hat sich das Projekt weiterentwickelt, nun sollen die Kritierien des One-Planet-Living-Programms konsequent umgesetzt und damit ein nachhaltiger ökologischer Fußabdruck hinterlassen werden. Der „ökologische Fußabdruck" ist ein vom Global Footprint Network entwickelter Maßstab, mit dem sich ermitteln lässt, wie viel Land und Wasser benötigt werden, um die Ressourcen zu produzieren, die verbraucht werden, und um Abfälle zu beseitigen. Die Architekten erklären: „In den feuchtigkeitsregulierenden Lehmdecken sorgen Rohre für die Verteilung der Wärme, die Mensch und Maschine abstrahlen, vor allem aber auch für die Verteilung kühler Luft. Horizontale Holzlamellen regulieren das einströmende Licht. Alle Materialien wurden auf ihre Umweltverträglichkeit überprüft; zudem durfte für ihre Produktion keine Kinderarbeit eingesetzt worden sein. Und natürlich wurde der Raum auch für Tiere gestaltet: ‚vogelfreundliche Dachziegel' und ‚Fledermauskeller'." Das ehemalige Herzstück des Altbaus von 1954 wurde abgerissen, um Platz für einen „amorphen", zentral gelegenen Pavillon zu schaffen. Eine Solarkraftanlage auf dem Dach liefert Strom, sämtliche Heizungsanlagen werden mit Pflanzenöl betrieben. Das Gebäude ist energietechnisch autark und CO_2-emissionsfrei.

WWF-Pays-Bas a lancé la construction d'un nouveau siège sur le site d'un ancien laboratoire situé dans la réserve naturelle de Schoonoord en 2003. Son but initial était de créer un immeuble à empreinte carbone neutre. Depuis, le projet a évolué pour mettre en œuvre les principes de One Planet Living et s'efforce d'atteindre un niveau d'empreinte pleinement écologique. Ce principe « d'empreinte écologique » est un outil mis au point par le Global Footprint Network qui mesure la quantité de terre et d'eau nécessaire pour produire les ressources consommées et l'absorption des déchets. Comme l'explique l'architecte : « Dans les plafonds de torchis à humidité stabilisée, la circulation continue d'air dans des tubes de verre diffuse la chaleur humaine ou produite mécaniquement et – plus important encore – le refroidissement. Des volets horizontaux en bois permettent la pénétration d'un maximum de lumière naturelle dans le bâtiment. Tous les matériaux ont été sélectionnés en fonction de leur impact sur l'environnement et des conditions de leur fabrication (travail des enfants). La vie sauvage a bien sûr été prise en compte : "Des tuiles de toiture favorables aux oiseaux", et des "caves pour chauves-souris" ». L'ancien centre du bâtiment, construit en 1954, a été démoli pour laisser place à un pavillon central « amorphe ». Le poste de production d'énergie solaire placé sur le toit et toutes les installations fonctionnent à l'huile végétale. Le bâtiment est autonome sur le plan énergétique et n'émet pas de CO_2.

Essentially an ecologically conscious office building, the WWF headquarters is highlighted in its natural setting, with a more organic form at its heart, surrounded by rectangular office wings.

Das WWF-Gebäude, ein gemäß den Prinzipien der Nachhaltigkeit entwickelter Bau, fällt in seiner landschaftlichen Umgebung durch ein organisches Gebilde auf, das sein Zentrum bildet und von rechtwinkligen Büroflügeln flankiert wird.

Immeuble de bureaux répondant aux principes du développement durable, le siège du WWF s'intègre dans son cadre naturel par une forme organique centrale se projetant entre deux ailes orthogonales.

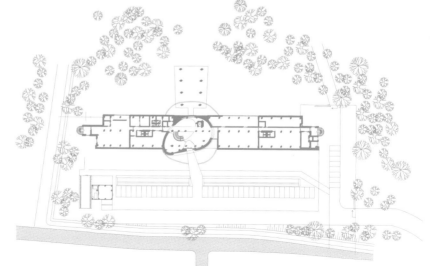

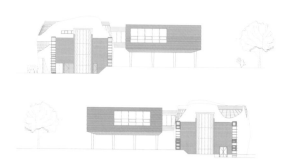

Transparent, curving surfaces mark the entrance and stairway seen in the images to the right and below. Curving walls emphasize the more organic aspects of the design.

Transparente, geschwungene Linien prägen den Eingangsbereich und das Treppenhaus, wie rechts und unten zu sehen. Geschwungene Wände unterstreichen die organischen Aspekte des Entwurfs.

Des parois de verre incurvées encerclent l'entrée et la cage d'escalier que l'on aperçoit à droite et en bas. Ces courbes renforcent les aspects organiques du projet.

ROSWAG & JANKOWSKI

Ziegert I Roswag I Seiler Architekten Ingenieure
Roswag Architekten
Schlesische Straße 26, Aufgang A / 10997 Berlin, Germany
E-mail: info@zrs-berlin.de / Web: www.zrs-berlin.de

werk A architektur
Guntram Jankowski, Dipl. Ing. Architekt
Lehrter Straße 57 / Haus 4 / 10557 Berlin, Germany
E-mail: kontakt@werk-a-architektur.de / Web: www.werk-a-architektur.de

Eike Roswag, born in 1969 in Gießen, Germany, studied Architecture and received a Dipl.-Ing. degree at the Technical University in Berlin. Natural building materials and earthen construction form the core competencies of his office, under the umbrella of Ziegert I Roswag I Seiler Architekten Ingenieure, located in Berlin. His wide-ranging projects include a timber-frame factory building for Artis in Berlin; a rammed-earth house in Brandenburg; school projects in Africa and Pakistan; and a historical building renovation in Abu Dhabi. In collaboration with Anna Heringer he realized the Handmade School in Rudrapur (Dinajpur, Bangladesh, 2005, published on page 126), which was honored with the 2007 Aga Khan Award for Architecture. Westend Grün (Westend Green, Berlin, published here) is one of the jointly realized projects of Roswag & Jankowski Architekten (2006–09). Guntram Jankowski was born in 1972 in Gräfelfing, Germany, and studied Architecture at the Technical University in Berlin. In 2003 he founded werk A architektur; from 2006 to 2009 he was a partner at **ROSWAG & JANKOWSKI ARCHITEKTEN**. His projects include Spindler & Klatt, a club and restaurant (Berlin, 2006); a timber-frame fire station (Neuseddin, 2008); Jahili Fort, a historical fort conversion with museum and visitor center (Al-Ain, Abu Dhabi, 2008); Haus am See (Friedrichswalde 2010); The Grand, a restaurant and bar (Berlin, 2012); and Atelierhaus am See (Friedrichswalde, Jankowski).

Eike Roswag, 1969 in Gießen geboren, schloss sein Architekturstudium an der TU Berlin als Diplom-Ingenieur ab. Natürliche Baustoffe und der Schwerpunkt Lehmbau bilden die Kernkompetenz seines Architekturbüros unter dem Dach Ziegert I Roswag I Seiler Architekten Ingenieure mit Sitz in Berlin. Die Projekte spannen einen Bogen von dem in Holzbauweise errichteten Betriebsgebäude für Artis in Berlin, einem Stampflehmhaus in Brandenburg über Schulprojekte in Afrika und Pakistan zu Baudenkmälern auf der Arabischen Halbinsel. Mit Anna Heringer realisierte er die Handmade School in Rudrapur (Dinajpur, Bangladesch, 2005, vorgestellt auf Seite 179–83), die 2007 mit dem Aga-Khan-Preis für Architektur ausgezeichnet wurde. Westend Grün (Berlin, hier vorgestellt) ist eines der gemeinsam unter Roswag & Jankowski (2006–2009) realisierten Projekte. Guntram Jankowski wurde 1972 in Gräfelfing bei München geboren und studierte Architektur an der Technischen Universität Berlin. 2003 folgte die Gründung von werk A architektur, von 2006 bis 2009 war er Partner bei **ROSWAG & JANKOWSKI ARCHITEKTEN**. Zu seinen Projekten zählen das Spindler & Klatt, Club und Restaurant (Berlin, 2006), die Feuerwehr Neuseddin, der Neubau des Gerätehauses in Holzbauweise (Neuseddin, 2008), das Jahili Fort, der Umbau eines Lehmsteinforts zum Museum mit Besucherzentrum (Al-Ain, Abu Dhabi, 2008), das Haus am See (Friedrichswalde, 2010), The Grand, Restaurant und Bar (Berlin, 2012) sowie das Atelierhaus am See (Friedrichswalde, 2012).

Eike Roswag, né en 1969 à Gießen, Allemagne, est Dipl.-Ing. Architect de l'Université Polytechnique de Berlin. Le travail sur des projets utilisant des matériaux naturels, et notamment en terre, fait partie de la compétence clé de son bureau d'architectes Ziegert I Roswag I Seiler Architekten Ingenieure à Berlin. Ses projets comprennent la conception d'un bâtiment d'entreprise en bois pour Artis à Berlin, une maison en béton de pierre à Brandebourg, des écoles en Afrique et au Pakistan ainsi que des constructions historiques sur la péninsule arabe. Avec Anna Heringer, il a réalisé l'école de Rudrapur (Dinajpur, Bangladesh, 2005, publiée pages 179–83), qui a reçu le prix Aga Khan d'architecture en 2007. Le Westend Grün (Berlin, 2006–07, publié ici) est une réalisation commune de Roswag & Jankowski. Guntram Jankowski, né en 1972, à Gräfelfing, Allemagne, a lui aussi étudié l'architecture à l'Université Polytechnique de Berlin. Il fonde werk A architektur en 2003 puis est associé de 2006 à 2009 à **ROSWAG & JANKOWSKI ARCHITEKTEN**. Ses projets comprennent le Spindler & Klatt, club et restaurant (Berlin, 2006), la construction en bois de la caserne des pompiers de Neuseddin (Neuseddin, 2008), fort Al Jahili, la réhabilitation d'un fort en briques de terre en musée avec un centre d'accueil pour les visiteurs (Al-Ain, Abu Dhabi, 2008), Haus am See (Friedrichswalde, 2010), The Grand, restaurant et bar (Berlin, 2012) ainsi que Atelierhaus am See (Friedrichswalde, 2012).

WESTEND GRÜN (WESTEND GREEN)

Berlin, Germany, 2006–07

Floor area: 187 m². Clients: Julia and Alexander von Seltmann. Cost: not disclosed

The rehabilitation of a 1930s building severely damaged during World War II started with the removal of a roof added after the war and continued with the reorganization of the entire structure, with new openings and connections added throughout. The new inner walls of the first floor are made of "mud bricks and brown mud plaster covered with white mud." Eike Roswag says: "We call the project the White Mud House. It has all the positive functions of mud buildings insofar as humidity control and fresh air are concerned. It is a very 'healthy' type of construction carried out with natural materials and no chemical-based paints or glues." The exterior is covered with 10-centimeter-thick reed thermal insulation covered with white lime plaster. This is the first building in Berlin to use such methods, which may well be inspired by Roswag's work in the developing world. A heat pump is used to reduce energy requirements, allowing the building to use only 60% of the power mandated by German standards for new buildings.

Die Sanierung des im Zweiten Weltkrieg schwer beschädigten Hauses aus den 1930er-Jahren begann mit der Demontage des nach dem Krieg aufgestockten Dachs und setzte sich in der Neuorganisation des gesamten Gebäudes fort. Hierbei wurden neue Fenster- und Türöffnungen und Raumverbindungen eingefügt. Die Innenwände im ersten Stock wurden aus „Lehmziegeln und braunem Lehmputz mit weißem Lehmoberputz" gearbeitet. Eike Roswag erklärt: „Wir nennen das Haus ‚Weißes Lehmhaus'. Es hat sämtliche positiven Eigenschaften von Lehmbauten, was Feuchtigkeitskontrolle und Frischluftzufuhr betrifft. Es ist eine sehr ‚gesunde' Bauweise mit natürlichen Baumaterialien und Farben und Klebstoffen auf chemiefreier Basis." Den Außenbau umhüllt eine 10 cm starke Dämmschicht aus Schilfrohr mit weißem Kalkputz. Es ist das erste Haus dieser Art in Berlin, dessen Methoden durchaus von Roswags Engagement in Entwicklungsländern inspiriert sein mögen. Eine Wärmepumpe senkt den Energiebedarf, sodass das Haus nur 60 % der nach deutschen Richtlinien für Neubauten bemessenen Energiemenge verbraucht.

La réhabilitation de cette construction des années 1930, sévèrement endommagée pendant la Seconde Guerre Mondiale, a commencé par la suppression de la toiture ajoutée après la guerre et s'est poursuivie par la réorganisation de la structure tout entière, ce qui a permis de créer de nouvelles ouvertures et connexions. Les murs intérieurs du premier niveau sont « en briques de terre et torchis de terre brune recouvert de pisé blanc… Nous avons appelé ce projet "la maison en torchis blanc". Elle présente toutes les fonctions positives des constructions en terre en termes de contrôle de l'humidité et d'aération naturelle. C'est un type de construction très "sain" réalisé avec des matériaux naturels sans peintures ni colles chimiques », explique l'architecte. L'extérieur est recouvert d'une isolation thermique de 10 cm d'épaisseur en roseaux recouverts d'enduit au mortier de chaux blanc. C'est la première construction berlinoise à faire appel à ces méthodes, peut-être inspirées de l'expérience de Roswag dans les pays en voie de développement. Une pompe à chaleur réduit la consommation d'énergie, et permet à la maison de n'utiliser que 60 % de l'énergie préconisée dans les nouvelles constructions en Allemagne.

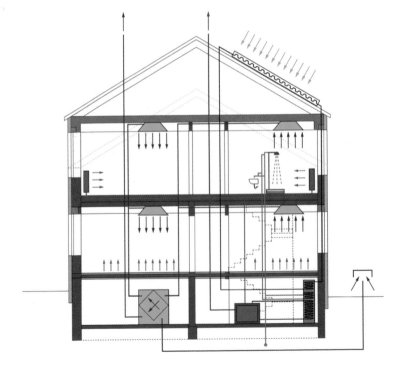

As seen from the outside, the building looks like an almost ordinary older house, but its thermally insulated surface, and indeed the heat transfer methods used by the architects as seen in the diagram to the left, make it decidedly green.

Von außen mag das Haus wie ein gewöhnlicher Altbau wirken, doch seine wärmeisolierte Außenhaut und insbesondere die Prinzipien der Wärmeübertragung (siehe Diagramm, links), die die Architekten hier anwenden, machen es zu einem ausgesprochen ‚grünen' Bau.

Vue de l'extérieur, la maison semble presque ordinaire, mais ses façades à isolation thermique et sa gestion des différences de températures (voir plan ci-contre), en font une véritable création environnementale.

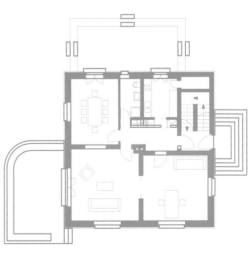

RURAL STUDIO

Rural Studio
College of Architecture, Design and Construction / Auburn University School of Architecture
P.O. Box 278 / Newbern, AL 36765 / USA
Tel: +1 334 624 4483 / Fax: +1 334 624 6015
E-mail: rstudio@auburn.edu / Web: www.ruralstudio.org

Samuel Mockbee, born in 1945, founded Mockbee/Coker Architects, based in Canton, Mississippi, and in Memphis, Tennessee, with Coleman Coker in 1978. The firm completed a number of structures, including the Barton House and the Cook House, both located in Mississippi. They enjoy considerable reknown in the region, established through their contemporary interpretations of local architecture. Samuel Mockbee taught at Yale, at the University of Oklahoma, and was a Professor of Architecture at Auburn University beginning in 1991. He created the **RURAL STUDIO** with Dennis K. Ruth in 1993 to improve living conditions in rural Alabama and to include hands-on experience in architectural pedagogy, while "extending the study of architecture into a socially responsible context." Three programs, lasting from a semester to a year, are organized for students at Auburn. Mockbee died in 2001, but it was immediately decided that the work of the Rural Studio would continue. The studio is today under the direction of Professor Andrew Freear, who was born in Yorkshire, England. He graduated from the Polytechnic of Central London and the Architectural Association in London. He taught at the University of Illinois before joining Auburn University. Completed community projects include the Akron Senior Center in Hale County (2001–02); the Lee County AIDS Alabama House (2002–03); and the Perry Lakes Pedestrian Bridge (2003–04). Other completed houses include Lucy House in Mason's Bend and Shiles House, both completed in Hale County in 2001–02; the Music Man House (Hale County, 2002–03); Christine's House (Mason's Bend, 2005–06, published here); and the St. Luke's Church Renovation in Old Cahawba (2006–08), all in Alabama, USA.

Samuel Mockbee, geboren 1945, gründete 1978 gemeinsam mit Coleman Coker sein Büro Mockbee/Coker Architects mit Sitz in Canton, Mississippi, und Memphis, Tennessee. Das Büro realisierte zahlreiche Bauten, darunter das Haus Barton sowie das Haus Cook, beide in Mississippi. Durch ihre zeitgenössische Interpretation ortstypischer Architektur erwarb sich das Büro einen beachtlichen Ruf in der Region. Samuel Mockbee lehrte in Yale sowie an der Universität Oklahoma und war seit 1991 Professor für Architektur an der Universität Auburn in Alabama. 1993 gründete er mit Dennis K. Ruth das Büro **RURAL STUDIO**, um die Lebensbedingungen in ländlichen Gegenden Alabamas zu verbessern. Zugleich ging es ihm darum, praktische Erfahrungen in Architekturpädagogik zu vermitteln und „das Architekturstudium in den sozial verantwortlichen Bereich zu erweitern". Studenten an der Universität Auburn werden drei Programme mit einer Dauer von einem Semester bis zu einem Jahr angeboten. Mockbee starb 2001, doch man beschloss sofort, die Arbeit von Rural Studio fortzusetzen. Heute wird das Studio von Professor Andrew Freear geleitet, der in Yorkshire geboren wurde. Er studierte an der Polytechnic of Central London und der Architectural Association in London. Bevor er nach Auburn kam, lehrte er an der Universität von Illinois. Zu den realisierten Gemeinschaftsprojekten zählen u. a. das Akron Senior Center in Hale County (2001–02), das Lee County AIDS Alabama House (2002–03) sowie die Perry-Lakes-Fußgängerbrücke (2003–04). Andere Hausbauten sind das Lucy House in Mason's Bend und das Shiles House (beide 2001–02 in Hale County fertiggestellt), das Music Man House (Hale County, 2002–03), Christine's House (Mason's Bend, 2005–06, hier vorgestellt) sowie die Sanierung der Kirche St. Luke's in Old Cahawba (2006–08), alle in Alabama.

Samuel Mockbee, né en 1945, a fondé Mockbee/Coker Architects avec Coleman Coker en 1978. L'agence basée à Canton, Mississippi, et Memphis, Tennessee, a réalisé un certain nombre de projets dont la maison Barton et la maison Cook, toutes deux dans le Mississippi. Elle bénéficie d'une importante réputation dans la région grâce à ses interprétations contemporaines de l'architecture locale. Samuel Mockbee a enseigné à Yale, à l'université de l'Oklahoma et a été professeur d'architecture à l'université Auburn à partir de 1991. Il a créé **RURAL STUDIO** avec Dennis K. Ruth, en 1993, pour améliorer les conditions de vie dans l'Alabama rural et mettre en pratique une expérience directe du chantier dans sa pédagogie, tout en « étendant l'étude de l'architecture dans un contexte social responsable ». Trois programmes, d'une durée d'un semestre à un an, sont organisés à Auburn pour les étudiants. Mockbee est mort en 2001, mais il a été immédiatement décidé que Rural Studio devait continuer. Il est aujourd'hui placé sous la direction du professeur Andrew Freear, né dans le Yorkshire en Grande-Bretagne. Il est diplômé de la London Polytechnic et de l'Architectural Association de Londres. Il a enseigné à l'université de l'Illinois, avant de rejoindre celle d'Auburn. Parmi les projets communautaires achevés figurent le Centre Akron Senior dans le comté de Hale County (2001–02) ; l'AIDS Alabama House dans le comté de Lee (2002–03) et la passerelle piétonnière du lac Perry (2003–04). Parmi leurs maisons réalisées : la maison Lucy à Mason's Bend et la maison Shiles (comté de Hale, 2001–02) ; la maison Music Man (comté de Hale, 2002–03) ; la maison de Christine (Mason's Bend, 2005–06), publiée ici, et la rénovation de l'église St. Luc à Old Cahawba (2006–08), le tout en Alabama, États-Unis.

CHRISTINE'S HOUSE

Mason's Bend, Alabama, USA, 2005–06

Floor area: 83 m². Client: Christine Green. Cost: not disclosed
Project Architects: Amy Green Bullington, Stephen Long. Project Instructor and Rural Studio Director: Andrew Freear
Structural Engineer: Joe Farruggia. Environmental Engineer: Paul Stroller

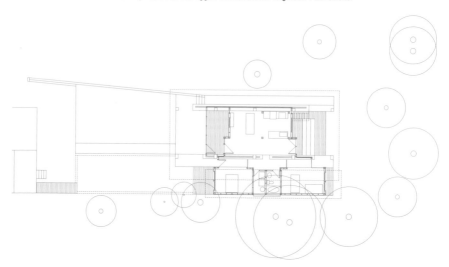

Like other Rural Studio work, Christine's House was an Auburn University architectural thesis. Both the young architects involved in this house, Amy Green Bullington and Stephen Long, received their B.Arch degrees from Auburn in 2005. They took advantage of the area's abundant red clay—mixing 70% earth, 25% pulped newspaper and 5% Portland cement, poured into cardboard boxes of various sizes—to make bricks for two main walls of the house. As Amy Bullington explains: "This hybrid adobe mix, a simple modification to traditional brick making, requires few special skills and little equipment, and its high insulation value (R33 for a 30.5 cm wall) is attractive in terms of long-term client cost." A wind tower inspired by Middle Eastern designs was placed over the kitchen of the house to encourage airflow. The students carefully studied the social patterns of Mason's Bend, where a number of other Rural Studio projects have been built, so that this new addition would fit into its surroundings. Aside from the economical construction design, a clear interest in sustainability has informed this project.

Wie andere Projekte von Rural Studio war auch Christine's House eine Abschlussarbeit in Architektur an der Universität Auburn. Die zwei an der Planung des Hauses beteiligten jungen Architekten, Amy Green Bullington und Stephen Long, erlangten ihre B.-Arch.-Abschlüsse 2005. Sie nutzten die in der Gegend verbreitete rote Tonerde, um aus einer Mischung aus 70 % Erde, 25 % Pappmaschee aus Altpapier und 5 % Portlandzement, die sie in Pappkartons unterschiedlicher Größe gossen, Ziegel für die beiden Hauptwände des Hauses herzustellen. Amy Bullington erklärt: „Dieser hybride Lehmziegelmix ist eine einfache Modifikation der traditionellen Ziegelfertigung und erfordert kaum besondere Fertigkeiten oder technische Ausrüstung; sein hoher Dämmfaktor (R33 bei einer 30,5 cm starken Wand) macht ihn für den Auftraggeber attraktiv im Hinblick auf Langzeitkosten." Ein von der nahöstlichen Tradition inspirierter Windturm wurde über der Küche installiert und fördert die Belüftung. Die Studenten hatten sich intensiv mit dem Sozialgefüge in Mason's Bend auseinandergesetzt, wo Rural Studio bereits zahlreiche andere Projekte realisiert hat, sodass sich der neueste Bau sinnvoll einfügt. Abgesehen von der sparsamen Bauweise ist das Projekt auch von einem Interesse an Nachhaltigkeit geprägt.

Comme d'autres travaux de Rural Studio, la « maison de Christine » est en réalité l'aboutissement d'une thèse d'architecture préparée à l'université Auburn. Les deux jeunes architectes impliqués dans ce projet, Amy Green Bullington et Stephen Long, ont reçu leur diplôme de B. Arch d'Auburn en 2005. Ils ont profité de la présence abondante d'argile rouge dans la région pour fabriquer des briques de diverses dimensions en mélangeant 70 % d'argile, 25 % de pulpe de papier et 5 % de ciment Portland. Elles constituent les deux murs principaux. Comme l'explique Amy Bullington : « Ce mélange hybride d'adobes, simple modification du processus traditionnel de fabrication des briques, demande peu de compétence ou d'équipement, et son pouvoir élevé d'isolation (taux d'isolation très élevé de R33 pour un mur de 30,5 cm d'épaisseur) est séduisant sur le plan du coût à long terme pour le client. » Une tour à vent, inspirée d'une typologie moyen-orientale, a été installée au-dessus de la cuisine pour faciliter la ventilation naturelle. Les étudiants ont soigneusement étudié les rapports sociaux de Mason's Bend, où un certain nombre de projets de Rural Studio ont été réalisés, pour que cette nouvelle construction s'intègre de façon appropriée. En dehors des aspects économiques de sa construction, ce projet est clairement placé sous le signe de la durabilité.

The emphasis on natural, locally obtained materials and simple methods of aeration make the house, a very basic structure, ecologically sound.

Die Konzentration auf natürliche, lokal verfügbare Materialien und einfache Belüftungsmethoden machen das Haus, eine sehr einfache Konstruktion, zu einem ökologisch verträglichen Bau.

L'accent mis sur les matériaux naturels locaux et des méthodes d'aération simples fait de cette construction très basique un exemple de solution écologique.

HIROSHI SAMBUICHI

Hiroshi Sambuichi Architects
8-3-302 Nakajima Naka-ku
730-0811 Hiroshima
Japan

Tel: +81 82 544 1417
Fax: +81 82 544 1418
E-mail: samb@d2.dion.ne.jp

HIROSHI SAMBUICHI was born in 1968. He graduated from the Department of Architecture in the Faculty of Science and Technology at Tokyo University of Science. After working for Shinichi Ogawa & Associates, he established Sambuichi Architects and began design work in Hiroshima. His work includes the Running Green Project (Yamaguchi, 2001); Air House (Yamaguchi, 2001); Miwa-gama (Yamaguchi, 2002); Sloping North House (Yamaguchi, 2003); Stone House (Shimane, 2005–07); and the Inujima Art Project Seirensho (Okayama, 2006–08, published here), all in Japan.

HIROSHI SAMBUICHI wurde 1968 geboren. Sein Architekturstudium schloss er an der Fakultät für Naturwissenschaften und Technik an der Tokyo University of Science ab. Nachdem er zunächst für Shinichi Ogawa & Associates gearbeitet hatte, gründete er sein Büro Sambuichi Architects in Hiroshima. Zu seinen Projekten zählen u. a.: Running Green Project (Yamaguchi, 2001), Air House (Yamaguchi, 2001), Miwa-gama (Yamaguchi, 2002), Sloping North House (Yamaguchi, 2003), Stone House (Shimane, 2005–07) sowie das Inujima Art Project Seirensho (Inujima, Okayama, 2006–08, hier vorgestellt), alle in Japan.

Né en 1968, **HIROSHI SAMBUICHI** est diplômé du département d'architecture de la Faculté des sciences et technologies de l'Université des sciences de Tokyo. Après avoir travaillé pour Shinichi Ogawa & Associates, il a fondé l'agence Sambuichi Architects et commencé à travailler à Hiroshima. Ses réalisations comprennent le Running Green Project (Yamaguchi, 2001) ; l'Air House (Yamaguchi, 2001) ; Miwa-Gama (Yamaguchi, 2002) ; la Sloping North House (Yamaguchi, 2003) ; la Stone House (Shimane, 2005–07) et le projet artistique de la raffinerie (*seirensho*) à Inujima (Okayama, 2006–08, publié ici), le tout au Japon.

INUJIMA ART PROJECT SEIRENSHO

Inujima, Okayama, Japan, 2006–08

Area: 790 m². Client: Soichiro Fukutake. Cost: not disclosed

This one-story wood-and-steel structure is located on a 5212-square-meter site on the small Inland Sea island of Inujima. The client, Soichiro Fukutake, is the head of the Benesse Corporation, which is also at the origin of Tadao Ando's projects on the nearby island of Naoshima. Like Naoshima, the island was marked by an industrial presence, in this case a copper refinery that operated between 1909 and 1919, leaving only ruins behind. The architect says: "I thought that all the existing materials are regenerable resources, such as the old architecture of the ruins, the geography, open spaces, the infrastructure of the factories, wastes, and so on. There are six different levels of height on the site, and I considered these as landscapes for making use of the necessary potential energy. I decided to use levels one to four in this project, and planned architectural figures to utilize and activate chimneys and accumulate energy for years and years." He used waste slag in the floor and walls. Timber is used above ground, as it was in the original plant, and the slag used in the floors contains iron oxide from the plant. The museum contains four main spaces, a cooling corridor that uses the heat of the earth, a sun gallery that collects the energy of the sun, an energy hall, and the chimney, and a landscape "controlling the circulation of vegetation and water." Rather than "large hidden machinery," the architect has used the energy of the earth and sun to "power" this museum.

Der einstöckige Bau aus Holz und Stahl liegt auf einem 5212 m² großen Grundstück auf der kleinen Insel Inujima in der Seto-Inlandsee. Soichiro Fukutake, Bauherr des Projekts und Direktor der Firma Benesse, war schon Auftraggeber der Tadao-Ando-Bauten auf der nahe gelegenen Insel Naoshima. Wie Naoshima so ist auch Inujima von seiner industriellen Vorgeschichte geprägt, in diesem Fall von einer Kupferraffinerie, die zwischen 1909 und 1919 in Betrieb war und von der noch Ruinen erhalten sind. Der Architekt erklärt: „Meine Überlegung war, alle vorhandenen Materialien als erneuerbare Ressourcen zu verstehen – die Architektur der Ruinen, die Geografie, die offenen Räume, die Infrastruktur der Fabriken, den Schutt und so weiter. Das Gelände hat sechs Höhenniveaus, die ich als Landschaften und potenzielle Energieerzeuger interpretiert habe. Ich beschloss, die Niveaus eins bis vier in das Projekt zu integrieren und entwarf eine Architekturkonstellation, in der sich die Schornsteine aktivieren und nutzen lassen, um so Energie auf Jahre hinaus speichern zu können." Für Böden und Wände griff der Architekt auf alte Schlacken zurück. Über Grund wurde wie in der alten Fabrik mit Holz gearbeitet. Die Schlacken der Bodenbeläge enthalten Eisenoxid aus dem alten Werk. Zum Museum gehören vier Bereiche, ein Kühlkorridor, der mit Erdwärme arbeitet, eine Sonnengalerie, die Solarenergie erzeugt, eine Energiehalle mit Schornstein und eine Landschaft, die „den Kreislauf von Vegetation und Wasser steuert". Statt „aufwendiger Technik hinter den Kulissen" nutzt der Architekt Erde und Sonne, um sein Museum mit Energie zu versorgen.

Cette construction en bois et acier d'un seul niveau est implantée sur un terrain de 5212 m² sur la petite île d'Inujima, dans la Mer intérieure du Japon. Le client, Soichiro Fukutake – qui dirige la Benesse Corporation – est par ailleurs à l'initiative des projets de Tadao Ando sur l'île voisine de Naoshima. Comme à Naoshima, les lieux étaient marqués par la présence d'une raffinerie de cuivre qui avait opéré de 1909 à 1919 et laissé une friche de ruines industrielles. Selon l'architecte : « J'ai pensé que tous ces matériaux abandonnés étaient des ressources réutilisables, de même que l'architecture ancienne de ces ruines, la géographie, les espaces ouverts, l'infrastructure des usines, les déchets, etc. Il existe six niveaux de hauteur sur le site que j'ai considérés comme un paysage dont il fallait extraire le potentiel énergétique nécessaire. J'ai décidé d'investir les niveaux 1 à 4, et j'ai conçu des formes architecturales pour utiliser et activer les cheminées et l'énergie accumulée depuis des années et des années. » Hiroshi Sambuichi s'est servi de scories pour les sols (mâchefer chargé d'oxyde de fer) et les murs. Le bois est utilisé pour les structures au-dessus du sol, comme dans l'usine originelle. Le musée contient quatre volumes principaux, un corridor de refroidissement qui utilise la chaleur de la terre, une galerie solaire qui collecte l'énergie du soleil, un hall de l'énergie et la cheminée, et un paysage aménagé « contrôlant la circulation de la végétation et de l'eau ». Plutôt qu'une « grosse machinerie dissimulée », l'architecte s'est servi de l'énergie de la terre et du soleil pour « ancrer » cette réalisation.

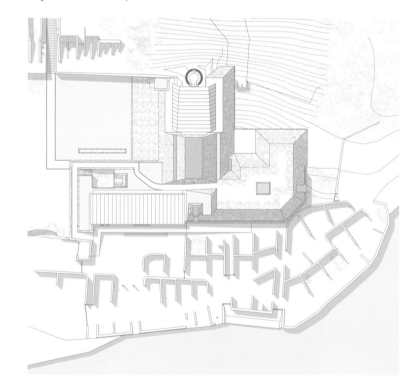

The museum occupies the site of a former copper refinery on a small, remote island, giving the ruins a certain poetic presence.

Das Museum liegt auf einer kleinen entlegenen Insel, auf dem Gelände einer ehemaligen Kupferraffinerie. Den Ruinen eignet geradezu etwas Poetisches.

Le musée occupe le site d'une ancienne raffinerie de cuivre située sur une petite île isolée. Les ruines dégagent une certaine poésie.

The tall smokestack of the former refinery marks the location of the museum. The architect has deftly combined new elements with the existing architecture.

Der große Schornstein der ehemaligen Raffinerie markiert den Standort des Museums. Gekonnt kombiniert der Architekt neue Elemente mit bestehender Architektur.

La haute cheminée de l'ancienne raffinerie signale le site du musée. L'architecte a habilement associé des éléments architecturaux anciens à des composants nouveaux.

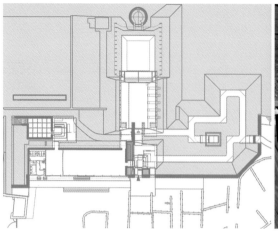

Hiroshi Sambuichi has used natural light and energy to the exclusion of artificial sources that would have been hard to come by on this abandoned site. He mixes existing spaces and elements with new ones in a way that makes it difficult to distinguish one from the other.

Hiroshi Sambuichi nutzt natürliche Licht- und Energiequellen und verzichtet auf künstliche Energie, die an diesem entlegenen Standort auch kaum verfügbar wäre. Er kombiniert bestehende Räumlichkeiten und Elemente so geschickt mit neuen, dass kaum Unterschiede erkennbar sind.

Hiroshi Sambuichi s'est servi de la lumière et de l'énergie naturelles à l'exclusion de toute source artificielle, difficile à mettre en œuvre sur un site aussi isolé. Il a mixé les volumes existants à de nouveaux éléments d'une telle façon qu'il est difficile de les distinguer.

Located near the island of Naoshima, where Tadao Ando has built numerous art-related projects for the same client, the museum is intended to bring this abandoned industrial site back to life.

Das Museum – unweit der Insel Naoshima, auf der Tadao Ando verschiedene Kunstprojekte für denselben Auftraggeber realisierte – will das verlassene Industriegelände wieder zum Leben erwecken.

Situé non loin de l'île de Naoshima sur laquelle Tadao Ando a réalisé de nombreux projets d'ordre artistique pour le même client, ce musée devrait redonner vie à ce site industriel abandonné.

ADRIAN SMITH + GORDON GILL ARCHITECTURE

Adrian Smith + Gordon Gill Architecture LLP
111 West Monroe, Suite 2300
Chicago, IL 60603
USA

Tel: +1 312 920 1888
Fax: +1 312 920 1775
E-mail: info@smithgill.com
Web: www.smithgill.com

Adrian Smith received his B.Arch degree from the University of Illinois (Chicago, 1969). He was a design partner in the office of Skidmore, Owings & Merrill (SOM) LLP from 1980 to 2003. He was Chief Executive Officer of the SOM Partnership (1993–95) and Chairman of the SOM Foundation (1990–95), and remained a consulting design partner at the firm until 2006. He is well known as the designer of towers such as the Burj Dubai (Dubai, UAE, 2006–09), the tallest building in the world. Gordon Gill was an Associate Partner at SOM LLP and a Director of Design for VOA Associates, before creating **ADRIAN SMITH + GORDON GILL ARCHITECTURE** with Adrian Smith in 2006. He was the designer of "the world's first net-zero energy skyscraper, the Pearl River Tower." Robert Forest received his B.Arch degree from Carleton University (Ottawa, Canada, 1994) and is the management partner for the Masdar Headquarters. The firm's work includes 1 Dubai (Dubai); Burj Dubai Gatehouses and Function Island (Dubai); the Grand Boulevard at Burj Dubai (Dubai); the Mansion at Burj Dubai (Dubai); 1 Park Avenue (Dubai); Park Gate (Dubai); Masdar Headquarters (Masdar City just outside of Abu Dhabi, 2008–10, published here); Sears Tower Sustainable Systems (Chicago, Illinois, USA); Vancouver Residential Development (Vancouver, Canada); and the Verde Residences and Offices (Dubai), all in the United Arab Emirates unless stated otherwise.

Adrian Smith erwarb seinen B.Arch. an der Universität Illinois (Chicago, 1969). Von 1980 bis 2003 war er als Partner bei Skidmore, Owings & Merrill (SOM) LLP für den Entwurf zuständig. Er war Hauptgeschäftsführer der SOM-Partnerschaft (1993–95) und Vorsitzender der SOM Foundation (1990–95) und blieb dem Büro bis 2006 als beratender Partner in Entwurfsfragen verbunden. Bekannt wurde er mit seinen Hochhausbauten wie dem Burj Dubai (Dubai, 2006–09), dem höchsten Gebäude der Welt. Gordon Gill war assoziierter Partner bei SOM LLP und Chefdesigner bei VOA Associates, bevor er 2006 mit Adrian Smith das Büro **ADRIAN SMITH + GORDON GILL ARCHITECTURE** gründete. Er entwarf den „ersten Nullenergie-Wolkenkratzer, den Pearl River Tower". Robert Forest erwarb seinen B.Arch. an der Universität Carleton (Ottawa, Kanada, 1994) und ist Managementpartner für das Masdar-Headquarters-Projekt. Projekte des Büros sind u. a. 1 Dubai (Dubai), Pförtnerhäuser und Event-Insel für den Burj Dubai (Dubai), The Grand Boulevard für das Burj Dubai (Dubai), The Mansion für das Burj Dubai (Dubai), 1 Park Avenue (Dubai), Park Gate (Dubai), die Masdar Headquarters (Masdar City am Rande von Abu Dhabi, 2008–10, hier vorgestellt), Sears Tower Sustainable Systems (Chicago, Illinois, USA), ein Wohnbauprojekt in Vancouver (Kanada) sowie die Wohn- und Büroanlage Verde (Dubai), alle in den Vereinigten Arabischen Emiraten, sofern nicht anders angegeben.

Adrian Smith est B. Arch de l'université de l'Illinois (Chicago, 1969). Il a été partenaire chargé de projet chez Skidmore, Owings & Merrill (SOM) LLP de 1980 à 2003, directeur exécutif principal de SOM Partnership (1993–95) et président de la SOM Foundation (1990–95) pour qui il sera consultant en design jusqu'en 2006. Il est particulièrement connu pour être l'auteur de tours, dont le Burj Dubai (Dubaï, EAU, 2006–09), l'immeuble le plus haut du monde. Gordon Gill a été partenaire associé de SOM LLP et directeur des projets pour VOA Associates, avant de fonder l'agence **ADRIAN SMITH + GORDON GILL ARCHITECTURE** avec Adrian Smith en 2006. Il a conçu le « premier gratte-ciel zéro-énergie au monde, la Pearl River Tower ». Robert Forest est B. Arch de l'université Carleton (Ottawa, Canada, 1994) et associé responsable du siège social de Masdar. Les réalisations du cabinet comprennent : 1 Dubai ; les Gatehouses et Function Island (tours portes de sécurité et lieu événementiel) de Burj Dubai ; le Grand Boulevard à Burj Dubai ; The Mansion à Burj Dubai ; 1 Park Avenue (Dubai) ; Park Gate (Dubai) ; le complexe résidentiel et de bureaux Verde (Dubai) ; le siège social de Masdar (Masdar City, en périphérie d'Abu Dhabi, 2008–10, publié ici) : la Sears Tower Sustainable Systems (Chicago, Illinois, États-Unis) et Vancouver Residential Development (Vancouver, Canada), toutes aux Émirats arabes unis, sauf exception.

MASDAR HEADQUARTERS

Abu Dhabi, United Arab Emirâtes, 2008–10

*Floor area: 88 000 m². Client: The Masdar Initiative, subsidiary of Abu Dhabi Future Energy Company. Cost: not disclosed
Collaboration: Les Ventsch (Director of Design), Ying Liu (Senior Designer), Environmental Systems Design (MEP Engineering),
Thornton Tomasetti (Structural Engineering)*

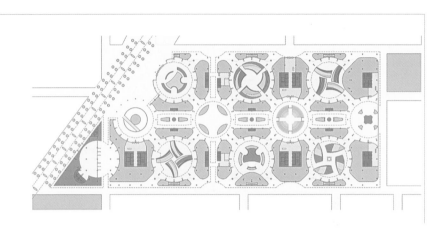

Masdar City is to be "the world's first zero-carbon, zero-waste city fully powered by renewable energy." The headquarters building, being designed by Adrian Smith + Gordon Gill Architecture, "will be the world's first large-scale, mixed-use 'positive energy' building, producing more energy than it consumes." Even more surprising, the building is intended to produce no waste, either liquid or solid. The structure is to include 6300 square meters of retail space, 78 000 square meters of office space, and 28 500 square meters of roof space. A large roof canopy and shaded green roofs are a first element of the sustainability strategy, as are glazed, insulating outer walls. The roof shade will have a large surface covered with photovoltaic cells, and solar thermal tubes are used to supply the building with air conditioning. Water use is strictly controlled by the most sophisticated means. Wind cones supply ventilation and direct warm air out of the building, while allowing light in. According to the architects: "The building's form is sculpted in response to an extensive environmental analysis to optimize system performance. Sustainable materials are utilized throughout and were selected based on life-cycle analysis."

Masdar wird die „erste CO_2-emissions- und abfallfreie Stadt der Welt [sein], die mit erneuerbaren Energien betrieben wird". Die eigentlichen Headquarters, entworfen von Adrian Smith + Gordon Gill Architecture, „werden das erste gemischt genutzte Gebäude mit einer ‚positiven Energiebilanz' sein, das mehr Energie produziert als verbraucht". Noch überraschender ist die Tatsache, dass das Gebäude darauf angelegt ist, weder feste noch flüssige Abfälle zu produzieren. Der Bau umfasst 6300 m² Gewerbefläche, 78 000 m² Bürofläche und 28 500 m² Dachfläche. Entscheidende Aspekte der nachhaltigen Strategie sind ein großes Baldachindach und schattige, begrünte Dachabschnitte ebenso wie eine dämmende, vorgebaute Außenhaut aus Glas. Ein erheblicher Teil der Dachfläche wird mit Solarmodulen ausgestattet, solarthermische Rohrleitungen klimatisieren das Gebäude. Der Wasserverbrauch wird mittels allerneuester Technik reguliert. Windtürme sorgen für Belüftung, dienen als Auslässe für warme Abluft und lassen zugleich Licht in den Bau. Die Architekten führen aus: „Die Form des Gebäudes ergab sich aus einer umfassenden Umweltanalyse, um die Leistung des Systems zu optimieren. Überall kamen nachhaltige Materialien zum Einsatz, die ihrer Ökobilanz entsprechend ausgewählt wurden."

Masdar City est « la première ville au monde zéro-carbone, zéro-déchets, entièrement alimentée par des énergies renouvelables ». L'immeuble du siège social du projet, conçu par Adrian Smith + Gordon Gill Architecture, « sera le premier immeuble construit au monde à la fois de grandes dimensions, mixte, à "énergie positive", c'est-à-dire produisant plus d'énergie qu'il n'en consomme ». Plus surprenant encore, il ne devrait produire aucun déchet, qu'il soit liquide ou solide. Il comptera 6300 m² de commerces de détail, 78 000 m² de bureaux et 28 500 m² de toitures aménagées. Un vaste auvent au niveau du toit et des toitures végétalisées ombragées sont les premiers éléments d'une stratégie de développement durable, de même que les murs extérieurs vitrés et isolés. Le toit sera recouvert en grande partie de cellules photovoltaïques et d'une installation d'énergie thermique solaire à tubes participant au conditionnement de l'air de l'immeuble. L'utilisation de l'eau sera strictement contrôlée par les moyens les plus sophistiqués. Des cônes à vent fourniront la ventilation naturelle et évacueront l'air chaud, tout en facilitant la pénétration de la lumière naturelle. Selon les architectes : « La forme sculptée du bâtiment est une réponse à l'analyse environnementale approfondie d'optimisation de la performance d'ensemble. Des matériaux durables seront mis en œuvre dans l'ensemble de la construction et sélectionnés en fonction de leur cycle de vie. »

The Masdar Headquarters combines an underlying Euclidian block structure with a surprising undulating roof shade that houses photovoltaic cells in large numbers, rendering the energy independence of the structure greater.

Die Masdar Headquarters kombinieren einen Unterbau in Form eines euklidischen Blocks mit einem überraschenden, gewölbten Baldachindach, auf dem großflächig Solarzellen installiert werden. Hierdurch wird der Bau von seinem Umfeld energetisch unabhängiger.

Le siège de Masdar associe un bloc de géométrie euclidienne à une toiture étonnamment ondulée équipée d'une multitude de cellules photovoltaïques qui accroissent l'autonomie énergétique de la structure.

Dr. Sultan Al Jaber, CEO of Masdar and client of this project, states: "In line with the Abu Dhabi 2030 Development Plan, Masdar is choosing to emphasize sustainability over height."

Dr. Sultan Al Jaber, Hauptgeschäftsführer von Masdar und Bauherr des Projekts, merkt an: „Entsprechend dem Entwicklungsplan Abu Dhabi 2030 wird in Masdar Nachhaltigkeit größer geschrieben als Gebäudehöhe."

Le Dr. Sultan Al Jabern, directeur général de Masdar et commanditaire du projet a déclaré : « Suivant le Plan de développement 2030 d'Abu Dhabi, Masdar a préféré le développement durable à la course à la hauteur. »

WERNER SOBEK

Werner Sobek Stuttgart GmbH & Co. KG
Albstr. 14
70597 Stuttgart
Germany

Tel: +49 711 767 500
Fax: +49 711 767 5044
E-mail: stuttgart@wernersobek.com
Web: www.wernersobek.com

WERNER SOBEK was born in 1953 in Aalen, Germany. He studied Architecture and Civil Engineering at the University of Stuttgart (1974–80) and did postgraduate research in "Wide-Span Lightweight Structures" at the University of Stuttgart (1980–86). He received his Ph.D. in Civil Engineering at the same university in 1987. He worked as a structural engineer in the office of Schlaich, Bergermann & Partner (Stuttgart, 1987–91), before creating his own office in 1991. Since 1995 he has been a Professor at the University of Stuttgart, where he succeeded Frei Otto as Director of the Institute for Lightweight Structures. His projects include École Nationale d'Art Décoratif, with Finn Geipel and Nicolas Michelin (Limoges, France, 1991–94); Façade Interbank, with Hans Hollein (Lima, Peru, 1996–99); Private Residence R128 (Stuttgart, Germany, 1998–2000); New Bangkok International Airport, with Murphy/Jahn (Thailand, 1995–2004); Mercedes-Benz Museum, with UNStudio (Stuttgart, Germany, 2003–06); H16 (Tieringen, Germany, 2005–06, published here); Papal Altar (Munich, Germany, 2006); and fair pavilions for Audi and BMW. In 2007 WSGreenTechnologies was cofounded by Klaus Sedlbauer and Werner Sobek in Stuttgart. WSGreenTechnologies "offers integrated planning of buildings taking into consideration all phases of construction, use, and deconstruction. This comprises also thermal, acoustic, and visual comfort, as well as questions of biocompatibility, insofar as possible emissions of the building materials used."

WERNER SOBEK wurde 1953 in Aalen, Baden-Württemberg, geboren. Er studierte Architektur und Bauingenieurwesen an der Universität Stuttgart (1974–80) und arbeitete nach seinem Abschluss an einer Forschungsarbeit zum Thema „Flächentragwerke und Leichtbaukonstruktionen" an der Universität Stuttgart (1980–86). 1987 promovierte er an derselben Hochschule. Er arbeitete zunächst als Statiker bei Schlaich, Bergermann & Partner (Stuttgart, 1987–91) und gründete 1991 sein eigenes Büro. Seit 1995 ist er Professor an der Universität Stuttgart, wo er die Nachfolge von Frei Otto als Leiter des Instituts für Leichtbau antrat. Zu seinen Projekten zählen die École Nationale d'Art Décoratif mit Finn Geipel und Nicolas Michelin (Limoges, Frankreich, 1991–94), die Fassade der Interbank mit Hans Hollein (Lima, Peru, 1996–99), das Privatwohnhaus R128 (Stuttgart, 1998–2000), der neue internationale Flughafen Bangkok mit Murphy/Jahn (Thailand, 1995–2004), das Mercedes-Benz Museum mit UNStudio (Stuttgart, 2003–06), das H16 (Tieringen, 2005–06, hier vorgestellt), die Altarüberdachung für Papst Benedikt XVI. (München, 2006) sowie Messepavillons für Audi und BMW. 2007 gründeten Klaus Sedlbauer und Werner Sobek gemeinschaftlich die Firma WSGreenTechnologies in Stuttgart. WSGreenTechnologies „bietet einen integrierten Planungsprozess für alle Arten von Gebäuden. Dieser Planungsprozess berücksichtigt alle Phasen eines Lebenszyklus des Gebäudes. Die hierbei behandelten Fragen umfassen das thermische, akustische und visuelle Wohlbefinden sowie den Bereich der Biokompatibilität z. B. in Bezug auf mögliche Emissionen durch die in Betracht gezogenen Baustoffe."

WERNER SOBEK, né en 1953 à Aalen, Allemagne, a étudié l'architecture et l'ingénierie civile à l'université de Stuttgart (1974–80), et a effectué des recherches approfondies sur les « structures légères de grande portée » dans le même cadre (1980–86). Il a reçu son diplôme de Ph.D. en ingénierie civile de la même université en 1987. Il a été ingénieur structurel à l'agence Schlaich, Bergermann & Partner (Stuttgart, 1987–91), avant de créer sa propre structure en 1991. Depuis 1995, il est professeur à l'université de Stuttgart où il a succédé à Frei Otto au poste de directeur de l'Institut des structures légères. Parmi ses réalisations : l'École nationale d'art décoratif avec Finn Geipel et Nicolas Michelin (Limoges, France, 1991–94) ; la façade de l'Interbank avec Hans Hollein (Lima, Pérou, 1996–99) ; la maison R128 (Stuttgart, Allemagne, 1998–2000) ; le nouvel aéroport international de Bangkok avec Murphy/Jahn (Thaïlande, 1995–2004) ; le musée Mercedes-Benz avec UNStudio (Stuttgart, Allemagne, 2003–06) ; H16 (Tieringen, Allemagne, 2005–06, publié ici) ; l'autel pour Benoît XVI (Munich, Allemagne, 2006) et des pavillons de foire commerciale pour Audi et BMW. En 2007, Klaus Sedlbauer et Werner Sobek ont fondé WSGreenTechnologies à Stuttgart. WSGreenTechnologies « offre la programmation intégrée de bâtiments prenant en compte toutes les phases de la construction, de l'utilisation et de la déconstruction. Ceci comprend également le confort thermique, acoustique et visuel ainsi que les questions de biocompatibilité, dans la mesure de possibles émissions des matériaux utilisés dans la construction ».

H16

Tieringen, Germany, 2005–06

Floor area: 454 m². Client: Helmut and Georgia Link. Cost: not disclosed

Seen from a distance the house adapts a decidedly discreet profile, integrating glass and stone elements in an unexpected way.

Aus der Ferne gesehen beweist das Haus ein ausgesprochen diskretes Profil und kombiniert Elemente aus Glas und Stein auf überraschende Weise.

Vue à distance, la maison présente un profil volontairement discret, intégrant divers éléments en verre ou en pierre de façon inattendue.

This house is described as a logical progression and improvement on the widely published R128 house. Located south of Stuttgart, the structure seeks "maximum transparency and a minimum of structure, full recyclability … and zero emissions." Careful attention was also paid to the integration of the house into its site. An all-glass cube, shielded from the street by a hedge, contains an open living space, while a second, black cube, located below, houses private spaces. A third, light-colored cube, connected to the black cube by a steel terrace, contains the garage and utilities room. The supporting steel structure of the entire house can be dismantled "within a couple of days." The black volume is built with prefabricated architectural concrete sections. Geothermal heating with a heat pump, as well as photovoltaic panels, reduces energy consumption. The sophisticated climate control system also contributes to a minimum use of electricity. The architects write, not without a certain amount of pride: "H16 is a tribute to outstanding icons of modern architecture, such as the ones designed by Mies van der Rohe. The building combines sustainability (by zero emissions and full recyclability), state-of-the-art design, and first-class building technologies, thus making it an achievement from an architectural, technical, and aesthetic point of view.

Dieses Wohnhaus wurde als logische Fortführung und Verfeinerung des weithin bekannten R128 bezeichnet. Der im Süden von Stuttgart gelegene Bau strebt nach „maximaler Transparenz und einem Minimum an Struktur, vollständiger Reclyingfähigkeit … und Emissionsfreiheit". Besondere Aufmerksamkeit galt der Einbindung des Hauses in sein Umfeld. In einem voll verglasten Kubus, der zur Straße hin durch eine Hecke abgeschirmt ist, befindet sich ein offener Wohnbereich; in einem zweiten darunterliegenden schwarzen Kubus liegen private Räume. In einem dritten, hellgrauen Kubus, der über eine Stahlterrasse mit dem schwarzen Kubus verbunden ist, sind Garage und Haustechnik untergebracht. Das tragende Stahlgerüst des gesamten Hauses lässt sich „innerhalb weniger Tage" demontieren. Der schwarze Baukörper wurde aus Betonfertigbauteilen errichtet. Eine Erdwärmeheizung mit Wärmepumpe sowie Solarmodule reduzieren den Energieverbrauch. Auch das ausgefeilte Klimasteuerungssystem trägt zur Minimierung des Stromverbrauchs bei. Die Architekten schreiben nicht ohne Stolz: „H16 ist eine Hommage an herausragende Ikonen der Architektur, wie etwa die Bauten Mies van der Rohes. Der Bau vereint Nachhaltigkeit (durch Emissionsfreiheit und vollständige Recycelbarkeit) mit anspruchsvollem Design und erstklassigen Bauverfahren, was es zu einer Leistung in architektonischer, technischer und ästhetischer Hinsicht macht."

Cette maison est présentée comme la progression logique et le perfectionnement du projet de la maison R128 largement publié. Située au sud de Stuttgart, elle recherche « un maximum de transparence et un minimum de structure, une recyclabilité totale… et zéro émissions ». Une grande attention a été portée à son intégration dans le site. Un cube entièrement vitré, protégé de la rue par une haie, contient un séjour ouvert, tandis qu'un second cube, noir cette fois, situé en dessous, abrite les chambres. Un troisième cube, de couleur claire, connecté au précédent par une terrasse en acier contient un garage et des pièces de service. La structure en acier qui soutient l'ensemble de la maison peut être démontée « en deux jours ». Le volume noir est en béton architectural préfabriqué. Un chauffage géothermique à pompe à chaleur ainsi que des panneaux photovoltaïques réduisent la consommation d'électricité. Le système sophistiqué de contrôle de la climatisation contribue également à ces économies. Les architectes précisent, non sans une certaine fierté : « H16 est un hommage aux icônes les plus célèbres de l'architecture moderne, comme celles conçues par Mies van der Rohe. Cette construction combine la durabilité (zéro émissions et recyclabilité totale), une conception d'avant-garde et des technologies de construction de haut niveau, qui en font un accomplissement sur les plans architecturaux, techniques et esthétiques. »

Seen from below, the glass box forming the upper level almost seems to
float on its base.

Von unten betrachtet scheint die
Glasbox der oberen Etage fast über
ihrem Sockel zu schweben.

Vu en contre-plongée, le cube vitré
du niveau supérieur semble flotter
au-dessus de sa base.

The upper volume of the house is an extremely light box made of glass, extending out to a wooden deck.

Le volume supérieur est une boîte vitrée extrêmement légère, qui se prolonge par une terrasse en bois.

Der obere Baukörper des Hauses ist eine extrem leichte Box aus Glas, an die sich eine Holzterrasse anschließt.

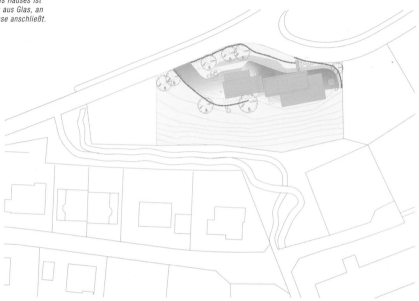

As might be expected, the interior of the house is very bright and open, an impression emphasized here by the choice of modern furniture.

Wie zu erwarten, ist das Interieur des Hauses hell und offen, ein Eindruck, der hier durch die Wahl moderner Möbel noch unterstrichen wird.

Comme on peut l'imaginer, l'intérieur de la maison est très ouvert et lumineux, impression renforcée par le choix d'un mobilier moderne.

If anything, the house proves that a
very modern house with large window
surfaces need not be considered
ecologically wasteful—in particular
with an engineer such as Werner
Sobek as its author.

*Das Haus stellt unter Beweis, dass
ein explizit moderner Bau mit großen
Fensterflächen keineswegs mit
Energieverschwendung einhergehen
muss – insbesondere, wenn ein
Ingenieur wie Werner Sobek für den
Bau verantwortlich zeichnet.*

*La maison prouve, entre autres,
qu'une résidence très moderne à
grandes baies vitrées peut éviter
les gaspillages énergétiques, en particulier lorsqu'un ingénieur comme
Werner Sobek en est l'auteur.*

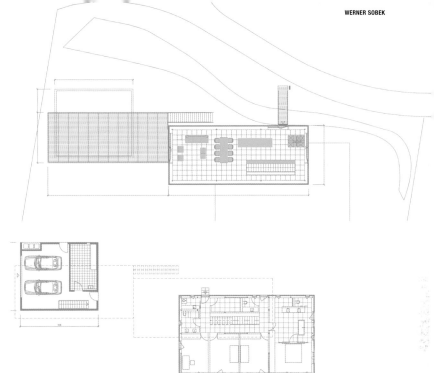

GERMÁN DEL SOL

Germán del Sol, Arquitecto
Camino Las Flores 11441
Las Condes, Santiago
Chile

Tel: +562 214 12 14
Fax: +562 214 11 47
E-mail: contacto@germandelsol.cl
Web: www.germandelsol.cl

GERMÁN DEL SOL was born in Santiago, Chile, in 1949. He graduated in 1973 from the Escuela Técnica Superior de Arquitectura de Barcelona, Spain. He created his own firm in Barcelona (1973–79) before returning to Santiago, where he worked on his own (1980–83), before spending two years in the office of R. Elmore in Palo Alto, California (1984–86). He then returned to his own practice in Santiago, where he has been based since 1986. Between 1988 and 1998, he created and directed Explora, a company dedicated to creating new travel destinations in remote places in South America. Between 1995 and 1998, he created and directed "Viña Gracia," a new Chilean vineyard. Germán del Sol then created and directed a new hot springs complex, next to the Villarrica Vulcano, in Pucón (Chile, 2001–05). His built work includes the Hotel Explora en Atacama (San Pedro de Atacama, 1998); horse stables (San Pedro de Atacama, 1999); saunas and pools (Atacama, 2000); Puritama Hot Springs Complex (Atacama, 2000); Geometricas Hot Springs Complex (Villarrica, 2004); Hotel Remota (Puerto Natales, Patagonia, 2005–06, published here); and Remota Spot (Patagonia, 2007), all in Chile. In 2008 he completed an apartment building in Vallecas (Madrid). He won the National Association of Chilean Architects Award in 2006.

GERMÁN DEL SOL wurde 1949 in Santiago, Chile, geboren. Sein Studium schloss er 1973 an der Escuela Técnica Superior de Arquitectura de Barcelona in Spanien ab. Nachdem er zunächst in Barcelona ein eigenes Büro betrieben hatte (1973–79), kehrte er nach Santiago zurück, wo er selbstständig arbeitete (1980–83), bevor er zwei Jahre lang für R. Elmore in Palo Alto, Kalifornien, tätig war (1984–86). Schließlich kehrte er zu seinem eigenen Büro in Santiago zurück, von wo aus er seit 1986 arbeitet. Von 1988 bis 1998 leitete er die von ihm gegründete Agentur Explora, die sich auf die Erschließung neuer Reiseziele an abgelegenen Orten Südamerikas spezialisiert hatte. Von 1995 bis 1998 führte er das von ihm gegründete chilenische Weingut Viña Gracia. Schließlich baute und leitete Germán del Sol auch eine Hotelanlage an den Thermalquellen am Vulkan Villarrica in Pucón (Chile, 2001–05). Zu seinen realisierten Projekten zählen das Hotel Explora en Atacama (San Pedro de Atacama, 1998), Pferdeställe (San Pedro de Atacama, 1999), Saunen und Pools (Wüste Atacama, 2000), die Thermalquellen Puritama (Wüste Atacama, 2000), der Thermalquellen-komplex Geometricas (Villarrica, 2004), das Hotel Remota (Puerto Natales, Patagonien, 2005–06, hier vorgestellt) sowie Remota Spot (Patagonien, 2007), alle in Chile. 2008 konnte ein Apartmentgebäude in Vallecas (Madrid) fertiggestellt werden. 2006 wurde er mit dem Preis des Nationalen Architektenverbands in Chile ausgezeichnet.

GERMÁN DEL SOL, né à Santiago, Chili, en 1949, est diplômé de la Escuela Técnica Superior de Arquitectura de Barcelona, Espagne (1973). Il fonde son agence à Barcelone (1973–79), avant de revenir à Santiago où il travaille à son compte (1980–83). Il collabore deux années avec l'agence de R. Elmore à Palo Alto, en Californie (1984–86), puis retourne à Santiago. De 1988 à 1998, il crée et dirige Explora, société qui propose de nouvelles destinations de voyages dans des lieux isolés d'Amérique du Sud. Entre 1995 et 1998, il fonde et dirige « Viña Gracia », un nouveau domaine viticole. Il a ensuite créé et dirigé un nouveau complexe touristique autour de sources d'eau chaude près du volcan de Villarrica, à Pucón (Chili, 2001–05). Parmi ses réalisations, toutes au Chili : l'hôtel Explora à Atacama (San Pedro de Atacama, 1998) ; des écuries (San Pedro de Atacama, 1999) ; des saunas et piscines (Atacama, 2000) ; le complexe thermal de Puritama (Atacama, 2000) ; le complexe thermal Geometricas (Villarrica, 2004) ; l'hôtel Remota (Puerto Natales, Patagonie, 2005–06, publié ici) et Remota Spot (Patagonie, 2007). En 2008, il a achevé un immeuble d'appartements à Vallecas (Madrid). Il a remporté le prix de l'Association nationale des architectes chiliens en 2006.

HOTEL REMOTA

Puerto Natales, Patagonia, Chile, 2005–06

Floor area: 5215 m². Client: Immobiliaria mares del sur. Cost: $9.5 million
Collaboration: José Luis Ibañez, Francisca Schüler, Carlos Venegas

Inspired by the sheep farming buildings of Patagonia, the Hotel Remota has a central courtyard occupied only by several boulders at its center. The architect states: "Latin America has an ancient tradition of architecture that stands in the midst of nature, where shepherds or merchants used to pass or stay the night, or where people gather once in a while to celebrate their ancient rites." Germán del Sol describes Remota as resembling a "big black barn" from a distance with an unexpectedly refined interior. Pillars, slabs, and interior walls are made of concrete. Waterproof industrial plywood panels coated with a synthetic asphalt membrane and a 25-centimeter-thick layer of expanded polyurethane cover the building and act as insulation. Double-glazed thermal window panes "form a continuous sequence of vertical openings in the exterior walls." The natural grasses found on the site are allowed to grow wild around the building, and on its landscaped roof. The three buildings that form the hotel are connected by wooden corridors. Within, the architect has placed spartan geometric dark wood furniture made by carpenters on site from dead wood culled in the Patagonian lowlands near the sea. Low-energy light bulbs, low-water consumption bathroom fittings, and an orientation intended to make use of passive solar energy are part of the overall sustainability strategy employed.

Das Hotel Remota, inspiriert von den Schaffarmen Patagoniens, hat einen zentralen Innenhof, in dem nur einige Findlinge liegen. Der Architekt erklärt: „Lateinamerika hat eine uralte architektonische Tradition von Bauten, die inmitten der Landschaft liegen, dort, wo einst Schäfer oder Händler vorüberzogen und die Nacht verbrachten oder sich Menschen versammelten, um uralte Riten zu feiern." Germán del Sol zufolge wirkt Remota aus der Ferne wie eine „große schwarze Scheune" mit unerwartet raffiniertem Interieur. Die Stützen, Plattenelemente und Innenwände sind aus Beton. Verkleidet und gedämmt wurde der Bau mit wasserfesten industriellen Sperrholzpaneelen, die mit einer synthetischen Asphaltmembran und einer 25 cm starken Schicht aus Polyurethan-Hartschaum ummantelt sind. Doppelwärmeschutzfenster „bilden eine uniforme Sequenz vertikaler Öffnungen in den Außenwänden". Die auf dem Gelände beheimateten natürlichen Gräser wachsen wild um das Gebäude ebenso wie auf dem begrünten Dach. Die drei Baukörper sind durch Holzkorridore miteinander verbunden. Die Innenräume stattete der Architekt mit spartanischen geometrischen dunklen Holzmöbeln aus, die von Schreinern vor Ort aus totem Holz aus der patagonischen Tiefebene an der Küste gefertigt wurden. Energiesparlampen, wassersparende Installationen in den Bädern und die Ausrichtung des Baus für die passive Nutzung von Solarenergie sind Bestandteil der hier angewandten Nachhaltigkeitsstrategie.

Inspiré des formes des bergers de Patagonie, l'hôtel Remota se caractérise par une cour centrale uniquement occupée en son centre par quelques rochers. L'architecte explique ainsi son projet : « L'Amérique latine possède une tradition ancienne d'architecture en pleine nature, où bergers et colporteurs séjournaient ou passaient la nuit, où des gens se réunissaient de temps en temps pour célébrer des rites anciens. » Il considère Remota comme « une grosse grange noire » vue de loin, mais possédant un intérieur au raffinement inattendu. Les piliers, les dalles des sols et les murs intérieurs sont en béton. Le bâtiment est habillé et isolé par des panneaux industriels en contreplaqué à membrane d'asphalte synthétique et couche de polyuréthane expansé de 25 cm d'épaisseur. Des fenêtres à double vitrage de verre thermique « forment une séquence continue d'ouvertures verticales dans les murs extérieurs ». Les herbes naturelles trouvées sur le site grandissent librement autour du bâtiment et sur son toit végétalisé. Les trois constructions qui constituent l'hôtel sont réunies par des corridors en bois. À l'intérieur, l'architecte a disposé un mobilier en bois de formes géométriques spartiate, réalisé sur place par les menuisiers à l'aide de bois mort récupéré dans les marais patagoniens au bord de la mer. Des ampoules à basse consommation, des équipements de salles de bains qui économisent l'eau, et une orientation qui favorise l'utilisation passive de l'énergie solaire font partie de la stratégie de durabilité utilisée.

Lying low in the ground, with its three buildings connected by wooden corridors, the hotel has a somewhat austere appearance.

Das Hotel besteht aus drei durch Holzgänge verbundene Bauten. Es scheint sich dicht an den Boden zu kauern und wirkt geradezu streng.

Se détachant à peine du sol, les trois bâtiments de l'hôtel reliés par des corridors en bois sont d'aspect assez austère.

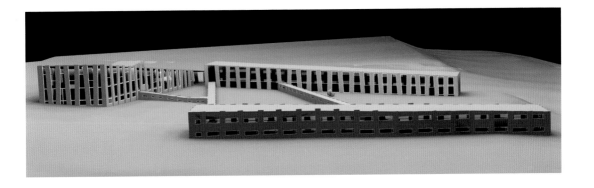

Even the landscaping of the hotel
participates in its overall impression
of frugality generated by the architects in this sparse natural setting.

Selbst die Gestaltung der Umgebung des Hotels trägt zum beinahe
spartanischen Gesamteindruck bei,
den die Architekten in dieser kargen
Landschaft geschaffen haben.

Même l'aménagement paysager
participe à l'impression générale
d'économie de moyens voulue
par les architectes pour ce cadre
naturel sévère.

Although simple, the interiors give a greater impression of warmth than the outside of the hotel.

Trotz seiner Schlichtheit vermittelt das Interieur mehr Wärme als die Außenansicht des Hotels.

Bien que sobres, les intérieurs sont plus chaleureux que l'aspect extérieur de l'hôtel.

STUDIO TAMASSOCIATI

studio tamassociati
2731 Dorsoduro
30123 Venice
Italy

Tel/Fax: +39 0415 226 974
E-mail: info@tamassociati.org
Web: www.tamassociati.org

Raul Pantaleo was born in Milan in 1962. He attended the IUAV (Istituto Universitario di Architettura di Venezia) in Italy, and holds an international certificate in Human Ecology obtained through postgraduate studies at the University of Padua. Massimo Lepore was born in Udine, Italy, in 1960. He graduated from the IUAV. He completed postgraduate studies in Urban and Environmental Requalification at the "Taller de Arquitectura y Urbanismo" (Municipality of Lleida, Spain). Simone Sfriso was born in London in 1966. She also graduated from the IUAV and now works as advisor and teaching assistant for courses in Urban Planning at the IUAV. They created **STUDIO TAMASSOCIATI** for "socially conscious design and communication" in 2001. Based in Venice, the firm works mainly for public institutions and NGOs. They develop projects for public spaces and hospital projects for NGOs in the Sudan (see the Salam Center for Cardiac Surgery, Soba Hilla, Khartoum, 2006–07, published here), Democratic Republic of Congo, Central African Republic, and Nicaragua. Their work includes Banca Popolare Etica headquarters (Padua, Italy, 2004–07); a redesign of the Marconi Square (San Giorgio Piacentino, Italy, 2007); San Giacomo del Martignone Urban Park (Anzola dell'Emilia, Italy, 2007); and a project for a children's hospital (Bangui, Central African Republic, 2007).

Raul Pantaleo wurde 1962 in Mailand geboren. Er besuchte das Istituto Universitario di Architettura di Venezia (IUAV) in Italien und erwarb mit Abschluss eines Postgraduiertenprogramms an der Universität Padua ein internationales Zertifikat in Ökologie. Massimo Lepore wurde 1960 in Udine geboren. Seinen Abschluss machte er ebenfalls am IUAV. Er absolvierte ein Postgraduiertenprogramm in urbaner und ökologischer Wiederaufbereitung an der Taller de Arquitectura y Urbanismo (Lleida, Spanien). Simone Sfriso wurde 1966 in London geboren. Auch sie machte ihren Abschluss am IUAV und ist dort inzwischen als Beraterin und Lehrassistentin für Stadtplanung tätig. Gemeinsam gründeten sie 2001 das **STUDIO TAMASSOCIATI** für „sozial verantwortliche Planung und Kommunikation". Die in Venedig ansässige Firma arbeitet hauptsächlich für öffentliche Träger und Nichtregierungsorganisationen (NGOs). Sie arbeiten an Projekten für öffentliche Einrichtungen und Krankenhäuser von NGOs im Sudan (Zentrum für Herzchirurgie „Salam", Soba Hilla, Khartoum, 2006–07, hier vorgestellt), in der Demokratischen Republik Kongo, der Zentralafrikanischen Republik und Nicaragua. Weitere Projekte sind u. a. der Hauptsitz der Banca Popolare Etica (Padua, Italien, 2004–07), die Umgestaltung der Piazza Marconi (San Giorgio Piacentino, Italien, 2007), der Stadtpark in San Giacomo del Martignone (Anzola dell'Emilia, Italien, 2007) sowie ein Kinderkrankenhausprojekt (Bangui, Zentralafrikanische Republik, 2007).

Raul Pantaleo, né à Milan en 1962, a étudié à Venise à l'IUAV (Istituto Universitario di Architettura di Venezia), et, après des études supérieures à l'université de Padoue, a passé un diplôme en écologie humaine. Massimo Lepore, né à Udine, Italie, en 1960, est également diplômé de l'IUAV de Venise. Il a effectué des études supérieures en requalification urbaine et environnementale au « Taller de Arquitectura y Urbanismo » (Lleida, Espagne). Simone Sfriso, née à Londres en 1966, est elle aussi diplômée de l'IUAV et travaille maintenant comme conseillère et assistante d'enseignement pour les cours d'urbanisme de l'IUAV. Ils ont créé ensemble le **STUDIO TAMASSOCIATI**, « conception et communication socialement responsables », en 2001. Basée à Venise, cette agence travaille principalement pour des institutions publiques et des ONG. Elle met au point des projets d'espaces publics et d'hôpitaux pour des ONG au Soudan (Centre Salam de chirurgie cardiaque, Soba Hilla, Khartoum, 2006–07, publié ici), en République démocratique du Congo, République centrafricaine et au Nicaragua. Parmi leurs interventions : le siège social de la Banca Popolare Etica (Padoue, Italie, 2004–07) ; la rénovation de la place Marconi (San Giorgio Piacentino, Italie, 2007) ; le parc urbain San Giacomo del Martignone (Anzola dell'Emilia, Italie, 2007) et un projet d'hôpital pour enfants (Bangui, République centrafricaine, 2007).

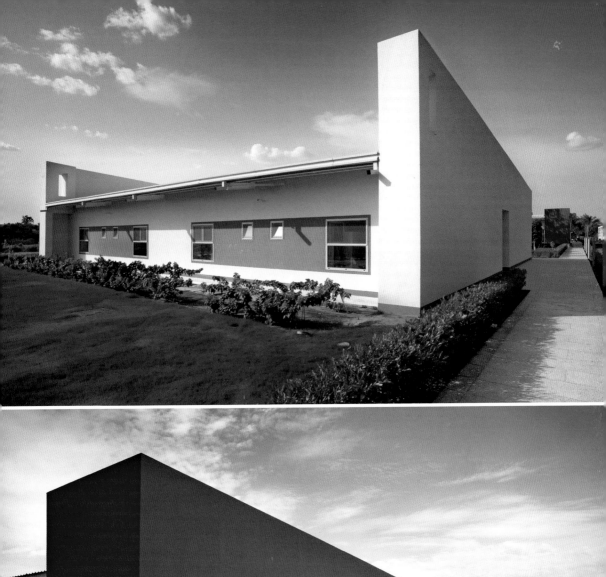

SALAM CENTER FOR CARDIAC SURGERY

Soba Hilla, Khartoum, Republic of Sudan, 2006–07

*Floor area: 11 000 m². Client: Emergency NGO. Cost: €6 million
Collaboration: Raul Pantaleo, Simone Sfriso, Massimo Lepore,
Sebastiano Crescini with Pietro Parrino and Gino Strada*

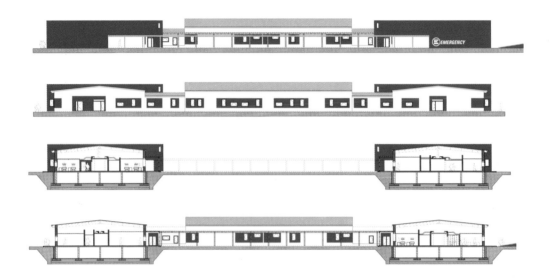

Emergency is an Italian NGO that provides free medical treatment to the civilian victims of war, landmines, and poverty. Emergency began work in North Darfur in 2004, and established their Center for Cardiac Surgery in Soba Hilla, 20 kilometers from Khartoum, in 2007. With a capacity of 63 beds and a 15-bed intensive-care unit, the center is organized around a "hollow" space formed by two existing mango trees. This traditional home design device, together with the low profile of the buildings, is intended to give people a sense that they are not lost when entering the facility. Studio tamassociati insists on the homelike atmosphere of the center, a decided contrast to many medical facilities and a useful initiative in this war-torn country. A 58-centimeter-thick wall made of two layers of bricks separated by an insulating air cavity, with small windows and high-performance glass panels, provides a first protection from local heat. Traditional thatched roofs are used for paths and rest areas. Some 1000 square meters of solar panels serve to greatly reduce energy consumption, while a system of tunnels and water vapor spray reduces ambient dust coming into the innovative chilling system. All of these measures are carefully thought-out reactions to the local situation, and to the architectural "honesty" of the project.

Emergency ist eine italienische NGO, die zivilen Opfern von Krieg, Landminen und Armut kostenlose ärztliche Hilfe bietet. Emergency ist seit 2004 in Nord-Darfur aktiv und gründete 2007 ein Zentrum für Herzchirurgie in Soba Hilla, 20 km südöstlich von Khartoum. Das Zentrum hat eine Kapazität von 63 Betten sowie eine Intensivstation mit 15 Betten und organisiert sich um einen offenen Hof, der um zwei vorhandene Mangobäume herum entstand. Die traditionelle Wohnbauform und niedrige Bauweise sollen verhindern, dass sich die Menschen verloren fühlen, wenn sie die Einrichtung betreten. Studio tamassociati legt besonderen Wert auf die häusliche Atmosphäre des Zentrums, ein bewusst gewählter Gegensatz zu den zahlreichen medizinischen Einrichtungen in diesem kriegsgebeutelten Land. 58 cm dicke Mauern aus zwei Backsteinschichten mit einer dazwischenliegenden isolierenden Luftschicht und kleinen Fenstern ebenso wie hochdämmende Glasscheiben sorgen für ausgezeichneten Schutz vor der Hitze. Pfade und Ruheplätze werden von traditionellen Grasdächern beschirmt. 1000 m² Solarmodule tragen dazu bei, den Energie-verbrauch drastisch zu senken. Ein Tunnel- und Wasserdampfsprühsystem mindert das Eindringen von Staub in das innovative Kühlsystem. Sämtliche Maßnahmen wurden sorgsam im Hinblick auf die Gegebenheiten vor Ort und die architektonische Authentizität des Projekts ausgearbeitet.

Emergency est une ONG italienne qui fournit des services médicaux gratuits aux victimes civiles de guerres, de mines et de la pauvreté. Elle a commencé à travailler au nord du Darfour en 2004 et a fondé un centre de chirurgie cardiaque à Soba Hilla, à 20 km de Khartoum en 2007. Avec une capacité de 63 lits et une unité de soins intensifs de 15 lits, ce centre s'organise autour d'un espace « en creux » formé par deux manguiers existants. Ce plan de maison traditionnelle ainsi que la faible hauteur des bâtiments veut donner aux patients le sentiment qu'ils ne sont pas perdus dans un univers étranger lorsqu'ils arrivent au Centre. Studio tamassociati insiste sur son atmosphère de maison, contraste marqué avec beaucoup d'installations médicales et initiative louable dans ce pays déchiré par la guerre. Un mur de 58 cm d'épaisseur composé de deux pans de briques séparés par une cavité d'air, de petites fenêtres et des panneaux de verre à haute performance offrent une protection de base contre la chaleur de la région. Les toitures traditionnelles en chaume sont utilisées pour ombrager les cheminements et les zones de repos. 1000 m² de panneaux solaires permettent de fortement réduire la consommation d'électricité achetée, tandis qu'un système de tunnels et de vaporisation d'eau diminue la pénétration de la poussière dans une installation innovante de refroidissement. Toutes ces mesures correspondent aux conditions locales et traduisent l'honnêteté architecturale de ce projet.

At first sight, the Salam Center appears to be surprisingly modern, in particular given its function and location near Khartoum.

Auf den ersten Blick wirkt das Salam Center überraschend modern, insbesondere angesichts seiner Aufgabe und Lage unweit von Khartoum.

À première vue, le centre Salam semble étonnamment moderne, en particulier si on considère sa fonction et son implantation à proximité de Khartoum.

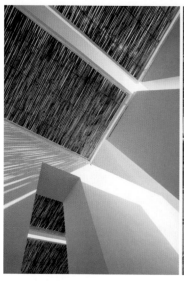

Some features of the design, like the screens seen here and the light, airy construction, make the appropriate nature of the intervention clearer.

Verschiedene Aspekte des Entwurfs wie die hier abgebildeten Sonnen-blenden und die leichte, luftige Bauart lassen die Angemessenheit dieser baulichen Intervention deut-licher werden.

Certaines caractéristiques du projet comme les pare-soleil visibles ici et le type de construction légère et aérée mis en œuvre expriment la nature bien adaptée de cette intervention.

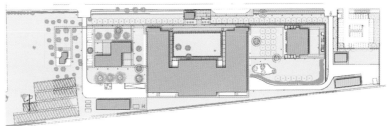

CHRIS TATE

Chris Tate Architecture Ltd.
Level 3, 93 The Strand
Parnell, Auckland
New Zealand

Tel: +64 21 608 996
E-mail: chris@christate.co.nz
Web: www.christate.co.nz

CHRIS TATE was born in 1971 in Auckland, New Zealand. He received a Bachelor of Social Science in Human Service from the Auckland College of Education (1994–97) and a Diploma in Architectural Technology from UNITEC Auckland (2004–05). He did social work for various agencies from 1990 to 2001, but during that period he also bought land on an island off the coast of Auckland and designed and built a house there. He left his social work in 2001 to manage the construction of a large house on the same island designed by Richard Priest. In 2006 he created Chris Tate Architecture and completed his first project, Forest House (Titirangi, Auckland, 2006, published here).

CHRIS TATE wurde 1971 in Auckland, Neuseeland, geboren. Er erwarb einen Bachelor in Sozialwissenschaften am Auckland College of Education (1994–97) und ein Diplom in Architektur an der UNITEC Auckland (2004–05). Von 1990 bis 2001 war er für verschiedene Organisationen im sozialen Bereich tätig, kaufte währenddessen aber auch Land auf einer Insel vor der Küste von Auckland und entwarf und baute dort ein Haus. 2001 gab er seine Tätigkeit als Sozialarbeiter auf, um auf derselben Insel die Aufsicht über den Bau eines großen Hauses zu übernehmen, das er für Richard Priest entworfen hatte. 2006 gründete er Chris Tate Architecture und realisierte sein erstes Projekt, das Forest House (Titirangi, Auckland, 2006, hier vorgestellt).

CHRIS TATE, né en 1971 à Auckland, en Nouvelle-Zélande, est Bachelor en sciences humaines et sociales du Auckland College of Education (1994–97), et diplômé en technologie architecturale de UNITEC Auckland (2004–05). Il a participé à différentes interventions sociales pour diverses agences de 1990 à 2001, et pendant cette période s'est acheté un terrain sur une île de la côte d'Auckland où il s'est construit une maison. Il a quitté son travail dans les services sociaux pour diriger la construction d'une vaste maison conçue par Richard Priest sur la même île. En 2006, il a fondé l'agence Chris Tate Architecture et a achevé son premier projet, Forest House (Titirangi, Auckland, 2006, publié ici).

FOREST HOUSE

Titirangi, Auckland, New Zealand, 2006

Floor area: 100 m². Client: Chris Tate. Cost: €150 000

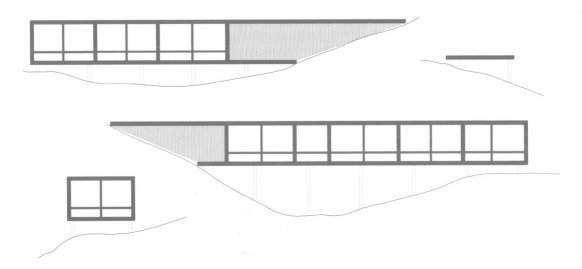

This house was built on a densely forested and steep 800-square-meter lot. Entering the house, visitors are required to descend 45 steps to reach the entrance. According to Chris Tate: "The site is slip sensitive, flood prone, and is protected by the local building authority as a 'Protected Environment.'" Including one bedroom, a study and a bathroom, with an open-plan living, dining, and kitchen area, the house is intended as "an interpretation of Philip Johnson's 1949 Glass House" (New Canaan, Connecticut, USA). A building platform was created on 16 poles across a gully and this glass box was set on it, cantilevered in all directions "to create a floating feeling." The precise site was selected to minimize tree removal, and New Zealand native trees were planted after construction. The house was designed to stop at a large Pururi (arched tree), saving it from being cut. A black-and-white color scheme was chosen in order to contrast with the green forest environment. Tate was allowed to build on the site because of the "low environmental impact" of the design. The floor inside the house is made of rough eucalyptus wood painted in high-gloss white.

Das Haus wurde auf ein dicht bewaldetes, steiles 800 m² großes Grundstück gebaut. Besucher müssen zuerst 45 Stufen hinabsteigen, um zum Hauseingang zu gelangen. Chris Tate erklärt: „Das Grundstück ist erdrutsch- und überschwemmungsgefährdet und wurde von der örtlichen Baubehörde als Naturschutzgebiet ausgewiesen." Das Haus mit einem Schlafzimmer, Arbeitszimmer, Bad und einem offenen Wohn-, Ess- und Küchenbereich wurde als „Interpretation von Philip Johnsons Glass House von 1949" (New Canaan, Connecticut, USA) gestaltet. Über einem Regenwasserablauf wurde eine Gebäudeplattform auf 16 Stützen aufgeständert. Hierauf wurde der Glaskubus platziert. Dieser kragt nach allen Seiten aus, um „einen schwebenden Eindruck" zu vermitteln. Die Lage des Baugrunds wurde so gewählt, dass nicht zu viele Bäume gefällt werden mussten; auch ein großer Pururi-Baum konnte stehen bleiben. Nach Bauabschluss wurden heimische Bäume angepflanzt. Schwarz und Weiß stehen in Kontrast zur grünen Waldumgebung. Tate erhielt seine Baugenehmigung auch wegen des „geringen Eingriffs in die Umwelt". Der Boden im Innern des Hauses wurde aus rohem Eukalyptusholz gefertigt und glänzend weiß lackiert.

Cette maison a été édifiée sur un terrain de 800 m², incliné et abondamment planté d'arbres. Pour entrer, le visiteur doit d'abord descendre 45 marches. Selon Chris Tate : « Le site, qui pourrait être sujet à des glissements de terrain et des inondations, est classé par la réglementation locale en "environnement protégé" ». Comprenant une chambre, un bureau et une salle de bains, un séjour de plan ouvert, une zone pour la préparation et la prise des repas, la maison se veut « une interprétation de la Maison de verre de Philip Johnson » (1949, New Canaan, Connecticut, États-Unis). Une plate-forme située au-dessus d'un ravin a d'abord été mise en place. Elle repose sur 16 pieux et soutient la boîte de verre, elle-même en porte-à-faux dans toutes les directions « pour créer une sensation de flottement ». L'implantation précise a été déterminée de façon à limiter le nombre d'arbres à supprimer. Des arbres d'essences locales ont été replantés après le chantier. La maison s'est volontairement arrêtée devant un grand pururi (arbre arqué) pour ne pas avoir à le couper. Le noir et le blanc ont été choisis pour contraster avec l'environnement forestier vert. Tate a eu le droit de construire sur ce terrain parce que le projet n'exerçait qu'un « faible impact environnemental ». Le sol intérieur est en planches brutes d'eucalyptus peintes en blanc laqué brillant.

The Forest House is indeed carefully inserted into its site, abutting the earth on one side, bridging a gully, and entirely surrounded by existing trees.

Das Forest Haus wurde außerordentlich umsichtig in sein Umfeld integriert – auf der einen Seite am Boden „andockend", überbrückt es einen Regenwasserablauf und ist rundum von Bäumen umgeben.

La « maison de la forêt » est soigneusement insérée dans son site, butant contre le relief d'un côté, franchissant un ruisseau et entièrement entourée d'arbres.

The interior of the house retains a modern if not modernist spirit, rendered more surprising by the almost invasive presence of nature all around its windows.

Das Interieur ist modern, wenn nicht modernistisch gehalten, was angesichts der geradezu invasiven Präsenz der Natur vor den Fenstern umso überraschender wirkt.

L'intérieur de la maison conserve un esprit moderne, voire moderniste, rendu plus étonnant encore par la présence presque envahissante de la nature devant les fenêtres.

TNA

TNA Co., Ltd.
9–7–3F Sumiyoshityou
Sinjuku-ku, Tokyo 162–0065
Japan

Tel: +81 3 3225 1901
Fax: +81 3 3225 1902
E-mail: mail@tna-arch.com
Web: www.tna-arch.com

Makoto Takei was born in Tokyo in 1974. He graduated from the Department of Architecture at Tokai University in 1997. Between 1997 and 1999 he was at the Tsukamoto Laboratory, Graduate School of Science and Engineering, Tokyo Institute of Technology, and worked with Atelier Bow-Wow. Between 1999 and 2000 he worked in the office of Tezuka Architects, before establishing **TNA** (Takei-Nabeshima-Architects) with Chie Nabeshima. Chie Nabeshima was born in Kanagawa in 1975 and graduated from the course in Habitation and Space Design, Department of Architecture and Architectural Engineering, College of Industrial Technology, Nihon University (1998), before working at Tezuka Architects (1998–2005) and cofounding TNA. Their projects include the Wood Wear House (Hayama, Kanagawa, 2005); Color Concrete House (Yokohama, Kanagawa, 2005); Ring House (Karuizawa, Nagano, 2006); Wood Ship Café (Hayama, Kanagawa, 2007); and the Mosaic House (Meguro-ku, Tokyo, 2006–07, published here), all in Japan.

Makoto Takei wurde 1974 in Tokio geboren. Sein Studium an der Fakultät für Architektur der Tokai-Universität schloss er 1997 ab. Von 1997 bis 1999 war er am Tsukamoto-Labor der Graduiertenschule für Natur- und Ingenieurwissenschaften am Tokyo Institute of Technology tätig und arbeitete für das Atelier Bow-Wow. Von 1999 bis 2000 arbeitete er für Tezuka Architects, bevor er mit Chie Nabeshima das Büro **TNA** (Takei-Nabeshima-Architects) gründete. Chie Nabeshima wurde 1975 in Kanagawa geboren und machte ihren Abschluss in Wohn- und Raumgestaltung an der Fakultät für Architektur und Bauingenieurwesen am College für Industrietechnik der Universität Nihon (1998), bevor sie für Tezuka Architects (1998–2005) arbeitete und TNA mitbegründete. Zu ihren Projekten zählen das Wood Wear House (Hayama, Kanagawa, 2005), das Color Concrete House (Yokohama, Kanagawa, 2005), das Ring House (Karuizawa, Nagano, 2006), das Wood Ship Café (Hayama, Kanagawa, 2007) sowie das Mosaic House (Meguro-ku, Tokyo, 2006–07, hier vorgestellt).

Makoto Takei, né à Tokyo en 1974, est diplômé du Département d'architecture de l'université Tokai (1997). De 1997 à 1999, il a étudié au Laboratoire Tsukamoto de l'École supérieure de sciences et d'ingénierie de l'Institut de technologie de Tokyo, et a travaillé pour l'Atelier Bow-Wow. De 1999 à 2000, il a été employé par Tezuka Architects avant de fonder l'agence **TNA** (Takei-Nabeshima-Architects) avec Chie Nabeshima. Chie Nabeshima, née à Kanagawa en 1975, est diplômée de conception de logements et d'espaces du Département d'architecture et d'ingénierie architecturale du Collège de technologie industrielle de l'université Nihon (1998), avant de travailler pour Tezuka Architects (1998–2005) et de fonder TNA. Parmi leurs projets : la Wood Wear House (Hayama, Kanagawa, 2005) ; la Color Concrete House (Yokohama, Kanagawa, 2005) ; la Ring House (Karuizawa, Nagano, 2006) ; le Wood Ship Café (Hayama, Kanagawa, 2007) et la Mosaic House (Meguro-ku, Tokyo, 2006–07, publiée ici).

MOSAIC HOUSE

Meguro-ku, Tokyo, Japan, 2006–07

Floor area: 84.5 m². Client: not disclosed. Cost: not disclosed

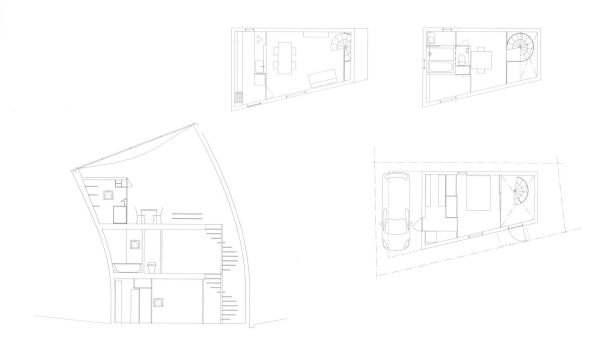

Built in a former parking lot for a couple with one child, this house is typical in its size of the numerous very small residences being designed in Japan, especially in densely built cities like Tokyo. Clad in white mosaic tile, the house appears to lean toward the "south sky like a sunflower." This orientation and the size of the skylight mean that the interior of the residence is flooded with light, despite its rather closed façades. The idea that nature can be present in the city and in architecture through such elements as light or wind is a particularly Japanese one, but one that is perfectly justified, especially in the urban matrix of Tokyo, where little space is left for nature in its more traditional representations (as in the gardens of the Imperial Palace). With this residence, or other realizations, such as their Ring House, the architects of TNA have shown a particular interest in nature and the environment, depending on location and their own sensitivity.

Die Größe des auf einem ehemaligen Parkplatz erbauten Hauses für ein Paar mit Kind ist typisch für die zahlreichen kleinen Wohnbauten, die in Japan entworfen werden, insbesondere in dicht besiedelten Städten wie Tokio. Das mit weißen Mosaikfliesen verblendete Haus neigt sich zum „südlichen Himmel wie eine Sonnenblume". Durch die Ausrichtung des Baus und die Größe des Oberlichtfensters sind die Innenräume trotz der eher geschlossenen Fassaden lichtdurchflutet. Der Gedanke, dass die Natur durch Elemente wie Licht oder Wind in Stadt und Architektur präsent sein kann, mag typisch japanisch sein, gerade in der urbanen Matrix Tokios ist er aber absolut gerechtfertigt, wo für die Natur und ihre traditionelleren Erscheinungsformen (etwa die Gärten des Kaiserpalasts) nur wenig Platz bleibt. Mit diesem Wohnhaus und anderen Projekten wie dem Ring House haben die Architekten von TNA je nach Lage der Grundstücke und mit dem ihnen eigenen Einfühlungsvermögen besonderes Interesse an Natur und Umwelt bewiesen.

Construite sur un ancien parking pour un couple et son enfant, cette maison est typiquement japonaise dans la petitesse de ses dimensions, fréquente dans les villes très densément construites comme Tokyo. Parée de mosaïque blanche, elle semble s'orienter vers le « Sud et le ciel comme un tournesol ». Cette orientation et la taille de la verrière signifient que l'intérieur est baigné de lumière malgré des façades assez fermées. L'idée que la nature puisse rester présente dans la ville et son architecture à travers des éléments tels que la lumière ou le vent est une vision très japonaise, mais parfaitement justifiée, en particulier dans la matrice urbaine tokyoïte où peu de place est laissée à la nature, même dans ses schémas traditionnels (comme les jardins du Palais impérial). Dans cette résidence et d'autres réalisations dont leur Ring House, les architectes de TNA montrent leur sensibilité particulière pour la nature et l'environnement en fonction du contexte.

The house quite literally takes a bow to the sky, channeling natural light inside while shielding it from excessive heat gain.

Das Haus verneigt sich buchstäblich vor dem Himmel, lässt Tageslicht in den Bau und schützt ihn zugleich vor allzu starker Wärmeentwicklung.

La maison s'incline littéralement devant le ciel, pour lui permettre de canaliser l'éclairage naturel vers l'intérieur tout en la protégeant d'un gain solaire excessif.

Contrary to external appearances
that show only a few small windows,
the house is flooded with light from
above.

Anders als die nur wenige kleine
Fenster zeigenden Außenaufnahmen
vermuten lassen, ist das Haus von
oben her lichtdurchflutet.

Contrairement aux apparences –
seules quelques petites fenêtres sont
visibles – la maison est illuminée de
lumière zénithale.

Furnished in sparse fashion, which is typical of Japan, the house has high spaces and is suffused constantly with natural light.

Das Haus ist sparsam möbliert, was für Japan typisch ist; seine hohen Räume erhalten den ganzen Tag über natürliches Licht.

La maison est meublée avec sobriété, à la japonaise, et ses hauts volumes bénéficient toute la journée de l'éclairage naturel.

UNSTUDIO

UNStudio
Stadhouderskade 113 / 1073 AJ Amsterdam / The Netherlands
Tel: +31 20 570 20 40 / Fax: +31 20 570 20 41
E-mail: info@unstudio.com / Web: www.unstudio.com

Ben van Berkel was born in Utrecht in 1957 and studied at the Rietveld Academy in Amsterdam and at the Architectural Association (AA) in London, receiving the AA Diploma with honors in 1987. After working briefly in the office of Santiago Calatrava in 1988, he set up his practice in Amsterdam with Caroline Bos. He has been a Visiting Professor at Columbia and a visiting critic at Harvard (1994). He was a Diploma Unit Master at the AA (1994–95). As well as the Erasmus Bridge in Rotterdam (inaugurated in 1996), **UNSTUDIO** built the Karbouw and ACOM office buildings (1989–93), the REMU Electricity Station (1989–93), all in Amersfoort; and housing projects and the Aedes East Gallery for Kristin Feireiss in Berlin. More recent projects include an extension of the Rijksmuseum Twente (Enschede, 1992–96); the Möbius House (Naarden, 1993–98); and Het Valkhof Museum (Nijmegen, 1998); NMR Laboratory (Utrecht, 1997–2000), all in the Netherlands; a switching station (Innsbruck, Austria, 1998–2001); an electrical substation (Innsbruck, Austria, 2002); the Mercedes-Benz Museum (Stuttgart, Germany, 2003–06); VilLA NM (Upstate New York, 2000–07); a music facility (Graz, Austria, 1998–2008); the Arnhem Station (Arnhem, the Netherlands, 1986–2011); the IBG (Informatie Beheer Groep) and Tax Offices (Groningen, the Netherlands, 2007–11); and Post Rotterdam (Rotterdam, the Netherlands, 2008–12), the last two published here. UNStudio was also a participant in the competition for the new World Trade Center in New York, in collaboration with Foreign Office Architects, Greg Lynn FORM, Imaginary Forces, Kevin Kennon, and Reiser + Umemoto, RUR, under the name of United Architects.

Ben van Berkel wurde 1957 in Utrecht geboren und studierte an der Rietveld-Akademie in Amsterdam und an der Architectural Association (AA) in London, wo er 1987 sein Diplom mit Auszeichnung erhielt. Nach kurzer Tätigkeit für Santiago Calatrava gründete er 1988 mit Caroline Bos sein Büro in Amsterdam. Er war Gastprofessor an der Columbia University in New York und Gastkritiker in Harvard (1994). 1994 bis 1995 war er Diploma Unit Master an der AA. Neben der 1996 eingeweihten Erasmusbrücke in Rotterdam baute **UNSTUDIO** in Amersfoort die Bürogebäude für Karbouw und ACOM (1989–93) sowie das Kraftwerk REMU (1989–93), in Berlin entstanden Wohnbauprojekte und die Galerie Aedes East für Kristin Feireiss. Zu ihren Projekten zählen außerdem ein Erweiterungsbau für das Rijksmuseum in Twente (Enschede, 1992–96), das Haus Möbius (Naarden, 1993–98), das Museum Het Valkhof (Nimwegen, 1998) und das Labor NMR (Utrecht, 1997–2000), alle in den Niederlanden, ein Umspannwerk (Innsbruck, 1998–2001), ein Elektrizitätswerk (Innsbruck, 2002), das Mercedes-Benz Museum (Stuttgart, 2003–06), die VilLA NM (im Bundesstaat New York, 2000–07), ein Musiktheater (Graz, Austria, 1998–2008), der Bahnhof Arnheim (1986–2011) sowie Büros für die IBG (Informatie Beheer Groep) und das Finanzamt (Groningen, 2007–11) und die Post in Rotterdam (2008–12); die beiden Letzteren werden hier vorgestellt. Darüber hinaus beteiligte sich UNStudio am Wettbewerb für das neue World Trade Center in New York unter dem Namen United Architects gemeinsam mit Foreign Office Architects, Greg Lynn FORM, Imaginary Forces, Kevin Kennon und Reiser + Umemoto, RUR.

Ben van Berkel, né à Utrecht en 1957, étudie à la Rietveld Academie d'Amsterdam ainsi qu'à l'Architectural Association (AA) de Londres qu'il quitte diplômé avec mention en 1987. Après avoir brièvement travaillé pour Santiago Calatrava en 1988, il ouvre son agence à Amsterdam, avec Caroline Bos. Il a été professeur invité à l'université Columbia, New York, critique invité à Harvard en 1994, et responsable d'unité pour le diplôme de l'AA en 1994–95. En dehors du pont Érasme à Rotterdam (inauguré en 1996), **UNSTUDIO** a construit, à Amersfoort, les immeubles de bureaux Karbouw et ACOM (1989–93), la sous-station électrique REMU (1989–93) ; ainsi que des logements et la galerie Aedes East de Kristin Feireiss à Berlin. Parmi leurs projets plus récents : l'extension du Rijksmuseum Twente (Enschede, 1992–96) ; la maison Möbius (Naarden, 1993–98) ; le musée Het Valkhof (Nimègue, 1998) et le laboratoire NMR (Utrecht, 1997–2000), tous aux Pays-Bas ; un poste d'aiguillage (Innsbruck, Autriche, 1998–2001) ; une station électrique (Innsbruck, Autriche, 2002) ; le musée Mercedes-Benz (Stuttgart, Allemagne, 2003–06) ; la VilLA NM (État de New York, 2000–07) ; une salle de musique (Graz, Autriche, 1998–2008) ; la gare d'Arnhem (Pays-Bas, 1986–2011) ; l'immeuble de l'IBG (Informatie Beheer Groep) et de l'administration fiscale (Groningue, Pays-Bas, 2007–11) et Post Rotterdam (2008–12), tous deux publiés ici. UNStudio a participé au concours pour le World Trade Center à New York, en collaboration avec Foreign Office Architects, Greg Lynn FORM, Imaginary Forces, Kevin Kennon et Reiser + Umemoto, RUR, sous le nom de United Architects.

IBG AND TAX OFFICES

Groningen, The Netherlands, 2007–11

Floor area: 45 000 m². Client: DUO2 Consortium. Cost: not disclosed
Collaboration: Ben van Berkel, Caroline Bos, Gerard Loozekoot, Lars Nixdorff

The architects demonstrate with this
design that even very large offices for
governmental organizations can be
ecologically sound, and indeed set an
example for the private sector.

Mit diesem Entwurf stellen die
Architekten unter Beweis, dass
selbst Bürogroßbauten für Behörden
ökologisch verträglich sein können
und dem privaten Sektor als gutes
Beispiel vorangehen können.

Les architectes prouvent par ce projet
que même de très grands immeubles
de bureaux pour des organismes
gouvernementaux peuvent bénéficier
de la logique écologique et donner
l'exemple au secteur privé.

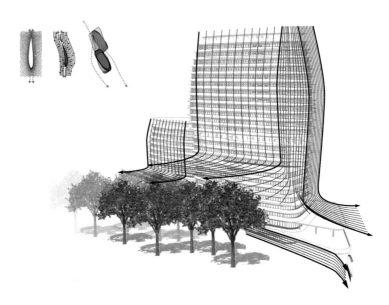

This design for the IBG (Informatie Beheer Groep) and Tax Offices is intended for 2500 employees and divided into spaces for the two users. Gardens, a central hall, and a pavilion for retail or commercial spaces bring those working in the building together in an informal way. In a proportion typical of the Netherlands, 1500 bicycles and 675 cars are to be accommodated in an underground garage. The architects explain: "An essential element in the design is the response to the location, adjacent to an important urban green space, known as the 'sterrenbos.' The aerodynamic form of the building has been achieved as the result of extensive sun and wind studies, which were carried out to ensure the minimum effect on this local green area." Biofuels and sunshading ensure that the building will be CO_2 neutral. UNStudio concludes: "This integrated approach to construction, material use, and management of the building fulfills government requirements stipulating that new buildings serve an exemplary function with regard to sustainable architecture."

Der Entwurf für die IBG (Informatie Beheer Groep) und das Finanzamt ist auf 2500 Mitarbeiter ausgelegt und in Räumlichkeiten für die verschiedenen Besuchergruppen unterteilt. Gärten, ein zentrales Foyer und ein Pavillon mit Ladenflächen bieten informelle Begegnungsmöglichkeiten für die Mitarbeiter. In einer Tiefgarage haben 1500 Fahrräder und 675 Pkws Platz – ein für die Niederlande typisches Verhältnis. Die Architekten erläutern: „Ein wesentliches Element des Entwurfs ist die Berücksichtigung des Standorts neben einer wichtigen städtischen Grünfläche, dem ‚Sterrenbos'. Die aerodynamische Form des Gebäudes ergab sich aus einer Reihe umfassender Untersuchungen zu Sonnenlichteinfall und Windverhältnissen, die durchgeführt wurden, um minimale Auswirkungen auf die örtliche Grünfläche sicherzustellen." Biobrennstoffe und Sonnenschutz sorgen dafür, dass das Gebäude CO_2-emissionsfrei bleibt. Abschließend merkt UNStudio an: „Diese integrierte Herangehensweise an Bau, Materialwahl und Gebäudemanagement entspricht Regierungsrichtlinien, die festschreiben, dass Neubauten im Sinne einer nachhaltigen Architektur vorbildlich sein müssen."

Ce projet pour les bureaux de l'administration fiscale et de l'IBG (Informatie Beheer Groep) est destiné à accueillir 2500 employés. Il est divisé en deux parties, une par client. Des jardins, un hall central et un pavillon pour des boutiques ou des espaces commerciaux réunissent ces deux parties de façon informelle. Dans une proportion typiquement néerlandaise, les parkings souterrains sont prévus pour 1500 vélos et 675 voitures. Pour l'architecte : « Un des éléments essentiels de ce projet est sa réponse au site, qui est adjacent à un vaste espace vert urbain, appelé le "sterrenbos". La forme aérodynamique du bâtiment est l'aboutissement d'études approfondies sur l'orientation solaire et la force des vents, afin de n'exercer qu'un impact minimum sur cet espace vert. » En terme d'émissions de CO_2, la neutralité de la construction est assurée par des protections solaires et l'utilisation de biofiouls. « Cette approche intégrée de la construction, de l'utilisation de matériaux et de la gestion du bâtiment répond aux demandes administratives stipulant que les nouvelles constructions doivent servir d'exemple dans le domaine de l'architecture durable. »

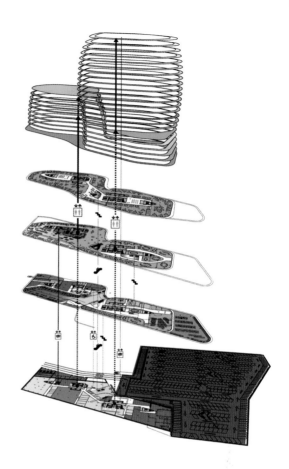

Using fluid forms generated for the overall design by studies of the wind and sun, the interior flows of the personnel are conceived to encourage casual contact and dialogue.

Die fließenden Formen gehen auf Studien zum Sonnenlichteinfall und zu den Windverhältnissen zurück. Die Bewegungsströme der Angestellten im Innenraum wurden so angelegt, dass informelle Begegnungen und Gespräche gefördert werden.

Dans un plan d'ensemble reposant sur des formes fluides issues d'études sur les vents et le soleil, les déplacements intérieurs du personnel ont été pensés pour faciliter les contacts et le dialogue.

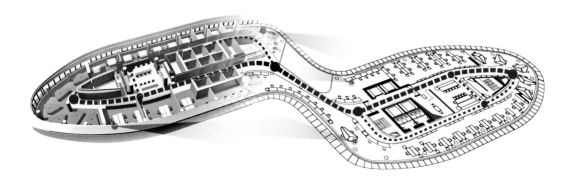

POST ROTTERDAM

Rotterdam, The Netherlands, 2008–12

Floor area: 44 000 m². Client: Delta Projectontwikkeling, SNS Property Finance, Redevco. Cost: not disclosed
Collaboration: Ben van Berkel, Caroline Bos, Gerard Loozekoot, Christian Bergmann

The roof in the central hall can be adjusted in accordance with the movements of the sun and has integrated photovoltaic cells to generate extra power for the complex.

Das Dach der Haupthalle lässt sich je nach Sonnenstand verändern und ist mit Solarmodulen ausgestattet, die zusätzliche Energie für den Komplex erzeugen.

La couverture du hall central peut se modifier en fonction de la course du soleil et intègre des cellules photovoltaïques qui produisent une partie de l'énergie utilisée par le complexe.

The architects speak in terms of "inclusive sustainability" for this "green shopping mall." "Sustainable architecture is today's foremost concern … With this project we aim to create the Netherlands' first sustainable urban retail and mixed-program complex. The integration of technical and design results in an inclusive design approach, which actively minimizes heat loads and contributes to a healthy environment." An existing structure is reused for the project, which aims for a LEED Platinum or Gold ranking. A large void above a courtyard provides natural ventilation and light. A roof on the central hall can be adjusted to direct light in specific directions and would have integrated photovoltaic cells, "which are now available in a variety of colors and degrees of translucency." The 70-meter-deep foundations below the tower allow the architects to send plastic tubes deep into the earth. Working with a vertical ground coupled chiller, the tubes allow the structure to draw either warmth or coolness out of the earth and to store the energy thus gained. The architects go a step further in their reflection, suggesting that some shops could specialize in health and nature awareness and that the public could thus be made to engage with the subject of sustainability.

Die Architekten sagen, dass die Nachhaltigkeit in dieser „grünen Shoppingmall" schon enthalten ist. „Heute gehört nachhaltige Architektur zu den wichtigsten Themen überhaupt … Mit diesem Projekt wollen wir den ersten nachhaltigen, urbanen, gemischt genutzten Komplex realisieren. Technische und gestalterische Erkenntnisse werden in einem ganzheitlichen Designansatz zusammengeführt, der aktiv zur Minimierung der Wärmebelastung und zu einer gesunden Umwelt beiträgt." Das Projekt integriert einen bestehenden Altbau und strebt eine LEED-Auszeichnung in Platin oder Gold an. Die erhebliche Raumhöhe über dem Hof sorgt für natürliche Belüftung und Lichteinfall. Das Dach über der zentralen Halle lässt sich so justieren, dass Licht in verschiedene Richtungen gelenkt werden kann, und soll mit integrierten Solarzellen ausgestattet werden, „die inzwischen in verschiedenen Farben und Transparenzgraden erhältlich sind". Da es erforderlich war, das Fundament für das Hochhaus bis zu 70 m tief zu legen, konnten die Architekten Kunststoffsonden tief in das Erdreich treiben. Angeschlossen an eine Erdwärmepumpe können die Sonden Wärme und Kälte aus dem Erdreich ziehen und die so gewonnene Energie speichern. Mit ihren Überlegungen gehen die Architekten sogar einen Schritt weiter und regen an, dass sich einige Läden auf Gesundheits- und Umweltbewusstsein spezialisieren und die Öffentlichkeit so für das Thema Nachhaltigkeit begeistern könnten.

Les architectes parlent de « durabilité inclusive » pour décrire ce « centre commercial vert ». « L'architecture durable est la principale préoccupation actuelle … Par ce projet, nous voulons créer le premier complexe mixte durable aux Pays-Bas. L'intégration de ces objectifs dans une approche poussée de la conception minimise les charges thermiques et contribue à un environnement plus sain. » Une construction existante a été réutilisée et le projet vise une notation LEED Platine ou Or. Un grand vide au-dessus d'une cour apporte la lumière et facilite la ventilation naturelle. Le toit au-dessus du hall central pourra s'orienter en fonction de la luminosité et sera équipé de cellules photovoltaïques intégrées « qui existent maintenant dans divers degrés de translucidité et de couleur ». La nécessité de creuser les fondations de la tour jusqu'à 70 m de profondeur a permis d'insérer dans le sol des tubes de plastique verticaux qui agissent comme refroidisseurs, et permettent d'exploiter, selon les saisons, la chaleur ou la fraîcheur du sol et d'emmagasiner l'énergie ainsi gagnée. Les architectes ont même suggéré que certains magasins pourraient se spécialiser dans la prise de conscience de la santé et de la nature, et que le public pourrait être appelé à participer aux efforts de développement durable.

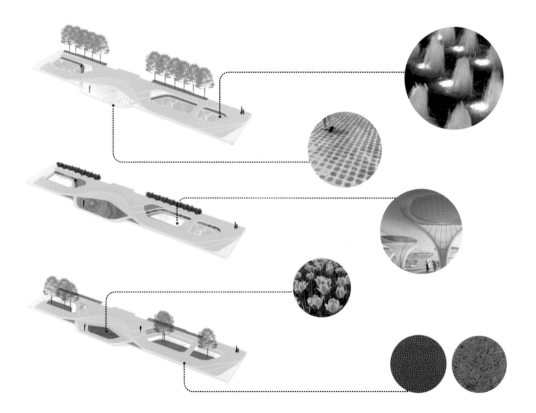

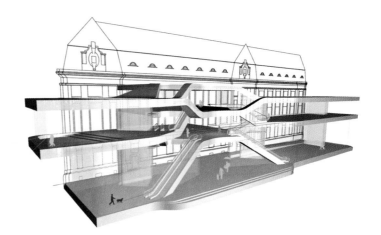

The perspective below emphasizes the external additions made by the architects to the existing structure. Geothermal sources are used for heating and cooling.

Die Abbildung unten lässt die Anbauten der Architekten an den Altbau erkennen. Zur Heizung und Klimatisierung des Baus wird Erd-wärme genutzt.

Le dessin ci-dessous montre les extensions réalisées par les architectes. La géothermie est utilisée pour le chauffage et le refroidissement.

MICHAEL VAN VALKENBURGH

Michael Van Valkenburgh Associates, Inc.
Landscape Architects, P.C.
16 Court Street, 11th Floor
Brooklyn, NY 11241
USA

Tel: 718 243 2044
Fax: 718 243 1293
E-mail: mvva_ny@mvvainc.com
Web: www.mvvainc.com

MICHAEL VAN VALKENBURGH received a B.S. degree from the Cornell University College of Agriculture (Ithaca, New York, 1973) and a Master of Landscape Architecture from the College of Fine Arts at the University of Illinois (Urbana-Champaign, 1977). He oversees both the New York and Cambridge, Massachusetts, offices of the firm and is involved in some way in every project. He was principal-in-charge for the ASLA Green Roof. Other firm principals are Matthew Urbanski, who is a lead designer for many of the firm's public projects, and Laura Solano, who is a specialist in landscape technology. Chris Counts, Project Designer and Project Manager of the project published here, received his Bachelor of Landscape Architecture from the University of Georgia, and his Master of Landscape Architecture from the Harvard GSD. He is a Senior Associate of the firm. Their work includes Harvard Yard Restoration (Cambridge, Massachusetts, 1992–2003); Tahari Courtyards (Millburn, New Jersey, 2002–03); Connecticut Water Treatment Facility (with Steven Holl, New Haven, Connecticut, 2001–05); the Teardrop Park (New York, New York, 1999–2006); and the ASLA Green Roof (Washington, D.C., 2005–06, published here), all in the USA.

MICHAEL VAN VALKENBURGH erwarb einen B. S. (Bachelor of Science) am College für Agrarwissenschaft der Cornell University (Ithaca, New York, 1973) sowie einen Master in Landschaftsarchitektur am College für bildende Künste der Universität von Illinois (Urbana-Champaign, 1977). Er betreut die Niederlassungen des Büros in New York und Cambridge, Massachusetts, und ist an jedem Projekt auf die eine oder andere Weise beteiligt. Für das ASLA Green Roof war er als Partner leitend verantwortlich. Weitere Partner sind Matthew Urbanski, Chefdesigner für zahlreiche öffentliche Projekte des Büros, und Laura Solano, Spezialistin für Landschaftsbau. Chris Counts, Projektdesigner und -manager des hier vorgestellten Projekts, erwarb seinen Bachelor in Landschaftsarchitektur an der Universität von Georgia und seinen Master in Landschaftsarchitektur an der Harvard Graduate School of Design. Er ist Seniorteilhaber des Büros. Zu den Projekten des Büros zählen u. a. die Sanierung des Harvard Yard (Cambridge, Massachusetts, 1992–2003), die Tahari-Höfe (Millburn, New Jersey, 2002–03), die Wasseraufbereitungsanlage Connecticut (mit Steven Holl, New Haven, Connecticut, 2001–05), der Teardrop Park (New York, 1999–2006) sowie das ASLA Green Roof (Washington, D. C., 2005–06, hier vorgestellt).

MICHAEL VAN VALKENBURGH est B. S. du Collège d'Agriculture de l'université Cornell (Ithaca, New York, 1973), et détient un mastère en paysagisme du Collège des Beaux-Arts de l'université de l'Illinois (Urbana-Champaign, 1977). Il dirige les bureaux de New York et de Cambridge, Massachusetts, de son agence, et s'implique dans chaque projet. Il a été responsable du projet de toit vert de l'ASLA. Les autres responsables de l'agence sont Matthew Urbanski, chargé des projets pour le secteur public, et Laura Solano, spécialiste des technologies du paysage. Chris Counts, concepteur et responsable de projets et de celui publié ici, est B. A en paysagisme de l'université de Géorgie, et M. A. de l'Harvard GSD. Il est associé senior de l'agence. Parmi leurs réalisations : la restauration du Yard de Harvard (Cambridge, Massachusetts, 1992–2003) ; les Tahari Courtyards (Millburn, New Jersey, 2002–03) ; les installations de traitement des eaux du Connecticut (avec Steven Holl, New Haven, Connecticut, 2001–05) ; le Teardrop Park (New York, 1999–2006) et le ASLA Green Roof (Washington, D. C., 2005–06, publié ici), toutes aux États-Unis.

ASLA GREEN ROOF
Washington, D.C., USA, 2005–06

Site area: 130 m². Client: American Society of Landscape Architects. Cost: $950 000
Collaboration: Michael Van Valkenburgh, Chris Counts, John Gidding, Gullivar Shepard, Stephen Noone, Robert Rock, Richard Hindle

Located in central Washington, D.C., this project, though small in area, is important because of the client—the American Society of Landscape Architects (ASLA). Mounds were created with lightweight materials at the north and south ends of the roof. The existence of these largely artificial hills on the roof naturally changes the visitor's perception of the space itself, but also of the Washington skyline. One of these "waves" was planted with low-growing varieties requiring little soil depth and the other, on the north, with "semi-intensive" (i.e., deeper rooted, taller) plants and almost two meters of soil. A special structural support suspended above the plants allows for a good number of people to be on the roof despite its high proportion of planted area. The architects write: "The project transcends its diminutive size because of the intense interest of the design community… It is designed with an educational pedagogy in mind, as it will be the launching pad for any future ASLA effort to teach the benefits of green roof technology."

Das im Zentrum von Washington, D.C., gelegene Projekt ist zwar flächenmäßig klein, wegen des Auftraggebers – der American Society of Landscape Architects (ASLA) – aber dennoch von Bedeutung. Am nördlichen und südlichen Ende des Dachs wurden mit Leichtbaumaterialien Böschungen angelegt. Diese überwiegend künstlichen Hügel auf dem Dach lassen die Besucher nicht nur den Ort selbst, sondern auch die Washingtoner Skyline anders wahrnehmen. Eine der beiden „Wellen" wurde mit niedrig wachsenden Pflanzen begrünt, die nur geringe Bodentiefe benötigen, die nördliche hingegen mit „semi-intensiver" (also tiefer wurzelnder, höherer) Bepflanzung und einer Bodentiefe von fast 2 m. Die über Teilen der Begrünung angebrachten und zu betretenden Abdeckungen machen es möglich, dass sich trotz des hohen Grünflächenanteils vergleichsweise viele Menschen auf dem Dach aufhalten können. Die Architekten schreiben: „Dank des starken Interesses in der Architekturgemeinde wächst das Projekt über seine winzige Größe hinaus… Es wurde mit didaktischen Hintergedanken entworfen, denn schließlich wird es Grundlage für zukünftige Bemühungen der ASLA sein, die Vorteile von Dachbegrünungen zu vermitteln."

Situé dans le centre de Washington, D.C., ce projet, bien que de faible surface, est important de par son client, The American Society of Landscape Architects (ASLA, Société américaine des architectes paysagistes). Des vallonnements ont été créés à l'aide de matériaux légers aux extrémités nord et sud de la toiture. L'existence de ces « collines », en grande partie artificielles, change naturellement la perception que le visiteur peut avoir de l'espace, mais aussi du panorama urbain de Washington. L'une de ces « vagues » a été plantée de variétés végétales de faible hauteur requérant peu de profondeur de sol, et l'autre, au nord, de plantes « semi-intensives » (à racines plus profondes) sur une épaisseur de sol de près de 2 m. Un support structurel spécial suspendu au-dessus des plantes permet au toit de recevoir un certain nombre de visiteurs malgré la forte présence des plantes. Selon les architectes : « Le projet transcende sa taille réduite par l'intense intérêt que lui porte la communauté professionnelle… Il est conçu dans un but pédagogique et éducatif, et sera la base de lancement des efforts futurs de l'ASLA pour enseigner les bénéfices de la technologie des toits végétalisés. »

The limited size of this green roof and weight constraints posed considerable challenges, but the designers succeeded in creating a convivial landscape environment where there had been only a flat surface before.

Die geringe Größe des begrünten Dachs und die gegebenen Belastungsgrenzen waren eine erhebliche Herausforderung. Dennoch gelang es den Gestaltern, ein freundliches Landschaftsumfeld zu schaffen, wo vorher nichts als eine ebene Freifläche war.

Les dimensions limitées de ce toit végétalisé et ses contraintes de poids ont posé de sérieux problèmes, mais les concepteurs ont réussi à créer un paysage convivial en remplacement d'une simple couverture plate.

WHY ARCHITECTURE

wHY Architecture
9520 Jefferson Boulevard
Studio C
Culver City, CA 90232
USA

Tel: +1 310 839 5106
Fax: +1 310 839 5107
E-mail: work@why-architecture.com
Web: www.why-architecture.com

WHY ARCHITECTURE was founded in 2003 by Yo-ichiro Hakomori and Kulapat Yantrasast. Hakomori received his M.Arch degree from UCLA, and his Doctorate from the University of Tokyo. Yantrasast, born in 1968 in Thailand, received his B.Arch degree in Thailand and his M.Arch degree and Ph.D. from the University of Tokyo. The two met at the University of Tokyo and they collaborated on several design competitions and research projects. After completing his studies, Hakomori worked for the late Frank Israel and for Arthur Erickson. Yantrasast became a key member of Tadao Ando's team in Osaka, working on the Modern Art Museum of Fort Worth, the Armani Teatro in Milan, the Foundation François Pinault for Contemporary Art in Paris, the Calder Museum project in Philadelphia, and the Clark Art Institute in Williamstown, Massachusetts. Their work includes the Grand Rapids Art Museum published here (Grand Rapids, Michigan, 2004–07); the Art Bridge (Los Angeles, California, 2008–09); the redesign of a number of galleries for the Art Institute of Chicago (2008–); and the Malibu Residence (Malibu, California, 2007–10), all in the USA.

WHY ARCHITECTURE wurde 2003 von Yo-ichiro Hakomori und Kulapat Yantrasast gegründet. Hakomori schloss sein Studium an der UCLA mit einem M.Arch. ab und promovierte an der Universität Tokio. Yantrasast, 1968 in Thailand geboren, erwarb seinen B.Arch. in Thailand und seinen M.Arch. an der Universität Tokio, wo er ebenfalls promovierte. Die beiden lernten sich an der Universität Tokio kennen, beteiligten sich zusammen an verschiedenen Wettbewerben und arbeiteten gemeinsam an Forschungsprojekten. Nach Abschluss seines Studiums arbeitete Hakomori für den inzwischen verstorbenen Frank Israel und für Arthur Erickson. Yantrasast wurde zu einer der Schlüsselfiguren in Tadao Andos Team in Osaka und war u. a. am Modern Art Museum in Fort Worth, Texas, dem Armani Teatro in Mailand, der Fondation François Pinault pour l'Art Contemporain in Paris, dem Calder-Museumsprojekt in Philadelphia sowie dem Clark Art Institute in Williamstown, Massachusetts, beteiligt. Zu den Projekten des Büros zählen das hier vorgestellte Grand Rapids Art Museum (Grand Rapids, Michigan, 2004–07), die Art Bridge (Los Angeles, Kalifornien, 2008–09), die Umgestaltung verschiedener Ausstellungsräume am Art Institute of Chicago (2008–) sowie die Malibu Residence (Malibu, Kalifornien, 2007–10).

L'agence **WHY ARCHITECTURE** a été fondée en 2003 par Yo-ichiro Hakomori et Kulapat Yantrasast. Hakomori est M.Arch d'UCLA et docteur de l'université de Tokyo. Yantrasast, né en 1968 en Thaïlande, a obtenu son B.Arch dans ce pays et son mastère et son doctorat à l'université de Tokyo. Ils se sont rencontrés à l'université et ont collaboré à l'occasion de plusieurs concours et projets de recherche. Après avoir achevé ses études, Hakomori à travaillé pour Frank Israël et pour Arthur Erickson. Yantrasast est devenu l'un des principaux collaborateurs de l'équipe de Tadao Ando à Osaka. Il a travaillé sur les projets du musée d'Art moderne de Fort Worth, le théâtre Armani à Milan, la Fondation François Pinault pour l'art contemporain à Paris ; le projet du musée Calder à Philadelphia ; et celui du Clark Art Institute à Williamstown, Massachusetts. Parmi leurs réalisations : le Grand Rapids Art Museum publié ici (Grand Rapids, Michigan, 2004–07) ; l'Art Bridge (Los Angeles, Californie, 2008–09) ; la rénovation d'un certain nombre de galeries pour l'Art Institute of Chicago (2008-) et la résidence Malibu (Malibu, Californie, 2007–10).

GRAND RAPIDS ART MUSEUM

Grand Rapids, Michigan, USA, 2004–07

Floor area: 11 613 m². Client: Grand Rapids Art Museum. Cost: $75 million
Architect of Record: Design Plus

The Grand Rapids Art Museum's new building, located in the city center, was the first art museum in the world to receive a LEED certification. This is not surprising given the necessary temperature, lighting, or humidity controls required in art museums. In fact, obtaining LEED certification was one condition of the 2001 donation by local philanthropist Peter Wege, a known defender of environmental causes. The facility includes approximately 5000 square meters of exhibition space. A large, sheltering canopy hovers over the facility and has its lobby, restaurant, education center, and pavilions "formed like fingers extending into the green of the park." The museum also faces a sculptural work by Maya Lin called *Ecliptic*, an oval square. The main museum space is a three-level gallery tower with natural overhead lighting for the top floor. The use of natural light in the structure is planned to reduce energy consumption where possible. Ten percent of the construction materials for the project were recycled, and rainwater is recycled for toilets, plant watering, and a reflecting pool. A vapor-mist air-conditioning system emits no hydrochlorofluorocarbons. With its strong, simple lines, the Grand Rapids Art Museum makes it clear that Kulapat Yantrasast learned from a master, in particular when he worked on the Modern Art Museum of Fort Worth.

Der Neubau des Grand Rapids Art Museum im Stadtzentrum war weltweit das erste Kunstmuseum, das eine LEED-Auszeichnung erhielt. Angesichts der in Kunstmuseen erforderlichen Steuerung von Temperatur-, Licht- und Luftfeuchtigkeitsverhältnissen erstaunt dies kaum. Tatsächlich war die Spende des ortsansässigen Philanthropen Peter Wege, der für sein Engagement in Umweltschutzfragen bekannt ist, daran gebunden, dass der Bau eine LEED-Zertifizierung erhielt. Die Einrichtung umfasst rund 5000 m² Ausstellungsfläche. Ein großes, schützendes Baldachindach schwebt über dem Bau. Lobby, Restaurant, museumspädagogische Einrichtungen und Pavillons wurden „wie Finger gestaltet, die in das Grün des Parks hineinragen". Dem Museum gegenüber befindet sich das „Ecliptic" betitelte Werk der Künstlerin Maya Lin, ein von ihr gestalteter ovaler Platz. Der zentrale Bereich des Museums ist ein dreistöckiger Turm mit Ausstellungsräumen, die vom obersten Stockwerk aus durch ein Oberlicht natürlich belichtet werden. Der Einsatz von natürlichem Licht soll den Energieverbrauch reduzieren. 10 % der Baumaterialien sind recycelt, Regenwasser wird aufbereitet und für Toiletten, die Bewässerung der Pflanzen und ein Wasserbecken genutzt. Durch die Verdunstungsklimaanlage wird kein FCKW emittiert. Mit seinen klaren, schlichten Linien macht das Grand Rapids Art Museum deutlich, dass Kulapat Yantrasast bei einem Meister in die Lehre gegangen ist, insbesondere während seiner Mitarbeit am Modern Art Museum in Fort Worth.

Le nouveau bâtiment du Grand Rapids Art Museum, situé en centre-ville, est le premier musée au monde à avoir reçu la certification LEED. Ce n'est pas surprenant, compte tenu de la problématique complexe de température, d'éclairage ou de contrôle de l'humidité posée par un musée d'art. En fait, l'obtention de cette certification était la condition pour recevoir une donation du philanthrope local, Peter Wege, défenseur connu de la cause environnementale. Les installations comptent 5000 m² environ d'espaces d'expositions. Un vaste auvent est suspendu au-dessus du musée dont le hall d'accueil, le restaurant, le centre éducatif et les pavillons « forment comme des doigts qui s'étendent vers l'espace vert du parc ». Le musée fait face à une place de forme ovale intitulée « Ecliptic » et conçue par l'artiste Maya Lin. Le volume principal est une tour de galeries de trois niveaux à éclairage zénithal. La lumière naturelle permet de diminuer la consommation d'électricité. Dix pour cent des matériaux de construction sont d'origine recyclée, et l'eau de pluie est récupérée pour les toilettes, l'arrosage des plantes et un bassin. Un système de conditionnement de l'air à émission de brouillard artificiel n'émet aucun hydrofluorocarbone. Par ses lignes simples et puissantes, ce musée témoigne de l'influence du maître auprès duquel Kulapat Yantrasast a appris, en particulier lorsqu'il travaillait sur le projet du musée d'Art moderne de Fort Worth.

The entrance to the Grand Rapids Art Museum is clearly signaled by its great overhanging canopy roof.

Der Eingang zum Grand Rapids Art Museum wird von einem monumentalen, ausgreifenden Vordach markiert.

L'entrée du musée est fortement signalée par son grand toit en porte-à-faux.

The architects have engaged in a careful assemblage of essentially Euclidean volumes, keeping in mind the ecological concerns of the client at all times.

Die Architekten schufen eine ausgewogene Komposition aus einfachen euklidischen Körpern und behielten dabei stets die ökologischen Vorgaben des Mäzens im Blick.

Les architectes ont réalisé un assemblage soigné de volumes essentiellement euclidiens en tenant compte en permanence des préoccupations écologiques de leur client.

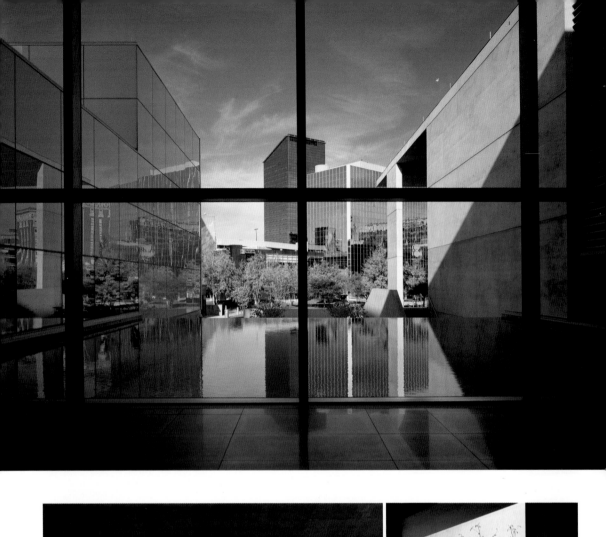

A grand entry sequence with its
ramped stairway may recall some
gestures of Tadao Ando. Left, a large
window opens the museum to the
nearby city center.

Der beeindruckende Eingangbereich
mit seiner rampenförmigen Treppe
mag an Gesten Tadao Andos erinnern.
Ein großes Fenster (links) öffnet
das Museum zum nahe gelegenen
Stadtzentrum.

L'impressionnante séquence d'entrée
et le grand escalier pourraient rappe-
ler certains gestes de Tadao Ando.
À gauche, une grande baie ouvre sur
le centre-ville tout proche.

KEN YEANG

T. R. Hamzah & Yeang Sdn. Bhd.
8 Jalan 1, Taman Sri Ukay
Off Jalan Ulu Kelang
68000 Ampang, Selangor
Malaysia

Tel: +60 3 4257 1948/1969
Fax: +60 3 4256 1005/9330
E-mail: trhy@tm.net.my
Web: www.trhamzahyeang.com

Born in 1948 in Penang, Malaysia, **KEN YEANG** attended the Architectural Association in London, 1966–71, and Cambridge University (Wolfson College), 1971–75. Much of his subsequent work was based on his Ph.D. dissertation in Cambridge on ecological design. His work (with Tengku Robert Hamzah as T. R. Hamzah & Yeang, created in 1976 in Kuala Lumpur) includes the Menara Mesiniaga Tower (Malaysia, 1989–92, a recipient of the 1995 Aga Khan Award for Architecture); the MBF Tower (Penang, Malaysia, 1990–93); a tower in Ho Chi Minh City (Vietnam, 1992–94); the Tokyo-Nara Tower (Tokyo, Japan, 1997); and the Menara UMNO (Penang, Malaysia, 1998). Further work includes the Mewah Oils Headquarters (Selangor, Malaysia, 2001–03, published here), and The New National Library Board Building (Singapore, 2001–05, also published here). His published books include *The Architecture of Malaysia* (Pepin Press, Kuala Lumpur, 1992) and *The Skyscraper, Bioclimatically Considered: A Design Primer* (AD, London, 1997). Ken Yeang was President of the Malaysian Institute of Architects from 1983 to 1986. Yeang and his firm have developed a substantial reputation for designing ecologically responsible buildings on a large scale and for master planning work in numerous countries, including UAE and China.

KEN YEANG wurde 1948 in Penang in Malaysia geboren und studierte 1966 bis 1971 an der Architectural Association in London sowie 1971 bis 1975 an der Universität Cambridge (Wolfson College). Ein Großteil seines späteren Werks baute auf seiner in Cambridge entstandenen Dissertation zum Thema ökologisches Planen auf. Zu seinen Projekten (mit Tengku Robert Hamzah als T. R. Hamzah & Yeang, Bürogründung 1976 in Kuala Lumpur) zählen der Menara Mesiniaga Tower (Malaysia, 1989–92, 1995 mit dem Aga-Khan-Preis für Architektur ausgezeichnet), der MBF Tower (Penang, Malaysia, 1990–93), ein Hochhaus in Ho-Chi-Minh-Stadt (Vietnam, 1992–94), der Tokyo-Nara Tower (Tokio, Japan, 1997) sowie das Menara UMNO (Penang, Malaysia, 1998). Weitere Arbeiten sind u. a. die Zentrale für Mewah Oils (Selangor, Malaysia, 2001–03) sowie das New National Library Board Building (Singapur, 2001–05), die beide hier vorgestellt werden. Zu seinen Veröffentlichungen zählen *The Architecture of Malaysia* (Pepin Press, Kuala Lumpur 1992) und *The Skyscraper, Bioclimatically Considered: A Design Primer* (AD, London 1997). Ken Yeang war von 1983 bis 1986 Präsident des Malaysischen Architekteninstituts. Yeang und sein Büro haben sich einen besonderen Ruf für die Gestaltung umweltverträglicher Großbauten erworben sowie für die Entwicklung von Masterplänen in zahlreichen Ländern, darunter auch die Vereinigten Arabischen Emirate und China.

Né en 1948 à Penang, Malaisie, **KEN YEANG** a étudié à l'Architectural Association de Londres (1966–71), et à l'université de Cambridge (Wolfson College, 1971–75). Une grande partie de ses travaux ultérieurs est issue de sa thèse de doctorat sur la conception écologique présentée à Cambridge. Ses réalisations (avec Tengku Robert Hamzah pour l'agence T. R. Hamzah & Yeang, créée en 1976 à Kuala Lumpur) comprennent la tour Menara Mesiniaga (Malaisie, 1989–92), Prix Aga Khan d'architecture 1995 ; la tour MBF (Penang, Malaisie,1990–93) ; une tour à Ho Chi Minh-Ville (Vietnam, 1992–94) ; la tour Tokyo-Nara (Tokyo, Japon, 1997) et le Menara UMNO (Penang, Malaisie, 1998). Il a conçu le siège de Mewah Oils (Selangor, Malaisie, 2001–03, publié ici) ; et le nouveau bâtiment de l'administration de la Bibliothèque nationale (Singapour, 2001–05, également publié ici). Parmi ses publications : *The Architecture of Malaysia* (Pepin Press, Kuala Lumpur, 1992), et *The Skyscraper, Bioclimatically Considered : A Design Primer* (AD, Londres, 1997). Ken Yeang a été président de l'Institut des architectes malais de 1983 à 1986. Son agence et lui ont acquis une réputation grandissante dans la conception d'immeubles écologiques et de plans d'urbanisme dans de nombreux pays, incluant Émirats arabes unis et la Chine.

MEWAH OILS HEADQUARTERS

Pulau Indah Park, Port Klang, Selangor, Malaysia, 2001–03

Floor area: 16 379 m². Client: Mewah Oils Sdn Bhd. Cost: £2 million

The project is the headquarters building for a Singapore-based company that produces palm-oil products and specialty fats. The program is for a four-story office (overall height 34 meters) with a four-story packing plant, and a 32-meter-high single-volume space to house an automated warehouse. As the architects explain: "The warehouse forms a towering backdrop to the north. The office block forms a thin southern frontage in an extruded form that is penetrated along its entire long section by a landscaped ramp connecting the ground floor vegetation to the roof garden and terrace. The inner public space is given full expression in the form of the building. The atrium volume is naturally ventilated by clerestories which open onto the roof gardens, at the upper western end." A linear, cascading watercourse lines the ramp hall. Ken Yeang has always been very concerned with ecological issues and in this instance, as he says, "what could have been a regular industrial plant and office is transformed into an ecological 'green-lung' that enhances the well-being of the building's users and the biomass of the site."

Dieses Projekt ist die Firmenzentrale für einen in Singapur ansässigen Hersteller von Palmölprodukten und Spezialfetten. Das Programm umfasst einen vierstöckigen Bürobau (insgesamt 34 m hoch), eine vierstöckige Verpackungsanlage sowie eine 32 m hohe Halle, in der ein automatisiertes Lager untergebracht ist. Die Architekten erläutern: „Das Lager türmt sich als gewaltige Kulisse nach Norden hin auf. Nach Süden hin bildet der Büroblock eine schmale, sich vom übrigen Gebäude abhebende Fassadenfront, die über die gesamte Länge von einer begrünten Rampe durchschnitten wird, die die ebenerdige Bepflanzung mit Dachgarten und -terrasse verbindet. Der innen liegende öffentliche Raum findet in der formalen Gestaltung des Baus umfassenden Ausdruck. Das Atrium wird am oberen westlichen Ende durch Obergadenfenster, die sich zum Dachgarten hin öffnen, natürlich belüftet." Ein linearer, über Stufen rinnender Wasserlauf säumt die Halle unter der Rampe. Ken Yeang hat sich schon immer intensiv mit ökologischen Fragen befasst. In diesem Fall, sagt er, „wurde das, was ein üblicher Werks- und Bürobau hätte sein können, zu einer ökologischen ‚grünen Lunge', die das Wohlbefinden der Nutzer des Gebäudes steigert und für mehr Biomasse auf dem Gelände sorgt".

Ce projet concerne le siège d'une société de Singapour spécialisée dans les produits à base d'huile de palme et les graisses. Le programme consiste en un bâtiment de bureaux de quatre niveaux de 34 m de haut, et une usine de conditionnement (de quatre niveaux également) et un volume de 32 m de haut, qui est un entrepôt automatisé. L'architecte explique que « l'entrepôt forme une masse importante au nord. Au sud, les bureaux sont protégés par une façade mince de forme extrudée, pénétrée sur toute sa longueur par une rampe paysagée qui connecte la végétation du rez-de-chaussée au jardin en toiture et à la terrasse. L'espace public intérieur trouve sa pleine expression dans la forme du bâtiment. Le volume de l'atrium est naturellement ventilé par des verrières découpées dans le jardin en toiture, à l'extrémité supérieure ouest. » Un petit ruisseau en cascade double la rampe. Ken Yeang a toujours été très concerné par les enjeux écologiques, et, à cet égard, il précise que « ce qui aurait pu n'être qu'un ensemble banal de bureaux et d'usine s'est transformé en un "poumon vert" écologique qui améliore le bien-être de ses usagers et la biomasse du site ».

Ken Yeang has long integrated green ideas into his architecture. Here, as the images below and above show, he has brought vegetation into and onto the building.

Ken Yeang integriert schon lange grüne Konzepte in seine Architektur. Wie die Abbildungen unten und oben zeigen, spielt die Begrünung hier sowohl im als auch am Bau eine Rolle.

Ken Yeang a depuis longtemps mis en pratique des concepts écologiques dans son architecture. Ici, comme le montrent les images, il a intégré la végétation dans et sur le bâtiment.

THE NEW NATIONAL LIBRARY BOARD BUILDING

Singapore, 2001–05

Floor area: 30 979 m². Client: National Library Board, Singapore. Cost: £80 million
Architect of Record: D. P. Architects, Singapore

The client provided the architect with a set of planning principles as the basis for design. The project should be an open, hospitable, and conducive learning environment for the people of Singapore; a national and civic institution with a distinctive character, reflecting Singapore's multicultural heritage and its aspirations to be a leading nation; user friendly, comprehensible to visitors and convenient for everyday staff use; an efficient building with integrated systems; a building for the tropical climate. The resulting 16-story 98-meter-high tower consists of two blocks separated by a semi-enclosed internal street. The larger block contains the library collections. The small, curved block contains exhibition, auditorium, and multimedia space. Sunshading blades, six meters deep in some locations, provide the aesthetic and functional base for the building's envelope. Over 6300 square meters are designated as green space throughout the library. Optimized day lighting and solar orientation, natural ventilation where possible, use of green or recycled materials for carpets and wall fabrics, and other strategies have been employed to make the structure ecologically responsible. Simulations were conducted on the energy consumption and building performance of the design and results showed an energy consumption rate of around 185 kWh/m²/year, which is less than typical commercial office towers (230 kWh/m²/year) in Singapore.

Der Auftraggeber gab dem Architekten eine ganze Reihe von Planungsvorgaben für die Gestaltung des Entwurfs an die Hand. Dazu gehörten: die Schaffung eines Orts, der den Bürgern Singapurs ein offenes, freundliches und förderliches Lernumfeld bieten sollte; eine nationale, öffentliche Institution mit unverwechselbarem Charakter, die das multikulturelle Erbe Singapurs und sein Streben, eine führende Nation zu sein, widerspiegelt; benutzerfreundlich, nachvollziehbar für Besucher und praktisch für die tägliche Arbeit der Angestellten; ein effizientes Gebäude mit integrierten Systemen, das dem tropischen Klima angemessen ist. Das daraufhin geplante 16-stöckige, 98 m hohe Haus besteht aus zwei Blöcken, die von einer halb umbauten Straße in seinem Inneren getrennt werden. Im größeren Block befinden sich die Bibliotheksbestände. Der kleinere, geschwungene Block umfasst Ausstellungsräume, ein Auditorium und einen Multimediaraum. Sonnenschutzlamellen, an manchen Stellen 6 m tief, bilden die ästhetische und funktionale Grundlage für die Gebäudehaut. Über 6300 m² der Bibliothek wurden als Grünfläche konzipiert. Um den Komplex ökologisch so verantwortungsvoll wie möglich zu gestalten, kamen Strategien wie optimierte Tageslichtnutzung und Ausrichtung des Baus nach der Sonneneinstrahlung, weitestgehende natürliche Belüftung, grüne oder recycelte Materialien für Bodenbeläge und Wandtextilien zum Einsatz. Simulationen des Energieverbrauchs und der Energieeffizienz ergaben einen Energieverbrauch von rund 185 kWh/m² pro Jahr, was unter dem Verbrauch vergleichbarer Bürohochhäuser in Singapur liegt (230 kWh/m² pro Jahr).

Le client avait précisé dans son programme les principes de base qu'il entendait voir respecter. Ce nouveau bâtiment devait être un lieu ouvert, accueillant et adapté à l'éducation, destiné au peuple de Singapour ; une institution publique nationale à caractère particulier, reflétant le patrimoine multiculturel de la ville et ses ambitions nationales ; un lieu convivial, d'appropriation facile par les visiteurs et pratique pour le personnel ; enfin un bâtiment efficace à systèmes intégrés, prévu pour le climat tropical. La tour de seize niveaux et 98 m de haut se compose de deux blocs séparés par une rue intérieure semi-protégée. Le bloc le plus important contient les collections de livres. Le petit bloc incurvé contient des espaces d'expositions et multimédias, et un auditorium. Des brise-soleil de 6 m de profondeur à certains endroits constituent fonctionnellement et esthétiquement l'enveloppe de la bibliothèque. Plus de 6300 m² d'espaces verts ont été prévus à l'intérieur du bâtiment. L'éclairage naturel optimisé, l'orientation solaire, la ventilation naturelle partout où elle était possible, des matériaux verts ou recyclés pour les moquettes et revêtements muraux, et d'autres stratégies ont été utilisées pour rendre durable cette nouvelle structure. Des simulations sur la consommation d'énergie et les performances du bâtiment ont été menées pendant la phase de conception et les résultats ont montré une consommation de 185 kWh/m² par an, soit moins que la consommation typique des tours de Singapour qui s'élève à 230 kWh/m² par an.

Sunshading blades and the generous presence of vegetation inside the building are visible signs of Ken Yeang's green design.

Sonnenschutzlamellen und die großzügige Begrünung im Inneren des Gebäudes zeugen von Ken Yeangs ‚grüner' Gestaltung.

Les lames de protections solaires et la présence généreuse de la végétation dans l'immeuble expriment l'approche écologique de Ken Yeang.

ZOKA ZOLA

Zoka Zola architecture + urban design
1737 West Ohio Street
Chicago, IL 60622
USA

Tel: +1 312 491 9431
Fax: +1 312 491 9432
E-mail: info@zokazola.com
Web: www.zokazola.com

ZOKA ZOLA was born in Rijeka, Croatia. She studied architecture at Zagreb University in Croatia and at the Architectural Association (AA) in London. She worked for David Chipperfield Architects, Sir Michael Hopkins + Partners, OMA in London; Professor Vittorio De Feo, Professor Francesco Cellini, Professor Paolo Portoghesi in Rome; and Professor Wilhelm Holzbauer in Vienna. Having qualified as an architect in the United Kingdom in 1990, Zola established her own studio in London. In 1995, she received the Young Architect of the Year Award, an annual award. She has taught Architecture as a Senior Lecturer at the Brookes University in Oxford, and was a Unit Master at the AA in London. In 1997, Zoka Zola moved to Chicago, where she first worked at De Stefano and Partners and started teaching at the School of the Art Institute of Chicago. Later, she established her own studio in Chicago and designed her own house, completed in July 2002. Her residence won the Home of the Year Award as the best home in North America. Her work includes the Pfanner House (Chicago, Illinois, 2002); a mixed-use development with penthouse and rooftop garden (Chicago, Illinois, 2003); Zero Energy House (Chicago, Illinois, 2004); a 24-hour mixed-use development with shops, restaurants, housing, and hotels along the Chicago River (Chicago, Illinois, 2008); a competition for a 200-unit housing project (Rijeka, Croatia, 2008); Rafflesia Zero Energy House (Kuala Lumpur, Malaysia, 2007–09, published here); and Solar Tower (Chicago, Illinois, 2007–, also published here), all in the USA unless stated otherwise.

ZOKA ZOLA wurde im kroatischen Rijeka geboren. Sie studierte Architektur an der Universität Zagreb in Kroatien und an der Architectural Association (AA) in London. Sie arbeitete für David Chipperfield Architects, Sir Michael Hopkins + Partners und OMA in London, für Professor Vittorio De Feo, Professor Francesco Cellini und Professor Paolo Portoghesi in Rom sowie für Professor Wilhelm Holzbauer in Wien. Nachdem sie 1990 als Architektin in Großbritannien zugelassen wurde, eröffnete Zola ihr eigenes Büro in London. 1995 wurde sie mit dem Young Architect of the Year Award, einem jährlich vergebenen Preis, ausgezeichnet. Sie unterrichtete als Privatdozentin Architektur an der Brookes University in Oxford und war Unit Master an der AA in London. 1997 zog Zoka Zola nach Chicago, wo sie zunächst bei De Stefano and Partners arbeitete und schließlich begann, Architektur an der School of the Art Institute of Chicago zu unterrichten. Später gründete sie ihr eigenes Büro in Chicago und entwarf ihr eigenes Haus, das im Juli 2002 fertiggestellt wurde. Ihr Wohnhaus gewann den Home of the Year Award als bester Wohnbau in Nordamerika. Zu ihren Arbeiten zählen das Haus Pfanner (Chicago, Illinois, 2002), ein Komplex mit gemischter Nutzung, der auch über ein Penthouse und einen Dachgarten verfügt (Chicago, Illinois, 2003), das Nullenergiehaus (Chicago, Illinois, 2004), ein 24 Stunden geöffneter Komplex mit gemischter Nutzung mit Läden, Restaurants, Wohnungen und Hotels am Chicago River (Chicago, Illinois, 2008), ein Wettbewerbsbeitrag für ein Wohnbauprojekt mit 200 Einheiten (Rijeka, Kroatien, 2008), das Rafflesia-Nullenergiehaus (Kuala Lumpur, Malaysia, 2007–09, hier vorgestellt) sowie der Solar Tower (Chicago, Illinois, 2007–, ebenfalls hier vorgestellt).

ZOKA ZOLA, née à Rijeka en Croatie, a étudié l'architecture à l'université de Zagreb et à l'Architectural Association (AA) de Londres. Elle a travaillé à Londres pour David Chipperfield Architects, Sir Michael Hopkins + Partners, OMA ; le Professeur Vittorio De Feo, le Professeur Francesco Cellini, le Professeur Paolo Portoghesi à Rome et le Professeur Wilhelm Holzbauer à Vienne. Architecte qualifiée au Royaume-Uni (1990), elle a créé son agence à Londres. En 1995, elle a reçu le prix des Jeunes architectes de l'année. Elle a enseigné l'architecture comme Senior Lecturer à l'université Brookes à Oxford, et a été responsable d'unité à l'AA à Londres. En 1997, elle est partie pour Chicago où elle a d'abord travaillé pour De Stefano and Partners et commencé à enseigner à l'École de l'Art Institute. Plus tard, elle y a créé une agence et a conçu sa propre maison, achevée en juillet 2002, qui a remporté le Home of the Year Award, prix de la meilleure maison construite en Amérique du Nord. Parmi ses réalisations : la maison Pfanner (Chicago, Illinois, 2002) ; un immeuble mixte avec penthouse et jardin sur le toit (Chicago, Illinois, 2003) ; la maison Zero Energy (Chicago, Illinois, 2004) ; un immeuble mixte avec magasins, restaurants, logements et hôtels au bord de la Chicago River (Chicago, Illinois, 2008) ; un concours pour un projet de 200 logements (Rijeka, Croatie, 2008) ; la maison Rafflesia Zero Energy (Kuala Lumpur, Malaisie, 2007–09, publiée ici) et la tour Solar (Chicago, Illinois, 2007–, également publiée ici).

RAFFLESIA ZERO ENERGY HOUSE

Kuala Lumpur, Malaysia, 2007–09

Floor area: 145 m² (interior); 30 m² (exterior). Client: YTL
Cost: $250 000

This project was the winner of an invited competition against MAD (Beijing) and Graft (Berlin), amongst others. The architect explains: "The project is envisaged as the first showcase of sustainable zero energy housing in the world. The competition brief called for houses that work in harmony with the environment, are made from renewable materials, create their own energy, and recycle water." The house sits on 12 columns in order to allow "other species to develop around it." An analysis of wind patterns leads to the use of concave and convex walls to focus airflows. A 50-centimeter air void is set between the upper and lower roof to provide insulation from heat. Solar panels are located on 92% of the roof, generating enough electricity to run the house. Low-energy ceiling fans accelerate the existing, natural air movements. Seven independent zones allow users of the house to select their own air conditioning levels. As for the architectural design, Zoka Zola states: "Our winning design (unintentionally) looks like the Rafflesia, the largest flower in the world and a native to the rainforests of Malaysia." The house intends to integrate itself into the very specific, warm, and humid climate of Kuala Lumpur.

Das Projekt konnte sich in einem Wettbewerb gegen Büros wie MAD (Peking) und Graft (Berlin) durchsetzen. Die Architektin führt aus: „Das Projekt wurde als weltweit erstes Vorzeigeobjekt für nachhaltige Nullenergie-Wohnhausbauten ausgearbeitet. Laut Ausschreibungsprofil waren Häuser gefragt, die im Einklang mit der Umwelt funktionieren, aus erneuerbaren Materialien gefertigt werden, ihren eigenen Energiebedarf decken und Wasser wieder aufbereiten." Das Haus steht auf zwölf Stützen, die es möglich machen, dass sich „andere Spezies um den Bau ausbreiten können". Eine Windanalyse gab Anlass, mit konvexen und konkaven Wänden zu arbeiten, um die Luftströme zu bündeln. Als Dämmschutz vor der Hitze wurde zwischen Ober- und Unterseite des Dachs ein 50 cm tiefer Hohlraum integriert. 92 % der Dachfläche wurden mit Solarmodulen versehen, die ausreichend Strom für das Haus produzieren. Energiesparende Deckenventilatoren verstärken die bestehenden natürlichen Luftströme. Dank sieben unabhängiger Zonen ist es Bewohnern des Hauses möglich, die Klimatisierung bedarfsgerecht zu regulieren. Zum architektonischen Entwurf merkt Zoka Zola an: „Unser Siegerbeitrag sieht (unabsichtlich) aus wie eine Rafflesie; die Pflanze ist im Regenwald von Malaysia beheimatet und bildet mit die größten Blüten der Welt." Materialen und Bauweise sind auf das sehr spezifische feuchtwarme Klima von Kuala Lumpur abgestimmt.

Cette maison a remporté un concours sur invitation face, entre autres, à MAD (Pékin) et Graft (Berlin). « Ce projet a été envisagé comme la première vitrine d'une maison durable Zéro Énergie dans le monde. Le programme du concours portait sur des maisons capables de créer leur propre énergie et de recycler leur eau. » La maison repose sur douze colonnes qui permettent « à d'autres espèces de se développer autour d'elle », explique l'architecte. Une analyse des vents a abouti à l'adoption de murs concaves et convexes pour concentrer leurs flux. Un vide d'air de 50 cm est aménagé entre les deux couvertures pour protéger de la chaleur. Les panneaux solaires, qui occupent 92 % de la surface de la toiture, génèrent assez d'énergie pour alimenter toute la maison. Des ventilateurs en plafond à basse consommation d'énergie accélèrent les mouvements naturels de l'air. Sept zones indépendants permettent aux habitants de choisir leur propre niveau de climatisation. Sur la forme, Zoka Zola précise : « Notre projet ressemble (non intentionnellement) à la Rafflesia, la plus grande fleur du monde qui pousse dans les forêts humides de Malaisie. » La maison s'intègre d'elle-même dans le climat particulièrement spécifique, chaud et humide de Kuala Lumpur.

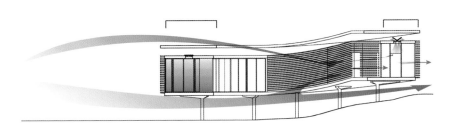

Although air conditioning is part of the design, it functions only as users require, encouraging the free flow of air through its volumes.

Obwohl der Entwurf auch eine Klima-anlage vorsieht, soll diese nur nach Bedarf von den Bewohnern genutzt werden. Luft soll ungehindert durch die Baukörper fließen können.

Bien que le projet utilise une climati-sation mécanique, celle-ci est conçue pour n'intervenir qu'en fonction des besoins des utilisateurs et mobiliser les flux de ventilation à travers les volumes.

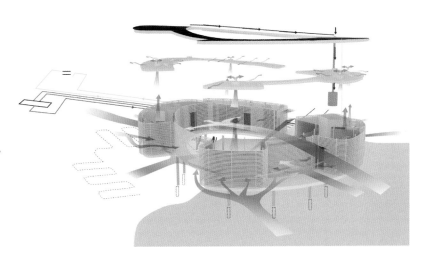

SOLAR TOWER

Chicago, Illinois, USA, 2007–

Floor area: 18 116 m². Client: not disclosed
Cost: not disclosed

This tower is intended to capture a maximum amount of solar power. Zoka Zola states: "A majority of the towers designed these days are extravagant formal propositions. Towers are in vogue but most of them are unconcerned with the issues of today or the future. In this way, the flood of towers designed these days is outdated. Architects must seize this time of the greatest responsibility and develop sustainable strategies for towers to use all the physical and social energies of their sites; especially because towers sustain the environment maybe better than any other building type." Essentially a research project, this tower could be modified to house a variety of activities and spaces without reducing its solar capacity. Sun-tracking solar panels are mounted on horizontal poles, a system that should increase their capacity by 30%–40%, or more, according to Zoka Zola. A subsidiary benefit of these panels is that they would shade the building's interior. The wind could also be used to generate further power. The complex surface of the building is described by the architect as a "cosmo-bio-logical-looking skin."

Das Hochhaus wurde konzipiert, um maximalen Nutzen aus der Solarenergie zu ziehen. Zoka Zola erläutert: „Ein Großteil der heutzutage entworfenen Hochhäuser ist formal extravagant. Hochhäuser sind in Mode, doch die meisten stehen den Fragen der Gegenwart und Zukunft unbeteiligt gegenüber. So gesehen ist die zurzeit entworfene Flut von Hochhäusern bereits überholt. Architekten müssen diese Zeit größerer Verantwortung nutzen, um nachhaltige Strategien für Hochhäuser zu entwickeln, die die gesamte physikalische und soziale Energie ihrer Standorte nutzen, gerade weil Hochhäuser der Umwelt wahrscheinlich zuträglicher sind als jeder andere Gebäudetyp." Das Hochhaus, im Grunde ein Forschungsprojekt, ließe sich für die verschiedensten Aktivitäten und Räumlichkeiten nutzen, ohne seine solarenergetische Kapazität einzuschränken. Die Solarmodule sind auf horizontalen Stangen montiert und richten sich nach dem Sonnenstand aus, ein System, das die Leistungsfähigkeit der Module Zoka Zola zufolge noch um 30 bis 40 % oder mehr steigern könnte. Ein positiver Nebeneffekt der Module ist es, dass sie dem Innern des Baus Schatten spenden. Darüber hinaus könnte Windkraft genutzt werden, um zusätzliche Energie zu erzeugen. Die komplexe Oberfläche des Gebäudes wurde von der Architektin als „kosmo-bio-logisch aussehende Haut" beschrieben.

Cette tour devrait capter le maximum possible d'énergie solaire. Zoka Zola explique qu'« une majorité des tours conçues de nos jours sont des propositions formelles extravagantes. Les tours sont à la mode, mais la plupart d'entre elles ne se sentent pas concernées par les enjeux d'aujourd'hui ou du futur. La grande masse des tours conçues actuellement est démodée. Les architectes doivent prendre en main leurs lourdes responsabilités et mettre au point des stratégies de développement durable pour les tours et utiliser toutes les énergies physiques et sociales de leur site, en particulier parce que les tours peuvent profiter de l'environnement peut-être mieux que n'importe quel autre type de bâtiment. » Essentiellement projet de recherche, cette tour pourrait se modifier pour accueillir diverses activités et formes d'espace sans réduire sa capacité solaire. Des panneaux solaires à orientation réglée sont montés sur des poteaux horizontaux, système qui devrait accroître leur capacité de 30 à 40 % voire plus, selon l'architecte. Un bénéfice subsidiaire de ces panneaux est qu'ils fourniraient également de l'ombre à l'intérieur du bâtiment. Le vent pourrait également servir à produire de l'électricité. La surface complexe de l'enveloppe est décrite par Zoka Zola comme « une peau d'aspect cosmobiologique ».

The Solar Tower is an experiment in maximizing the potential of an urban building to generate electricity, above and beyond any specific consideration of its internal use.

Der Solar Tower ist ein Experiment, um das Potenzial urbaner Bauten zur Energieerzeugung zu maximieren, unabhängig vom jeweiligen Bedarf des Gebäudes und gegebenenfalls darüber hinaus.

La Tour solaire est une expérimentation d'optimisation du potentiel d'un immeuble urbain dans la production d'électricité, au-delà de toute considération spécifique sur son usage interne.

INDEX OF ARCHITECTS, BUILDINGS, AND PLACES

CREDITS